Natural Born
SUCCESS

Natural Born
SUCCESS

Discover the Instinctive Drives™
that make you tick!

Paul Burgess

Wrightbooks

BICENTENNIAL
1807
WILEY
2007
BICENTENNIAL

First published 2007 by Wrightbooks
an imprint of John Wiley & Sons Australia, Ltd
42 McDougall Street, Milton, Qld 4064

Office also in Melbourne

Typeset in Berkeley LT 11.5/14.5pt

© Paul Burgess 2007

The moral rights of the author have been asserted

Burgess, Paul.

Natural born success: discover the instinctive drives that make you tick.

Includes index.

ISBN 9780731405824 (pbk.).

ISBN 073140582X (pbk.).

1. Personality tests. 2. Motivation (Psychology) - Testing.

I. Title.

616.89075

Story on pages 22 to 23 by Francie Baltazar-Schwartz
Pages 238 to 239 and 241 to 242 by Aron, A & Aron, EN, *Statistics for Psychology*, 1994, Pearson Education, Inc., Upper Saddle River, New Jersey
Cover image © Photodisc
Back cover photograph © Ken Holt. Reproduced with permission
Wiley Bicentennial Logo: Richard J Pacifico

Printed in the United States by Courier Westford, Inc.

10 9 8 7 6 5

Disclaimer

Contents

What people say about *Natural Born Success* and the *I.D. System*™

[The I.D. System™] has helped me re-craft my conversations with my team and peers, and it has helped me to become more self-aware of the impact of my style on others. Paul and I have recently discussed how to expand the use of I.D.™ to my wife and kids, with the goal of improving our communications as well ... So whether your team is a family, a self-managed work group, a couple, or—like mine—a business team, this book and the process it outlines can help you better understand who you are.

I particularly like the way Paul has written the book—using real-life examples with real-life people in real work situations as well as personal situations. He cleverly takes his points from concept to explanation to examples so that the learning sticks for the reader and they can associate the learning with specific situations which embeds it in their thinking and application on a day-to-day basis.

Randy Pond
Senior Vice President
Operations, Processes & Systems
Cisco Systems Inc.

In my work with psychometric test research in the field of organisational behaviour, I have not seen anything get so quickly to the core of what makes someone tick. In my observation, when applying the I.D. System™ to students and industry participants, the I.D.™ helps people to really get to know each other. I see it as extremely useful as a tool and process that quickly helps you understand the core of the human being—much deeper than any other aspect of personality or behaviour.

Anneke Fitzgerald (PhD)
Research Program Studies Coordinator
College of Business
University of Western Sydney (UWS)

As a leader, understanding my own I.D.™ and those of my team has freed up my time; we all now achieve much better outcomes because we know how to approach each other. As their boss, I now know how to work things through with them so they can do their job in way that also meets their needs—the first time—so there are now far fewer escalations back to me and better quality outcomes from them.

Jordan Hawke
Head of Retail Sales
Tower Australia Limited

When your team is running a hundred miles an hour it's very easy for people to be focused on themselves, on their own goals, their issues and not be thinking as much about working effectively with others. Silos emerge and the lack of involvement and connection mean that people end up feeling what they don't understand. They make judgements about what people should or shouldn't do and how they should or shouldn't behave. In this context the I.D.™ has been a very valuable tool for me and my team.

One of the things that I particularly like is that there is no inherent value judgement about one I.D.™ being better than another—so instead of people being preoccupied by what their 'profile' says about them they are free to focus on other people and how to get on with them. It has helped each of us understand the connections at a business level as well as at a personal level. The improvements in the way my team relate to and reach out to each other has been palpable.

The I.D.™ has brought significant self-realisation to the team, which has broken down barriers, improved communication and has had a big impact on our productivity.

Jim Hassell
Managing Director, Australasia
Sun Microsystems, Inc.

Acknowledgements

I always knew I would write this book—even though it has taken some fifteen years to complete and about thirteen years of false starts while I figured out a way to do it that would work for me. That way always has been—and probably always will be—for me to surround myself with outstanding people. To that end, I've lived a very 'serendipitous life'—the right people just seem to show up.

The initial encouragement and belief provided by Marg Bentley and Lyn Burgess was invaluable to me—as was their support and active involvement during the ensuing years in which the *I.D. System*™ was brought to life. It really was a team effort.

To the many staff members and consultants who have worked with me since then, you have all been pioneers—and I know you've felt the pain of that at times, just as much as you have also revelled in helping get something so exciting off the ground. In particular, I want to thank Don MacDonald, who has been with me since day one and whose support has never flinched. Gail Freeman and Al Ramos have also been there for virtually the whole journey—sharing all the triumphs and tribulations—so thank you.

What a gift Tracy Kennedy has been to me! What started as a four-month, international work-experience stint continued for four years—with Tracy quickly becoming my right-hand person. She was the first to facilitate our training programs and gain the I.D.™ 'black belt'—thereby giving everybody else the confidence that they could do it too. You helped build much of what we have today, Tracy. To Tracy's mother, Linda, thank you for steering your daughter in my direction and for your support and friendship through many tough years.

How do I acknowledge the extensive contribution of Greg Meyer? The tools and resources available now for people to not only understand their I.D.™, but also to use it have much to do with your passion and unique skill. You have protected me and I.D.™ in so many ways, but—most importantly—you have relentlessly ensured we are congruent to our vision. You also introduced Anneke Fitzgerald to the I.D. System™.

Anneke Fitzgerald (PhD) and her research team at the University of Western Sydney have also made a unique contribution. Their research has added that vital academic credibility piece that was missing for so long, and your faith in me and your passion for my vision has meant just as much.

To my many clients, our live experiences with you have given us the ingredients to pull together the substance that is now within this book. Please know that you have therefore made a significant difference. I want to specifically thank Cheryl MacNaught and Noel Whittaker—and their company—who have been clients right from the start, and who have always been very public in their support of both me and I.D.™ You have been an inspiration to me while writing this book.

I have a special relationship with Cisco Systems and enjoy working with the people there immensely. In particular, I want to thank Randy Pond for his active support and friendship and for the kind words he contributed to this book. You've taught me and inspired me far more than you realise. You challenge me to keep growing so I can always add fresh value to you, your team and your organisation. And thanks to Brad Cook for getting this amazing journey started, which was a whole seven years ago now!

To Greg Hodge, thank you for your stunning foreword. Our time together with the swimmers remains one of my favourite career highlights. Your ethics, skill and genuine care for the holistic development and wellbeing of elite athletes always inspired me to give you my best.

Acknowledgements

To my current team of staff and consultants, thank you for the passion, commitment and sheer hard work that you contribute every single day—I am so proud of you. You are amazing people and I love working with you. You set a great example of what a high-performance team really looks like. Thank you also to my manager, Peter Read, for your unswerving loyalty to me.

I needed a special person to help me write this book and I found that person in Karen McCreadie. I want everyone to know that Karen is a genius! Thank you, Karen, for your passion and your outstanding skill. Thank you also for working so patiently with me, meeting every deadline and making it so much fun.

As for my personal circle, I would—first and foremost—like to say thank you to my beautiful wife, Kim, whom I adore. I finally got this done! Can you believe it? I love sharing my life with you, and I totally appreciate your untiring patience and support, not just while this book has been written, but always. I know it's challenging at times being married to someone who is passionately driving a vision, but I often feel like I can only do it because I have you to come home to. I love you.

To my gorgeous kids, Laura, Mitchell, Jace and Sam, no father could love his children more nor be more proud of them than I am of you. Nor could he learn more from them or have more fun with them than I do with you. Thanks for giving it all back to me in spades—I love how that works. You inspire me every day to be—and give—my best.

I am also privileged to be stepfather to Kim's children—Matt, Sharn, Lindsay and Jarrad—an instant party! You are all so loving and accepting and you make it easy for us all to be together. You make our family fun.

To my siblings and their families—along with Mum and Dad—thank you for always believing in me and supporting me. Together with my faith, I'm sure they're the greatest gifts you could have given me.

Finally, to all my friends—they know who they are—you influence me more than you know. My life is so much richer because of you and I always cherish every minute we spend together. To all of you—and others who I'm not able to list here by name—I hope that you each know the very simple truth of my journey. I couldn't have done this without you.

Foreword

I first met Paul when he was working with a young athlete who was in my swim program at Sutherland Leisure Centre, in Sydney, Australia. This guy in a bright tie and colourful trouser braces turned up on pool deck to talk about 'Kate'. This was early in the 1990s. As a school teacher and swim coach I was extremely interested in human behaviour and how best I could motivate and challenge the kids in my classroom and swim squad. The I.D.™ principles made immediate sense to me. I needed to be involved. I was hooked.

I decided to introduce the I.D. System™ to twenty of our best teenage athletes and I believe it had a profound impact on the squad as a team, on each of the children who applied it (six of them went on to become Olympians or members of the Australian Swim team), on their families and certainly on my coaching and future career. In fact the one athlete whose father was skeptical and therefore did not participate in the program was the only one of these twenty who I believe was held back from being an Olympian and from having a successful tertiary education experience and career.

For me, the I.D.™ helped me better understand my own coaching style and how it impacted on each swimmer. It was insightful to realise how they interpreted my coaching style and my communication—athletes respond to coaches in different ways. It is not enough for the coach to present his or her training programs in one way. I clearly remember 'Steve', for whom too much information just confused him. His training (and results) improved dramatically when I pitched the manner of my delivery differently for him. Then there was 'Kathy' who needed to know every aspect of every part of the training sessions (even before they started) so she could plan her effort accordingly.

The self-awareness gained by each swimmer made it easier for them to have stronger self-belief and to be able to be more accepting of others. No longer did athletes complain because one athlete missed a few laps while others did more yards, or why some athletes needed much more of the coach's time for one-on-one instruction whereas others could function effectively with group talks. And, given how well I came to understand the kids, I was even able to help the parents communicate better with their children.

As I moved away from club coaching into managing the High Performance programs for the NSW Institute of Sport and later Australian Swimming, the impact of the *I.D. System*™ profoundly influenced the implementation of new and innovative programs. I wish that I had this book with me then, but I was fortunate to have Paul 'on hand' to steer me right when I was unsure or needed further schooling in getting the best out of the athletes.

Since Paul invites you to go straight to the section of the book which interests you, naturally I went to the section on kids and parenting. My children are adults with family of their own now so it was a bit of a 'retrospective' but it did also give me further insight into my new grandson and my daughter as a parent. Paul provides practical insights and strategies by using his own family experiences which will resonate loudly with many readers. The *I.D.*™ is presented in a fun and humorous way which all readers will enjoy regardless of their interest in the total book. Kids are interesting, challenging, unique and fun and all these leap out at you from the pages of the book, making it simultaneously informative and enjoyable.

From Paul's analogies and descriptions of parent behaviour I could readily identify myself and recall many other 'styles' I have seen over the years as a teacher and coach. This book will help you find out about yourself, your kids and others.

The I.D.™ is an important concept in today's complex world and allows greater flexibility for individuals, parents, teachers, coaches, team leaders and managers by providing us all with an accurate insight into the true person with whom we are interacting. I'm delighted that Paul has finally written this book and I strongly recommend you read it — better yet, apply it.

Greg Hodge
Former Head Coach
Swimming Australia
March 2007

Introduction

Our quest for happiness, fulfilment and success has been the topic of thousands — possibly millions — of books. It has spawned the explosion of personal development courses and workshops aimed at unleashing our hidden potential and finding our true purpose. What is it that makes people successful? Is there a pattern to success? Is there a pattern to failure? What is happiness? Is it possible to feel a sense of fulfilment most of the time? Can we really have it all?

There are a plethora of theories and ideologies that profess to have the answers. Some would say all you need to do is find your passion and discover what excites you and inspires you — those subjects that you lose yourself in as hours feel like minutes. It's a nice idea and it certainly makes sense, but how many people do you know who are genuinely passionate about something? And how many of those people are making a living in an area or field they love? Chances are you won't know many.

Surely if obtaining success and fulfilment is as simple as finding our passion, we should all be able to possess success and fulfilment. But finding our passion is more easily said than done, I can assure you! Many people who have found their passion did so quite unintentionally. I can't imagine there are many people who sat down one Saturday morning and said, 'Right. Time to find my passion', and then by mere reflection or consultation stumbled across it! Nonetheless I believe there are ways to get close to the bullseye on this one, and I cover that further in chapter 3. Suffice to say, however, that finding your passion is (by itself) not a panacea leading to success and fulfilment.

The other argument strongly advocated is that happiness and success can be found by using your unique talent or ability. You do have a talent or ability that is not shared by everyone. That we all have gifts that make us special is a nice idea, but if it was so easy to identify them, then people would know what they were particularly suited to and be using those gifts to successfully earn a living—and most people are clearly not doing that.

The fact remains that millions of people the world over still squash into train carriages at 7.30 am on their way to another day in a job they hate. Millions of people still feel trapped and miserable in a profession that robs them of self-esteem and joy. Millions of people continue the cycle that sees them come home from work thoroughly exhausted. They slump into the settee to escape into a couple of hours of mindless TV before falling asleep, only to wake the next day, dog tired, to start the process again.

Adages such as 'Do what you love and the money will follow' have sent us into a frenzy as we search for that elusive Holy Grail. Yet all this talk of finding our passion and locating our talent is not actually helping us find them—and even if it does, finding them does not necessarily lead to a life of success and happiness. There are thousands of theories and methodologies available, and the problem is not that they don't work—it is that they don't always work for everyone. Why not? How is it possible that two people can read the same book or attend the same course and achieve completely different results or outcomes from it? If the information helps to change one person's life, why does it not work for everyone? The fact is all these approaches may be valid—but not for everyone and not all the time. So there has to be something else at work.

This quandary fascinated me for years. What is it that makes someone successful? What makes someone happy? Why is happiness so different for different people? What leads to a sense of fulfilment? Does fulfilment mean different things to different people? If so, why?

The answers to all those questions and more are in this book. I believe the reason we are so often thwarted in our quest for fulfilment and success is that what we seek is too limiting. The concept that there is a specialist niche of some kind that we were born to fill is just too narrow for most of us to find. Especially if we are busy living life and don't have the luxury of spending hours in quiet contemplation. Consequently we are all scurrying around looking for our exact place in the world—the jigsaw puzzle in which our shape fits perfectly and everything suddenly falls into place and makes sense. But finding that niche is like looking for a needle in a million haystacks.

What if it isn't that specific? What if happiness and success are a product of how you live rather than what you do? What if happiness can be found in a multitude of places and professions

> *What if happiness and success are a product of how you live rather than what you do?*

that are radically different yet share certain characteristics? What if your destiny isn't to be a writer, for example, but instead to live an unstructured, creative life? Then whether you find that lifestyle as a writer, an accountant or a horse breeder wouldn't actually matter that much would it? What if we are searching for the wrong thing? If we just need to find the right haystack and not necessarily the needle within it? Wouldn't the search be significantly easier?

My research, which I share with you through this book, proves that we are indeed searching for the wrong thing. Yes, we do have gifts and talents that make us unique. And yes, it would be fun to be able to use those talents in everyday life. But talent alone is not the magic bullet. Neither is passion—I have met people over the years that are genuinely passionate about what they do, yet that alone does not make them happy or successful. I have also met people who believe they have a talent and have demonstrated it to amazing effect, and yet they are still not happy—at least not consistently. Certainly passion and talent helps, but to gain real, lasting fulfilment, it's also necessary to apply the skills—even the seemingly insignificant ones—that come naturally to you. For example, Steve Irwin proved himself to be extremely passionate about wildlife and conservation—and that passion took him a long way in his career; however, Steve's success was not only a product of his passion, but also a product of his other, quite-observable skills—such as his people and communication skills.

Passion or talent is one thing—*Instinctive Drives*™ (*I.D.*™) are quite another. It is *Instinctive Drive*™ (an underlying motivation) that offers you a blueprint for success and happiness. Finding out what instinctively motivates you and discovering your natural operating system can transform your life—and that's what *I.D.*™ is all about.

Your *I.D.*™ is your *Instinctive Drive*™; it is what motivates you to do the things you do and it never changes. By knowing the fundamental building blocks of your self and how they manifest in life, you are armed with the knowledge and insight to make decisions that will support your happiness and success rather than work against your grain. (If you turn to appendix C, you will find details about having your *I.D.*™ profile assessed by Link-up International at a special discounted price available only to readers.)

We have all experienced moments in which we were 'in stride'—some call it being 'in the zone'—yet if you think back to two or three instances of this in your life you were probably not doing the same thing each time. You might have felt in stride while you were on a sports field, in a meeting or perhaps while giving a presentation at a company event. Perhaps you were alone for some experiences, in a group for others, and sometimes at work or play? So how can things feel so natural and effortless in one situation and difficult and laborious a week later? *I.D.*™ unlocks that puzzle—it unlocks what makes you *you*.

Previously there have been two schools of thought on identity—one says that genetics or nature plays a major role in who we become, and the other proposes that nurture exerts more influence. Through the course of my research I profiled identical twins, and they had very different characteristics—which was evident even in the way they did things. I have also profiled people through generations of families and, again, they are very different—no correlations or patterns. So it can't just be genetic. If who we are is just about nurture then siblings brought up in the same way would have similar personalities, yet any parents with more than one child will tell you that their children are totally different—'like chalk and cheese' is the expression most parents use. I have four children who have the same parents and were brought up in the same way, yet they are each unique—and the characteristics that make them special were apparent within weeks of being born. So there has to be something else influencing who we become!

What if I was to tell you that the key to success and happiness is just a few pages away? What if you could find what you've been searching for wherever you choose to look? What if finding your passion is not the Holy Grail—some epic search that would lead you from one frustrating disappointment to the next? What if I was to tell you that happiness and success are not the product of finding your passion, but rather of understanding your own I.D.™ and living in a way that is congruent to your true self—that essential nature that makes you who you are? What if I was to tell you that you could eliminate stress in your life, regain your health and cut down medication or eliminate it? What if you could feel a sense of fulfilment and joy as a permanent experience, rather than as an occasional and random occurrence dependant on external forces beyond your control? What if I could show you a way to enjoy a sense of achievement, operate at peak performance, enjoy high self-esteem and self-worth and have oodles of energy—just by understanding the nuances of how you uniquely work best?

I can show you a system that will never let you down and a way of living that is suited to your essential nature that will result in your success, happiness and fulfilment.

Welcome to I.D. —Instinctive Drives™ —your pass key to happiness, consistent success and rewarding relationships.

Paul Burgess
Sydney
March 2007

Chapter 1

The I.D. System™

Before I introduce the *I.D. System™* I want to spend a little time explaining the development of it—where it came from and how its emergence came about. I discovered the four *Instinctive Drives™* in 1991 after much research. My extensive study was fuelled by my fascination about what makes people tick and what needs to happen for them to operate at their best.

Initially I explored a number of popular profiling systems because they promised answers about personality and the suitability of different personalities to specific situations. Yet my experience with these other techniques told me that although they were often interesting, they were not always accurate. Nor did they actually facilitate change or provide the recipients of the profile with any clear direction on how to use the newly discovered information. The other systems available did not seem to enable people to get to grips with the quirks of their personality or make any lasting impression or difference to the individual—other than providing interesting dinner-party conversation.

One model that particularly caught my attention, Kolbe, proposed to study natural talents and behaviour. I trained in this methodology and used it for several years because I felt it more closely reflected my own beliefs about human nature. I tried to use it to assist people to understand themselves better and therefore to assist them through periods of change—especially in the field of succession planning. What I found, however, was that the more I immersed myself in that product and the more people I introduced to its profiling technique, the more I found inconsistencies that caused me to question some of its fundamental assumptions. For some people it provided them with interesting information about themselves that seemed to validate parts of their character they had perhaps been wrestling with; for others it not only offered little value, but it also labelled them in a way that was totally contrary to their own personal experience and success. For example, I once worked with someone whose profile indicated that he would not be good or comfortable in sales. Yet he worked in that field, and, more importantly, he loved it and was good at it. I thought perhaps it was because he was new to the industry and that once the initial enthusiasm wore off he would indeed find that it was not a suitable career for him. So I visited him many months later to see if my theory had played out. It hadn't—he was having a ball! I knew he wasn't being overly zealous to prove a point because I interviewed his wife, boss and colleagues to see if what he was telling me was accurate in the eyes of those around him—and it was. Everyone I met told me how fantastic he was and how much he enjoyed the business. Yet his profile indicated that he would not be suitable to that profession.

This bothered me. A fundamental purpose of profiling is to enable organisations and individuals to make better career choices so that the individual is in the right place and the organisation doesn't waste money recruiting people who don't 'fit' that role. But if these methods of analysis are not always accurate, then surely that can be quite disastrous for the individual as well as the organisation—and it can indeed have significant legal consequences.

In contrast to other profiling systems—which pigeonhole people into roles or behaviours—the I.D. System™ provides people with an I.D.™ that gives them a blueprint for the life they will live. It doesn't tell them what profession they will pursue or whom they will marry, but it does tell them what will drive them, what will inspire them and what will make them happy and fulfilled. It indicates a natural, normal operating style.

What if my sales guy's employer had done his profile prior to him joining the company and decided based on that feedback that he wasn't right for the job? The guy in question would have missed out on a job he excels in and loves, and his employer would have missed out on a top-class salesperson. I was sure there was something else at work that was somehow being missed by this and many other existing profiling techniques. So I set out to find what was missing and in the process pulled my own thoughts and observations together to create my own proprietary model.

What I knew for sure was that many of the existing profiling tools—although interesting—were measuring behaviour—not drive or motivation. I was equally sure that we are not defined by our behaviour. Therefore looking solely at *what* someone does is not an accurate reflection of *who* that person is, and it is certainly not an accurate reflection of what he or she is capable of. What I was interested in was not *what* was done but *why* it was done. Take two list writers, for example, who both start their week with a 'to do list'. The behaviour is the same but the reason behind that behaviour could be very different. One could be motivated to write lists because it gives her a sense of control and order, whereas the other person may write lists to obtain a sense of achievement when he ticks the items off. They are characteristics of two different drives, yet the external behaviour is exactly the same. In other words, looking at the behaviour actually tells you nothing useful about the person at all.

> The behaviour is the same but the reason behind that behaviour could be very different

It was this type of paradox that was, in my opinion, causing the anomalies in many of the existing profiling tools. The other profiling tools were assessing behaviour and making assumptions based on it that were not always accurate. This was a critical distinction and one I was convinced lay at the heart of an alternative approach. Although it may seem like a minor point initially, it is not. If I was to watch what you do today, I would not be able to use that behaviour as an accurate prediction for what you will do tomorrow. If, on the other hand, I understand why you did what you did, then I would be much more able to accurately predict what you will do tomorrow because I understand your innate motivation.

Once you understand the *why* you become much more adept at successfully influencing the *what*. Not only that, but once you understand the why you can much more accurately predict behaviour and outcomes because you can appreciate the motivations that are sparking them. Not only does your motivation increase significantly, but your areas of competency, your ability to focus and your decision-making skills—including synthesising information and then taking action—also improve. This leads to increased productivity and an improved ability to resolve issues and build constructive, meaningful relationships. Also, your sense of achievement, fulfilment and self-worth are all positively affected because you can tap into your driving force—once you know what it is of course.

It's very difficult to tap into the wellspring of creativity, interest, enthusiasm and passion—the consequences of being motivated—if you don't know what drives your motivation. I was convinced, therefore, that if I could find a way to accurately and consistently highlight motivation—the *why* behind action and behaviour—then I would be able to offer the world a way of tapping into that wellspring at will. I envisioned a way for everyone to feel truly happy—and that would be very powerful indeed.

So convinced that this was the missing piece of the puzzle, I set about finding it. I began by simply talking to people about why they did what they did. Everyone I met was a potential research subject. I was obsessed by it and I would always delve more deeply than the initial answers my prospects gave me.

This process of continuing to ask a question over and over to get to greater levels of clarity is a technique I now call *level 4 questioning*. Level 4 questioning involves asking for the motive behind each answer, until you get down to a core truth.

So, for example, I would ask:

Q: 'Why did you choose to become an accountant?'
A: 'Because I've always loved numbers.'

Q: 'What is it about numbers that you like so much?'
A: 'They are not subjective.'

Q: 'What's wrong with subjectivity?'
A: 'Nothing—it's just that I prefer to work with absolutes.'

Q: 'Why are absolutes so important to you?'
A: 'Because there is no grey area. In accounting it's either right or it's wrong. I know when I'm right.'

As I continued to question everyone in my path, I discovered this same need to be right was common. I found that once people were probed for more detail they would indicate that they were fundamentally driven to 'get it right', 'make it right', 'keep it right' or 'do the right thing'. Perhaps I had found the first why? I certainly knew this motivation was true for me!

But being right wasn't the only motivator for people I interviewed. When I spoke to my wife at that time, Lyn, about her motivation for doing things, 'getting it right' had nothing to do with it. What motivated her was a desire for harmony; she was motivated to ensure everything fitted together and worked like clockwork. Again this seemed to play out with significant numbers of people I asked; a need for harmony seemed to be a very strong motivating force.

Margaret, the principal of my children's school and a member of the original *I.D.*™ development team, knew that neither of these things meant anything for her—nothing about them resonated. In fact what was really interesting was that they actually repelled and demotivated her. For Margaret thrived on the challenge of doing something new, of being thrown in at the deep end and of performing under pressure and working against the odds—where, invariably, she felt compelled to find a way forward. I distinctly remember us talking about this, and I could see the enthusiasm and energy 'turn on' before my eyes. I was sure this was the third piece of the puzzle.

I defined these motivating forces, in order of development, as the following:

- the *Instinctive Drive to Verify*™
- the *Instinctive Drive to Complete*™
- the *Instinctive Drive to Improvise*™.

I decided to call them *Instinctive Drives*™ because I knew what I was exploring was instinctive—and instinct, by definition, relates to how something drives us to be a certain way. Just as a soldier's dogtag is his or her ID, so too is *Instinctive Drive™* our internal identifier. It is our innate nature and it remains unaltered throughout our life—regardless of conditioning, upbringing, attitudes or beliefs. It wasn't until after I had been using the term for some time that someone pointed out Freud's concept of the *id*, which he believed was a part of the structure of the mind and the home of the primitive instincts and energies in the unconscious mind. In other words, *Instinctive Drive™* proved to be the perfect name.

By this stage virtually everyone I talked to began to relate to one or more of these three motivations. But then I met medical specialist Dr Howard Chilton, a director of neonatal care at the Royal Hospital for Women in Sydney. Part of his job was informing parents when their child had been diagnosed with a disability such as Down Syndrome. He told me about a couple who had received very sad news about their child and came back a couple of weeks later for a check-up. When he asked them how they were, their response was 'Yes, we're fine'. Dr Chilton told me that after hearing their response he just found it really difficult to communicate with them because he felt as though they weren't being completely honest with him. He understood that denial was a normal emotion to feel at difficult times, but for him it made moving forward in a positive way very hard to do. He said, 'If I am going to deal with people, there must be congruency, a genuineness, a certain level of congruency and honesty between how we relate to each other'. This was a motivation that did not fit into any of the initial three drives—it was something different. After extensive testing and empirical research I came to describe that instinct as the *Instinctive Drive to Authenticate™*.

I had now identified four *Instinctive Drives™*. Initially I had hoped that there would be more than four because I was aware that many profiling systems—such as Myers-Briggs, Kolbe, DISC and HBDI—also have four indicators. But every single person I spoke to would invariably be driven by at least one of these four *Instinctive Drives™*:

➪ the *Instinctive Drive to Verify™* (The need to make sure you're doing the right thing—and then doing it right.)

➪ the *Instinctive Drive to Authenticate™* (The need for your personal involvement and environment to be congruent and transparent.)

➪ the *Instinctive Drive to Complete™* (The need for harmony and efficiency in everything.)

⟫ the *Instinctive Drive to Improvise*™ (The need for excitement and animation to energise you to perform at your best.).

Interestingly, I found that people were often attracted to people and environments that reflected the opposite of their drive because it meant that there was a need for them to 'do their thing'. For example:

⟫ People who are driven to Verify would be attracted to problems or complexity because that gives them an opportunity to sort it out and make it right.

⟫ Those with the Authenticate drive would be attracted to things that are broken or unproductive because it gives them a chance to fix it and do something productive.

⟫ People who are driven to Complete wouldn't be able to resist a mess or a crisis because it is the classic opportunity for them to restore peace and harmony.

⟫ Those with the Improvise drive need to breathe life and hope into situations, so they can be found in places where there is little hope or excitement and where they can produce results against the odds!

As human beings we need to feel needed. It seems, therefore, that we are attracted to places and situations in which we can use our talents and abilities to make things better. Ironically once we have brought our gifts to a situation and fixed the crisis or injected enthusiasm into it, we are driven to find new environments where we can repeat that process.

Armed with these insights, I talked to Margaret about my observations. Her reaction to the *Instinctive Drive to Verify*™ and the *Instinctive Drive to Complete*™ alerted me to the possibility that there may be directions within each drive. It wasn't as if Margaret was neutral about her reaction to the idea of 'getting it right' or 'creating harmony'—indeed she actively distanced herself from it. Others talked about 'avoiding these things with a passion!' Clearly they seemed to draw energy from avoiding—as opposed to using—these drives. This led to the creation of 'Avoid' drives within each of the four drives:

⟫ The need to avoid the *Instinctive Drive to Verify*™ (The need for things to be simple and straightforward rather than complex, and the need to accept things 'as is'.)

⇴ The need to avoid the *Instinctive Drive to Authenticate*™ (The need for leverage, depth and ideals.)

⇴ The need to avoid the *Instinctive Drive to Complete*™ (The need for variety and spontaneity.)

⇴ The need to avoid the *Instinctive Drive to Improvise*™ (The need for certainty, logic and substance.).

I tested this theory and it was plain to see that each individual related to each one of the four drives in varying capacities. I ultimately found that everyone was either driven by an *Instinctive Drive*™, driven to actively avoid it or neutral to its influence. This explains why at the time of writing there were over 700 different combinations of *I.D.s*™.

I have been asked why there were not just eight drives. It would mean that it would be possible to score somewhere on each of the eight drives; however, that wasn't possible. For example, those driven to avoid the *Instinctive Drive to Verify*™ were always driven that way; none of them were ever driven to use the Verify drive. At times they exhibited one or two behaviours commonly associated with the Verify drive, but if I delved beneath the surface to understand why they did something, there was always a different motivation. For example, someone driven to Avoid Verify needs to avoid being interrogated, and that may compel them to pay attention to the detail and get things right—which would initially look like something someone driven to Verify would do. My point is that for someone to be classified as driven by an instinct, that person would need to demonstrate *all* the behaviours attached to that instinct and show that he or she strives to meet *all* the needs associated with that instinct.

Society's expectations

It became obvious to me when I started to discover *I.D.*™ that motivation was complicated and was never just about one thing. Society, religion, culture and upbringing often dictate that there is a certain way to be. If you were to buy a house, for example, the accepted wisdom on such a big decision would be to look at a number of different properties, study the market, think about it for a while and then make a considered judgement. Yet for people with particular *Instinctive Drives*™ that would be torture. I know of one such person who went out shopping one day to buy a pair of boots and came back with an apartment. It's a great story but it's also an authentic expression of who she is and a highly predictable experience based on her *I.D.*™.

There are social expectations around many issues. Parenting is a classic example in which there is an agreed 'profile' of what a 'good parent' looks like—a loving, dedicated, organised, conscientious, disciplined, forward-planning, involved individual. Yet not everyone parents the same way, and if you don't hit the accepted benchmarks it can be very hard. It's the same with studying—it is accepted that the 'right way' to study is to diligently and systematically revise all the way up to the exams. Yet for some people that simply doesn't work, and the only way for them to perform at their absolute best is to cram at the last minute under intense pressure because that's how they'll achieve the marks they need. But because it's not the 'right' way to study, they will probably feel enormous pressure to conform from their parents and teachers. The irony is that cramming and last-minute, high-pressure situations *is* the 'right' way for *that* person; by conforming to the stereotypical best-student persona, these types of people are actually doing themselves a huge disserve. The *I.D. System™* identifies these differences and allows people to navigate their own way through life based on what's 'right' for them—not necessarily what's 'right' for society.

Society, religion, culture and upbringing very often dictate that there is a certain way to be

Social expectations, and the degree to which we naturally align to them, are just one of the influences that can alter how our *I.D.™* manifests itself in our life—in short the degree to which we live true to ourselves or not. I refer to these external conditioning influences as 'onion skins' and will discuss them later in this chapter.

Regardless of *I.D.™* we all have to conform to various cultural expectations, laws and rules—and we all can. What drives each of us to do this, however, can be quite different. Some people clean their teeth everyday according to a certain routine. I bet they even do the same number of brush strokes! Yet those who are not as 'routine driven' and probably have a greater need for variety probably brush their teeth a different way each day and at a different time—but they still get it done.

We can all do the same tasks, but we will usually approach them with varying styles and levels of motivation. Yet we might each succeed at that same task. My point is that it all comes down to how we perceive a task or situation and whether that perception aligns to our *I.D.™* or not.

Components of the complete *I.D. System*™

As discussed earlier, it is important to remember that although I often discuss each drive separately for ease of understanding, a person's *I.D.*™ is actually made up of all four drives of different intensities and directions. This means there are many, many different *I.D.s*™. In addition, everyone is affected by conditioning, so it is even possible for two people with the same *I.D.*™ to be quite dissimilar. Clearly the *I.D. System*™ is more complex than it seems, so this chapter provides an easy to understand overview of the main features of it.

Intensity of Drives

An individual's *I.D.*™ is represented by four numbers. Those numbers reflect the intensity of each drive and determine how a combination of them plays out in life. For each drive there is a scale of 1 to 9, reflecting how strongly an individual is driven by that instinct. The information below shows the consequences of that scale for *I.Ds*™. A scale of:

▷ 1 to 4 indicates the individual is driven to avoid that *Instinctive Drive*™

▷ 5 indicates that the person is neutral towards that drive and is motivated neither to use nor avoid it

▷ 6 to 9 indicates the individual is driven to use that *Instinctive Drive*™.

Take my *I.D.*™ of 8147 as an example. The profile indicates I am:

▷ 8 in Verify (driven by the *Instinct to Verify*™)

▷ 1 in Authenticate (driven to Avoid the *Instinct to Authenticate*™)

▷ 4 in Complete (driven to Avoid the *Instinct to Complete*™)

▷ 7 in Improvise (driven by the *Instinct to Improvise*™).

My strongest score is a 1 in Authenticate and it is therefore my most intense drive. Remember that the intensity of your drive increases the further your score in that drive moves away from 5 in either direction. So my score of 1 is the most extreme 'avoid' ranking you can achieve, and my second most intense drive is in Verify, with a score of 8. Figure 1.1 shows my *I.D.*™ profile. An *I.D.*™ profile provides an easy-to-understand, visual representation of a person's unique combination of *Instinctive Drives*™.

Figure 1.1: my *I.D.*™ profile

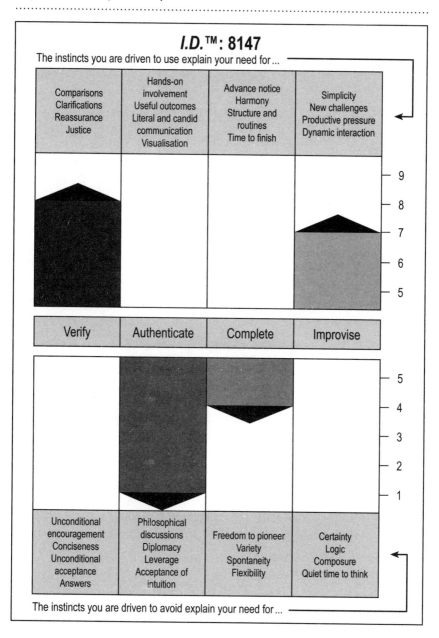

I.D.™: 8147

The instincts you are driven to use explain your need for...

Verify	Authenticate	Complete	Improvise
Comparisons Clarifications Reassurance Justice	Hands-on involvement Useful outcomes Literal and candid communication Visualisation	Advance notice Harmony Structure and routines Time to finish	Simplicity New challenges Productive pressure Dynamic interaction
Unconditional encouragement Conciseness Unconditional acceptance Answers	Philosophical discussions Diplomacy Leverage Acceptance of intuition	Freedom to pioneer Variety Spontaneity Flexibility	Certainty Logic Composure Quiet time to think

The instincts you are driven to avoid explain your need for...

Combination of drives

Your *I.D.*™ is determined by the combination of all four of your drives. So my 8 in Verify is affected by my scores in each of the other three *Instinctive Drives*™ and the same applies to each of my other 3 scores.

That's why the whole *I.D.*™ is used when understanding someone's true motivations, needs and talents, rather than simply referring to only one key instinct. For example, if I was 8174 instead of 8147, not only would my 8 in Verify present differently because of the change in the Complete and Improvise drives, but so also would my whole *I.D.* I would essentially be a completely different person.

Everyone has one score in each drive which indicates if you are driven to use, avoid or are neutral to that drives influence. All combinations of drives are possible, and none are better or worse than others—just different.

An *I.D.* cannot be guessed

Your *I.D.*™ score is determined by the *I.D.*™ questionnaire—an extensively researched and validated profiling instrument. Completing the questionnaire is the only accurate way to determine your *I.D.*™ Reading this book will certainly give you a good grasp of the concepts, but the only way to know for sure is to complete the *I.D.*™ questionnaire.

The *I.D.* is just one component of the comprehensive *I.D. System*™. The complete system includes a scoring algorithm, the resulting bar chart and *I.D.*™ report, a management strategy report and an extensive library of strategies for help in being 'in stride' in life, relationships and career challenges. It also includes associated models—the *Peak Performance Indicator*™ and the Onion Skin model—that provide a comprehensive understanding of the subtle connections between instinctive motivations (*I.D.*™) and behaviour and personality.

You can find the *I.D.*™ questionnaire as well as the latest research findings from the University of Western Sydney on the reliability and validity of the questionnaire on the Link-up International website at <www.idcentral.com.au>.

Identical *I.Ds* don't mean identical people

How your particular *I.D.*™ plays out in your life is very much dependent on your view of the world or, as I refer to them, your 'onions skins'. Onion skins are the layers of conditioning and personal experience that contribute over time to your perceptions of life. These layers represent your values, beliefs, confidence, self-esteem, upbringing, family environment, skills, knowledge and attitude.

Even though your *I.D.*™ doesn't change over time, some of your onion skins can and therefore your behaviour and personality can change.

Distribution of drives throughout the population

The four *Instinctive Drives*™ are equally represented throughout the general population. This challenges the many stereotyped roles and expectations that society has created—affecting everyone from boys and girls, men and women, husbands and wives, parents and children, to teachers and students, employers and employees, and leaders and their teams.

The Onion Skin model

Earlier in this chapter I mentioned the Onion Skin model. I use it to explain how nature (*I.D.*™) blends with nurture to determine how our *I.D.*™ influences our resulting actions, behaviour and personality.

The age-old 'nature versus nurture' debate assumes that human behaviour is predominantly determined by either nature or nurture—in other words, an either/or debate. Yet I believe our actions are a result of both influences—both nature and nurture. As figure 1.2 (overleaf) shows, the Onion Skin model uses layers of an onion to represent the nurture elements—or external conditioning influences—that combine with our nature (*I.D.*™) to determine the behaviour and personality we present to others. Like onions, human beings are also made up of layers, and at the core is the essential, natural self—*I.D.*™—which does not change over time. *I.D.*™ is a way of understanding what our nature is—what really drives us.

Surrounding the innate core of *I.D.*™ (at the centre of the onion) are much more flexible layers that combine to make you the person you are today.

These layers are the elements of your life that are influenced by nurture, and they explain why people with exactly the same *I.D.*™ can express themselves completely differently.

Take an *I.D.*™ with a strong Improvise drive, for example. Typically these people thrive on a challenge, positive energy and excitement. Living on the edge for them feels exhilarating; they don't see or worry as much about the risks, instead seeing the potential opportunities.

One Improvise person could meet those needs by becoming a cat burglar, while the other could fulfil them by becoming a venture capitalist. Both scenarios fulfil the need for excitement and challenge, yet how each person expresses that drive is dependent on elements of nurture explained by the Onion Skin model. How was he raised? Who were her major influencing forces? Where did he live? What did her parents do for a living and what did they expect from their child? How well did he do in school?

Figure 1.2: the Onion Skin model

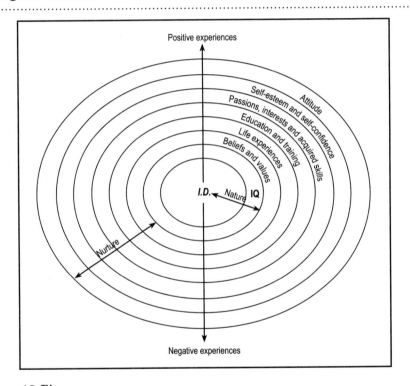

I.D.™

I.D.™ is constant and doesn't change over time. It is always true. However, how *Instinctive Drive*™ plays out in your life can change based on the influence of the other layers.

IQ

IQ in this context refers to intellectual capacity and natural abilities—such as artistic flair, memory, sports, design, dexterity, speaking or writing. These are relatively fixed. They can be impaired by age, illness or injury, and sometimes by low self-esteem or by you not using them enough. Sometimes abilities simply stay undiscovered!

Beliefs and values

Although beliefs and values are often perceived as stable, they can be influenced by people, experiences, education and the media.

Life experiences

Life experiences include defining moments and significant emotional events that can have either a positive or a negative impact. These influences vary on a daily basis.

Education and training

Education and training remains stable depending on ongoing relevance and application. Although new knowledge can alter them.

Passions, interests and acquired skills

These can change over time—especially if you are exposed to new experiences. But they remain fairly consistent for long periods.

Self-esteem and self-confidence

Self-esteem and self-confidence are partly innate in that some people naturally display higher levels of them than others. Society dictates what a self-confident person with high self-esteem should look like—but it is a stereotype that is based on certain drives. True self-esteem and self-confidence comes from within and is largely a consequence of the cumulative effect of other layers. This layer and the Attitude layer are deeper than the other nurture layers because they exert the most influence in daily life.

Attitude

Attitude is partly innate; however, it is also largely dependent on emotional intelligence (the ability to rise above circumstance and still feel in control over life). Of course attitude is influenced by the other layers.

....

In other words, life experiences, parental influences and education all shape the values and beliefs that then determine the way *I.D.*™ plays out. So what 'right' means to one Verify-driven person may mean something quite different to another person with the same *I.D.*™. Likewise, harmony to one Complete-driven person, may actually be disruptive to another Complete-driven person—indeed these definitions can even change for the same person over time. For example, I remember thinking that it was right to persevere in an argument until I 'won' by persuading the other person to see my point of view. Then someone helped me see that for me to 'win', the other person needed to 'lose', which, in effect, would cause me to lose too. So I was cleverly given a new perspective that would become one of my strongest guiding principles or new 'right' for dealing with debates in a relationship: 'Be wrong, so that others can be right'. Although I am still driven to 'get it right', my definition of it has changed. Herein lies the key to helping people achieve behaviour change—help them find a new definition!

Therefore to fully understand a person we need to understand their I.D.™ (of course), but we also need to understand these onion skin layers. To my knowledge there is no profile system that can accurately pinpoint those layers—and nor do I believe that there should be. It is those unique layers that set people apart, and I believe you can only discover and understand those layers in other people when you are in a relationship with them—it's what relationships are all about. I often explain it this way: the I.D.™ helps you know where someone lives—not just the country, but also the city, suburb and street—but to get inside that house you need to be invited. In other words, people need to invite you into their 'home' before they can reveal all the other rooms—their onion skin layers. So if truly relating to someone requires this level of relationship and investment of time, you might wonder what the value is of knowing their I.D.™ The answer is it gets you straight to the front door. How much time and energy would you waste if you knew the suburb that someone lived in, but didn't know where their actual house was!

My personal experience, that of my consultants and clients and all the anecdotal evidence that I've accumulated over the years clearly demonstrate that both nature *and* nurture are important in terms of how our lives turn out, and how we affect and are perceived by others.

I.D.™ is, in my opinion, more significant than the onion-skin layers because it:

➪   is the driving force

➪   doesn't change over time

➪   is ours (not derived from our parents or anyone else)

☞ is the natural operating system on which all the other components rely.

Above all you must be true to your *I.D.*™ if you are to reach all the potential that life holds for you. If you're not true to it, then you will live with some sense of compromise.

Unconscious nurturing

These nurture elements are made up of conscious and unconscious elements as well as passive and active influences; for example, training and education is an active influence, whereas conditioning is often passive and unconscious yet it can greatly influence how our *I.D.*™ presents in the world. All these influences can, of course, be either positive or negative.

A great deal of our conditioning is unconscious. Although conditioning is an ongoing process, most of the major conditioning takes place in our formative years. As children, we determine 'normal behaviour' by looking at our family and living conditions. What we believe as adults (unless we consciously choose to alter it) is greatly influenced by the beliefs, values and attitudes of the people we grew up with—our family, friends and teachers. What our parents or key role models believed was possible, their values and opinions, and their attitudes and expectations all have a significant impact on how we see the world. We are influenced by where we lived—the cultural, social and religious beliefs of our environment. We are conditioned by significant emotional events and by how we were treated as children—and whether we were loved and nurtured. All of these elements come together consciously and unconsciously to influence our view of the world and of ourselves. Often our *I.D.*™ does not align with cultural expectations or family norms and this too can add pressure to us—initially as children and later as adults—as we are made to feel different and even a little isolated as a result.

> As children, we determine 'normal behaviour' by looking at our family and living conditions

The good news, however, is that although you don't have much control over this process or the past, you can change the future and rewrite the scripts of your conditioning. The truer you become to your *I.D.*™, the better your life will become—to thine own self be true!

So what about the new-age notion that you can be anything we want to be? That you can change a great deal of your past conditioning to liberate yourself from imposed and outmoded limitations and expectations has led to an 'anything's possible' mentality. Although this is certainly true, I believe the real questions you need to be asking are not 'Can I do this?', but instead:

⇨ How do I do this in a way that is true to me?

⇨ Can I sustain it at an optimum level?

⇨ Is this the best use of my time and talent?

⇨ What price am I paying to do it?

⇨ What else could I be doing that would be more effective and fulfilling for me?

Conscious choice

Although conditioning will determine what we are exposed to—which in turn can influence our interests and passions—we have free choice when it comes to how our life turns out. So a city child who has never even seen a cow may still decide he wants to be a farmer, despite having no exposure to rural life. This interest could first have been piqued through TV documentaries, books or an uncle in Scotland who talks enthusiastically of his experiences as a boy growing up on a farm. In other words, school, friends and expanded horizons will all influence what we are interested in and passionate about—and that will affect how we interact with the world.

Training and education can also have a profound influence on how I.D.™ expresses itself in life. Feeding your mind, learning new skills and discovering new abilities influence your attitudes and ideas about the world, and this can challenge your original conditioning. Studying in a new town, city or even country, for example, can massively influence how you see things. If you moved to this new environment, not only would new knowledge expand your thinking, but access to other extra-curricula activities and new people would provide you with different ideas and philosophies. All of these things can alter your past conditioning and make you question long-held beliefs, perhaps realising that what you thought and were told isn't always true. These influences and the day-to-day experiences of your life will affect your attitude and perception. All these factors also come together to determine your confidence and self-esteem. Finding out who you really are, working out for yourself what you really believe and having conviction in that position feels good!

In my experience working with thousands of people over the last fifteen years, the onion skin layers that make the biggest difference between two similarly skilled, experienced and educated people are confidence, self-esteem and attitude. Interestingly, enough it is these three areas that are most affected when someone embarks on a journey of personal growth and development. Over the years I have met many people who have attended various workshops and had the opportunity to unravel some of their unconscious conditioning—and it is their attitude and confidence that rises as a result. You can't erase the past but you can always decide to view it differently!

I have one friend who has spent thousands of dollars and hours in workshops and courses. She's driven by the *Instinct to Improvise*™ and loves the energy and buzz of the seminar environment and enjoys learning. One of the things that used to irritate her about herself despite all the training was that her first response when asked to do something was always to say yes. She thought that—as an adult with more maturity and greater sense of responsibility—she should've learned to use a more considered approach with her decision making, yet once she did her I.D.™ and found she was driven very strongly by the *Instinct to Improvise*™, she realised that her supposed flaw was just a trait of the drive. Simply knowing she didn't posses a weakness completely changed her attitude to the behaviour.

People are often quick to think that characteristics of their personality are weaknesses or problems that need to be fixed. They look around and wonder what's wrong with them. I'm often asked, 'Why can't I trust people?', 'Why am I so unmotivated?', 'Why is it that some people just seem happy all the time' or 'Why am I so indecisive?' Although I don't have the answers to those questions, remember that there is no perfect I.D.™—none is better or worse than another. More importantly no I.D.™ has the license on trust, happiness or motivation. But if you understand your I.D.™ and make adjustments to the way you live and work based on those innate needs, then you will be happier. If you take a closer look at the elements of your life that have also influenced who you are today, make conscious changes to your attitude, open your mind and expand your horizons, then there is no end to what you can achieve. As Saint Francis of Assisi says, 'Grant me the serenity to accept the things I cannot change [*I.D.*™]; the courage to change the things I can [onion skins]; and the wisdom to know the difference [EQ]'.

The six needs of being human

In the course of developing the *I.D. System*™ I identified needs associated with each direction of each *Instinctive Drive*™ that must be met in order for people to perform at their best and feel fulfilled. I also found other needs that seemed to be relevant to every drive and direction—and indeed for every person. These needs relate to striving and fulfilment and are not necessarily organised within a hierarchy; they are needs that have to be met in order for people to be at their best and in stride.

I'm aware that many others before me have written about human needs—Abraham Maslow is well known for his Hierarchy of Needs and life coach Anthony Robbins also lists six human needs; however, they speak about those needs in terms of a hierarchy, the needs I'm referring to must be fulfilled simultaneously if we are to be at our best. I believe they include the following:

1   The need to *strive* (apply mental energy)

    ⤳   to achieve

    ⤳   to love

    ⤳   to be needed

2   The need to *have your efforts recognised*

    ⤳   to receive attention

    ⤳   to receive recognition

    ⤳   to receive love

3   The need to *strive your way* (using your *I.D.*™)

    ⤳   to avoid stress

    ⤳   to perform at your peak

    ⤳   to build self-esteem

4   The need to *be equal but unique*

　　↝ to be accepted and special

　　↝ to fit in, but stand out

5   The need to *develop cognitively*

　　↝ to have intelligence

　　↝ to possess experience

　　↝ to have skills

6   The need to *use all your cognitive capacity*

　　↝ to have multiple intelligences and expertise

　　↝ to possess experiences

　　↝ to have skills.

Everything we do as human beings is influenced by these needs. If they're not met through positive means, we will unfortunately find negative ways to meet them instead. For example, a troubled teenager joining a gang could simply be looking for a connection and significance because those things were not readily available at home.

Some people argue that the *I.D.*™ appears to simplify the obvious complexity of the human psyche — that simply reducing it to four simple drives is almost an insult to the variety of ingredients that make us tick. But those who have studied the *I.D. System*™ in its entirety soon see that it includes a level of sophistication that honours human beings as a complex species. I simply use the four drives as a starting point for explaining the *I.D. System*™ so that it is relatively easy for people to understand.

However, to understand the intricacies of the *I.D.*™, start with your *I.D.*™. Then add your combination of instincts and intensity of drives — leaving about 10 000 possibilities. Now add the onion skin layers — almost infinite combinations now. Finally, add the degree to which you are meeting the six basic human needs. The answer leaves you with a resulting personality, action or behaviour based upon all those complexities. So yes, it's not as simple as simply knowing the four drives. But as a starting place, it sure makes it possible for people to gain tremendous insight into a whole new world of untapped potential for them.

A story on attitude

Although knowing the intricacies of your *I.D.*™ is essential for reaching your full potential, having the right attitude is also important. Supporting this view is the following inspirational story on attitude that has been circulating the internet and reaching people around the world via email.

Jerry was the kind of guy who was always in a good mood and always had something positive to say. When someone asked him how he was doing, he would reply, 'If I were any better, I would be twins!'. He was a unique manager because he had several waiters who would follow him around from restaurant to restaurant. The waiters followed Jerry because of his attitude — he was a natural motivator. If an employee was having a bad day, Jerry would be there telling him or her how to look on the positive side of the situation.

Seeing this style really made me curious, so one day I went up to Jerry and said to him, 'I don't get it! You can't be a positive person all of the time. How do you do it?'

Jerry replied, 'Each morning I wake up and say to myself, Jerry, you have three choices today. You can choose to be in a good mood or you can choose to be a victim or I can choose to learn from it. I choose to learn from it. I choose the positive side of life.'

'Yeah, right. it's not that easy', I protested.

'Yes it is', Jerry replied. 'Life is all about choices. When you cut away all the junk, every situation is a choice. You choose how to react to situations. You choose how people will affect your mood. You choose to be in a good mood or a bad mood. The bottom line: it's your choice how you live life.'

I reflected on what Jerry said and soon thereafter left the restaurant industry to start my own business. We lost touch, but I often thought about him when I made a choice about life instead of reacting to it.

Several years later I heard that Jerry did something you are never supposed to do in the restaurant business: he left the back door open one morning and was held up at gunpoint by three armed robbers. While trying to open the safe, his hand, shaking from nervousness, slipped off the combination. The robbers panicked and shot him. Luckily Jerry was found relatively quickly and rushed to the local trauma centre. After eighteen hours of surgery and weeks of intensive care, Jerry was released from the hospital with fragments of the bullet still in his body. I saw Jerry about six months after the accident. When I asked him how he was and he replied, 'If I were any better I'd be twins. Want to see my scars?'

I declined to see his wound, but did ask him what had gone through his mind when the robbery took place. 'The first thing that went through my mind was that I should have locked the back door', Jerry replied. 'Then as I lay on the floor, I remember that I had two choices: I could choose to live or I could choose to die. I chose to live.'

'Weren't you scared? Did you lose consciousness?' I asked.

Jerry continued, 'The paramedics were great. They kept telling me I was going to be fine. But when they wheeled me into the emergency room and I saw the expression on the faces of the doctors and nurses, I got really scared. In their eyes, I read, "He's a dead man". I knew I needed to take action.'

'What did you do?' I asked.

'Well, there was a big burly nurse shouting questions at me', said Jerry. 'She asked if I was allergic to anything. I said I was. The doctors and nurses stopped working as they waited for my reply. I took a deep breath and yelled, "Bullets!" Over their laughter I told them, "I am choosing to live. Operate on me as if I am alive — not dead."'

Jerry lived thanks to the skill of his doctors, but also because of his amazing attitude. I learned from his story that we have the choice to live fully. After all, attitude is a major factor determining whether we tap into the power of our *I.D.*™ in a positive or a negative way.

If you want to change your attitude, change it, but it is a choice — one that is not made once, but every minute if necessary. It does take work, but the more you do it, the stronger that mental muscle becomes. Change happens in the instant you decide to do something differently — so change your mind.

Although your attitude can change and is totally under your control — your *I.D.*™ doesn't change. So find out what it is and then work on the onion skins so that you can be the best person you can possibly be. People who have chosen a path of self-discovery in addition to the *I.D.*™ have made exponential progress. They are able to see what can change and deal with that while honouring themselves for the unique being that they are — and while accepting themselves just as they are.

I.D.™ allows people to truly accept themselves just as they are. I have witnessed people who have been exposed to I.D.™ for the first time finally give themselves permission to be authentically true to their nature. Finally, after years of struggle and berating themselves for supposed 'flaws' in their character, they are able to see themselves in a new light and arrive at a place of deep personal acceptance. Although that may seem like a small thing, I have witnessed it enough times to know that its implications are life changing.

What we have to understand is that our I.D.™ represents our best route to experiencing a life of fulfilment and achievement. When we are in stride with that way of operating we gain amazing benefits — including creativity, good health, oodles of energy and productivity. But as we journey through life we are often pulled away from our instinctive 'best' way. Often the people doing the pulling are parents, teachers, employers and partners, keen that we maximise our chances and do our best. The parent that nags her child to turn the music down and study more diligently for her exams does so not out of malice but because she genuinely cares about her daughter and wants her to do well. Her understanding of effective studying is based on her own experiences and accepted wisdom. She does not realise that her daughter is innately different from her and that accepted wisdom and diligent study are academic suicide for the young student. What usually happens is that the daughter will conform and be miserable for the duration of the process; it is this type of experience that pulls us offcourse. The further away you get from your true north — your optimal operating style — the more stress and distress you will feel in all areas of your life.

Each of us is a unique human being and there is no one-size-fits-all approach to anything. What I.D.™ does is it allows you to discover your own blueprint for success and happiness. This awareness provides you with permission to be yourself. By knowing what makes you tick you can learn how to be more productive and happier. (They are not necessarily mutually exclusive!)

We will always have to do things in life that we would rather not do, and doing them may indeed go against our grain. The *I.D. System*™ isn't saying you can't or shouldn't do certain things, but rather that going against your *Instinctive Drives*™ is not the optimal way to succeed and that there's a way to achieve more success — even while you enjoy the process. When you go against your natural operating system you will compromise your effectiveness and fulfilment. If you know your *Instinctive Drive*™ you can simply make adjustments to how something is done so that you still get the job done without making yourself miserable in the process. By understanding your *I.D.*™ you will be able to use strategies that work with your essential nature rather than against it. This enables you to be much more productive, even with jobs you would normally struggle with.

This book is dedicated to helping you unravel the impact of *Instinctive Drives*™ upon your life. I will explore with you how they play out in your everyday life — in relationships, in business, in terms of your health and fitness, and in other important areas, such as finances and parenting. My hope is that you will smile as you recognise yourself and others in these pages — and perhaps by doing so you will be more forgiving of yourself and those around you.

It is my firm belief that if people understood their *I.D.*™ — how it plays out in their life and how other people with different *I.Ds*™ interpret their actions — the world would be a very different place. There would be more tolerance of difference and there would be more latitude for alternative approaches. Perhaps best of all, there would be less stress, better relationships, fewer divorces, better parents, more capable children (with greater self-esteem), a more skilled next generation, and more fulfilment, happiness and success. A sense of self-worth and self-acceptance would not just be for those lucky few — it would be the birthright of us all.

I.D.™ is so much more than just a profiling tool. It is a way of life, a language and a system of living that creates wealth, health, happiness and success — on your terms. And that is the *I.D's*™ greatest gift.

Chapter 2

The four Instinctive Drives™

I.D.™ holds the answer to what naturally works best for you so let's have a closer look at what each *Instinctive Drive™* is all about. Each drive (in both directions) has its own characteristics that offer both talents and vulnerabilities—depending on the situation. Often our greatest talent can also be our greatest vulnerability—in the wrong situation. For example, finding errors can be a great asset, but when it's the sole focus in a family it can make for a very critical environment. This book offers strategies that you can implement into your life to ensure you harness those talents while also managing your vulnerability.

The wonderful thing about I.D.™ is that it let's you understand your underlying motivations so you can consciously be in control of when and how you use your strengths and when and how you can minimise their impact in certain situations.

When you first saw the names of the four instincts, you might have jumped to a conclusion about what they mean due to your particular understanding of the words 'verify', 'authenticate', 'complete' and 'improvise'. It's important, however, that you don't confuse the names of the instincts with the verbs they seem to represent. Read on so that you can gauge the meanings of the words within the context of the *I.D. System*™. For example, don't be tempted to think that the *Instinctive Drive to Verify*™ is about needing to verify things, that the *Instinctive Drive to Complete*™ entails finishing tasks and seeing them through to completion or that the *Instinctive Drive to Improvise*™ is characterised by the ability to think on one's feet.

The *Instinctive Drives*™ refer to *why* people act or behave in a certain way and as such their implications are much deeper than they may appear. You need to understand, therefore, that the words used to describe your *Instinctive Drives*™ are all about motivational drives—not behaviours—and it's a very important distinction. There are many characteristics to each drive, and one word will never capture that diversity, however, for simplification and ease of understanding I have given each *Instinctive Drive*™ a one-word description.

Your drives are like a raging river inside your mind—they never, ever stop flowing. People driven by the *Instinct to Improvise*™ don't *decide* to improvise; rather, everything they do, depending on the intensity of the drive is affected by their drive to Improvise. It works in the same way for the other drives.

Although this book will cover the attributes and characteristics of each *Instinctive Drive* individually, it's imperative to remember that the *I.D.*™ consists of a combination of those four drives and their varying levels of intensity. Consequently what initially appears quite simple can in reality be quite complex when you start to look at how your particular *I.D.*™ will play out in life. It is the amalgamation and intensity of drives in your *I.D.*™ that determines how you meet and interact with the world.

In writing this book I've been very conscious that people will go about reading it in different ways, depending on their *I.Ds*™. Some will read it from front to back, others will digest bits and pieces according to their interests at the time and some will skim. Other readers, again, will be quite thorough and probably quite reflective on those pages that provoke and challenge them. Each approach will work just fine, but they all at least require a rudimentary understanding of the drives upfront, so that as you read the book—in your way—it will make sense from the word go. We are typically conditioned to believe that to gain the most out of reading a book you should start at the beginning and read until the end. But for certain *I.Ds*™ reading a book in the traditional way won't actually be the best way for them to digest all the value this book contains. If you have the urge to initially flick through the book and see what grabs you—do it! If you want to jump to different chapters and read backwards—do it! If you want to scribble in the margins—do it! On the other hand, if your best way *is* to read from front to back—do that. That's what *I.D.*™ is all about—finding your natural best way, applying it as often as possible to your life and not feeling guilty about it! This book is designed to accommodate all the different *I.Ds*™ so you can go about reading this book in whatever way best suits you and you will still gain great value from it.

Made up of four numbers, an individual *I.D.*™ always follows the same sequence:

1   The first number relates to the *Instinct to Verify*™.

2   The second number relates to the *Instinct to Authenticate*™.

3   The third number relates to the *Instinct to Complete*™.

4   The fourth number relates to the Instinct to Improvise™.

At times I will use real examples to show how a particular *I.D.*™ could manifest itself in real life. Although I will often describe actions and behaviours, remember that it is the motivation behind them that is most important. I may also surmise someone's strongest *Instinctive Drive*™ to add colour and interest to the stories, but please be aware that I don't advocate guessing *I.Ds*™. Even with my knowledge of the *I.D. System*™, I can't accurately guess someone's *I.D.*™ The only accurate method is via completion of the validated *I.D.*™ questionnaire (turn to appendix C for information about completing the questionnaire).

This chapter is only meant to give you a broad overview of the *Instinctive Drives*™ so that you can begin to see the differences and perhaps recognise yourself and others in the initial descriptions. It is only the tip of the iceberg and as we progress through the book I am confident that you will gain greater understanding and insight.

The *Instinctive Drive to Verify*™

It's Sunday afternoon and you've got a friendly golf game with a good friend. You've decided to try out a new course and have just pulled up outside the club, looking at your watch at least twice to ensure that you have the right time. Even though you're bang on time and know you're right, you had to check. You meet your friend and head out to the course. Your friend putts for a four at the first hole and misses; you can't help but offer guidance. You are sure that sound advice based on the extensive Greg Norman and Arnold Palmer videos you've studied will be welcomed. Instead you see his shoulders stiffen as he goes in for the shot.

You seem to frequently stretch the bonds of friendship because of your need to 'get it right'. You think that you are just trying to help your friends improve, but they feel like they are being criticised and couldn't possibly live up to your exacting standards.

You're a natural problem solver. Everything is a problem just busting to be fixed—and that includes your mate's golf swing! It's the same at home—your daughter came home from school thrilled with her 95 per cent in maths and it took every ounce of self-control and a few choice looks from your wife for you not to ask her about the 5 per cent she didn't get right! It's not as if you were trying to be negative—far from it—you just wanted to help.

If you are a Verify-driven person you will always need to check everything because you have to be absolutely sure you are right. You are motivated by improvement and the best way to become better at something is to find where you went wrong last time and fix it. Even if you were right about something initially, you'll find a way to make it better! The evolutionary process of improvement never stops for Verify people.

There are a range of attributes that come with this drive. Your mind instinctively makes comparisons, and so you naturally focus on the things that could be improved next time and measure your success based on your ability to do so.

Another natural trait is your ability to prioritise everything. Because you think things through and weigh up the options, you find comparing easy to do and can make decisions based on that. This is not a mental process, however—it's an instinct. You automatically rank everything in your life to gauge priorities. And it's not just tasks—you prioritise everything including your friends, deciding which of them is more important than the others. You even prioritise your family, working out which sibling you feel closer to. Of course if you are a Verify person, you will have a reason and justification for each one of these priorities.

Driven to avoid the *Instinct to Verify*™

You've just come back to work after the holiday of a lifetime. You visited eight countries in eight weeks, danced at the Rio Carnival and ran with the bulls in Pamplona, Spain. You ate at some of the most famous restaurants and watched spectacular sunsets. You swam with humpback whales and lay on white sandy beaches, met wonderful people and just had a magical time. You are super excited about it all and having lunch with your colleagues. One of them—someone who is driven to Verify—asks, 'What was your favourite experience?' All of a sudden your mind goes blank. You don't see things as favourite—to you the whole holiday was a package, and it was all incredible!

Your natural instinct is not to judge or prioritise because you don't see things in terms of 'better or best'. But your colleague continues to probe for an answer and almost appears irritated that you can't pinpoint one stand-out moment. Pressured, you respond, 'Okay, okay the Pyramids were amazing.' The fact is you did think the Pyramids were amazing, but so was everything else. As soon as someone tries to get you to prioritise and grade your experiences, the magic can start to drain away. You don't know what just happened because five minutes ago you were happily sharing your experiences and now you feel strangely flat. It's almost like you feel silly and inadequate for not being able to pinpoint your favourite moment. You just don't see life in those terms.

Indeed you realise that you are often surprised by the constant judgements of better or worse and good or bad that find their way everywhere—friends and colleagues' conversations, society, news—everywhere! You feel exhausted by it all. Life just is; there isn't necessarily best or better. To you things are just the way they are. Once your lunch break is over you are relieved to end the 'interrogation' and go back to your desk.

Those driven to avoid the *Instinct to Verify*™ don't categorise, compare or play favourites, and they see things in a pragmatic, accepting kind of way. This has its advantages and disadvantages too. Because everything just is, they don't question things as much as they sometimes probably should and tend to be non-confrontational. Confrontation usually occurs when someone violates another person's boundaries, values or rules—and if one doesn't have a clear idea of what those boundaries are, how can they be violated? The other reason for non-confrontation is to avoid interrogation. Those around people driven to avoid Verify will say, 'Why did you just accept that? Why didn't you speak up?', but they will shrug and answer, 'I don't know'. Avoid Verify people will tend to avoid speaking up in situations like this because they think, 'What's the point?'. They believe it is pointless to speak up if the action has no significant purpose other than proving a point.

This can be seen as a weakness by others who think the person didn't speak up because he or she was scared or intimidated, but it's not necessarily the case. Often those driven to avoid Verify just don't see something as a problem until someone else points it out to them, and even then they may still wonder what all the fuss is about! The important thing to remember is that asking those people driven to avoid Verify to justify their answer or position is going to cause them all sorts of stress; they won't know 'why' they chose a certain path or made a certain decision—but they will know it is right for them.

This issue of non-judgement and seeing things in their entirety rather than individually can mean that they tend to make sweeping generalisations. So in the example used here, the man either had a great holiday or he didn't. Avoid Verify people don't naturally split experiences into components to differentiate between the things they liked and didn't like; consequently, they wouldn't automatically say something like, 'The flight was awful but the hotel was great'. If encouraged to do so they can, but if something colours their experience then the whole experience is tainted by that.

We are brought up in a Verify world in which there is a standard of right and wrong, and one of those standards is that we owe it to other people, as a matter of courtesy, to be able to explain ourselves. But the truth is that people driven to avoid Verify find it very difficult to do so. Even though they will very often be right, they won't be able to explain why.

The *Instinctive Drive to Authenticate*™

It's your turn to cook dinner. Your partner calls at 5.17 pm to see if there is anything that she needs to pick up for you before coming home. You know it's 5.17 because the clock on the microwave blinks at you as you're on the phone. You ask how long she's going to be before she arrives. She says twenty minutes. To you that means your partner will arrive home at 5.37, and that you should put the pasta on at 5.27.

Your partner arrives home at 6.18 pm and shortly after is wearing the pasta instead of eating it. Besides from being soggy, your avoid Authenticate partner is confused and pretty upset too. To her, 'twenty minutes' is a guide time — a rough indication of arrival based on current information. To you 'twenty minutes' means twenty minutes — not nineteen minutes or twenty one minutes and certainly not forty one minutes! You are not angry because your partner was late — you would actually be just as cranky if she had been early — what irritates you is her lack of congruency. Your partner did not do what she said she would do, and as a consequence you feel let down and betrayed.

Needless to say a heated argument breaks out. There is no beating around the bush when things are on your mind; you have a way of putting issues on the table that can be perceived as confronting. Because you need — and will be — direct and upfront, often people feel like you are being insensitive.

Every drive has two dimensions: the way it causes people to operate and also the way people need to contribute. Being driven by the *Instinct to Authenticate*™ means that you are compelled to be authentic — real — and that means being congruent, productive and useful so that you can see tangible outcomes for your effort. This is why meetings can sometimes drive these people nuts. When colleagues sit around talking about issues, theories and options — even if it results in a healthy discussion that brings the team closer and resolves some problems, if nothing actually changes or is resolved and no action plan comes from it (especially a personal action plan) then Authenticate people will write off the meeting as a complete waste of time. A person driven by the *Instinct to Authenticate*™ judges progress by tangible change and physical reality — not ethereal ideas and concepts. In addition, he or she needs to deal with the real issue and are driven to make things real and relevant. There is nothing more fulfilling for those with the Authenticate drive than being productive and doing something useful that results in their effort being plain to see to them and those around them.

Those driven to Authenticate don't read between any lines; they don't actually see that there are gaps to interpret in the first place. They just see the lines themselves — in terms of the actual behaviour or spoken word — and not the meaning behind them. They won't interpret the nuances of language or body posture, and they won't mull over conversations deciphering fifteen alternative meanings for the last conversation they had. When a person driven by the *Instinct to Authenticate*™ hears someone speak he or she hears exactly literally what is said and that's it. Authenticate-driven people won't factor in tone of voice, body language, contexts or even colloquialisms. For example, I once took two of my children—who are both strongly driven by the *Instinct to Authenticate™*—to an outback-adventure show at which their Authenticate-driven need to take things literally made me chuckle. We were standing at the ticketing booth buying our tickets; after I'd thanked the woman behind the counter for the tickets, she replied, 'No problem. See you later'. Obviously she didn't mean it literally, but as a turn of phrase; Sam and Jace, on the other hand, took it literally and were quite shocked to hear that the stranger at the outback ticketing booth would see them later that day!

What is valuable for those with the Authenticate drive to understand is that sometimes doing nothing is the best way forward and that talking things through is a necessary and important part of creation, especially in teams—even if they do see the real issues before everyone else. When a person with an Authenticate drive can learn to respect other people's process and give the group leeway to express themselves, he or she becomes a great asset to any team.

Driven to avoid the *Instinct to Authenticate™*

You're in a meeting with your team and have explained an upcoming new project. You are absolutely sure that everyone is on board and is as committed and excited about it as you are. As you discuss what is going to happen next, one of your colleagues makes a comment that clearly demonstrates that she in fact doesn't understand or share your vision. This is a source of real confusion and irritation to you. As far as you are concerned your explanation was crystal clear and any ambiguity in your communication of the project would easily be picked up if she would just read between the lines.

Irritated, you explain what you think is obvious and realise that she is not the only one to be a little unclear about the way ahead. Indeed there are people in the group that interpreted your position in a number of different ways! You think, 'How is that possible? What is wrong with these people? Do I really have to spell everything out in black and white? Get with the program and read between the lines!'

For those driven to avoid the *Instinct to Authenticate™*, what you see is not what you get. In fact what you see is only a tiny sliver of what's really going on. Those driven to avoid the *Instinctive Drive to Authenticate™* expect that everyone will read between the lines, and they assume that others 'get it'; the reality is that half the people they communicate with on a daily basis don't. Those driven to Avoid Authenticate will spend their life saying, 'Yeah, but wasn't that obvious?', 'You know what I mean—right?' or 'Do I have to spell it out?' It is important for those driven to avoid Authenticate to form the habit of removing ambiguity from their communication. If they leave nothing to interpretation then everyone's life will be much easier.

Those people who are driven to avoid the *Instinct to Authenticate*™ are still driven by the notion of authenticity—but real for them means something very different to those driven to Authenticate. And it's very often not as tangible; for example, 'justice' is real to them and is not just a theory! Where people with the Authenticate drive are motivated by what's outside of themselves—things they can touch, feel and produce—people who are driven to avoid the *Instinct to Authenticate*™ are preoccupied with what's inside—thoughts, feelings, ideas and concepts. They are like an iceberg—most of their true character is hidden beneath the surface because their focus is on what's going on underneath. There is always so much more to what they say and do than is apparent to others. Unless others take the time to get to know them and delve to understand the deeper underlying motivations and philosophies behind everything that they think, feel and do, then they won't really know the real person.

The challenge for people driven to avoid the *Instinct to Authenticate*™ is that when they communicate there can often be quite a gap between what other people gain from the communication and what they are really trying to get across. As a result, they can appear to be very incongruent but can easily explain their actions and join the dots if asked to explain themselves. Once explained, the initial incongruence disappears and it makes perfect sense; however, not everyone takes the time to ask—and as a result the person driven to avoid the *Instinct to Authenticate*™ can often be misunderstood. So although it always makes perfect sense to them, it doesn't to others. They are not driven to have everything as out in the open as those with the Authenticate drive. Ironically, people driven to Avoid Authenticate think they are an open book and that their communication is obvious and clear. Part of the reason for that is their ability to read between the lines and digest more subtle forms of communication very well—and because this comes easily to them, they often assume that everyone else operates that way too, when of course they don't. But to those that do not interpret those nuances, an Avoid Authenticate person's conversation is like a word puzzle with some of the letters missing so they guess at the truth. Once people start guessing at motivations, expectations, outcomes and intent, it's a short road to discord.

Those driven to Avoid Authenticate will always have more going on inside than they can ever get out. If something is 'outside', it would be real, but while it remains inside, it stays in the realm of philosophy, ideas and feelings—and that is where the Avoid Authenticate is happiest. They could spend all their time telling someone about every thought and feeling they ever had—and as fast as they got them out, more would be flooding in. There is loneliness felt by Avoid Authenticates about this because they feel that no-one will ever really get to know them. It's like they want to share their iceberg, but they can't get it up out of the water! However, they will find some friends who will be able to 'dive beneath the surface' with them. These are the ones who do not waste time talking about the 'froth and bubble' of life; they are the friends who talk to Avoid Authenticates about philosophy or belief systems and lots of deep and meaningful issues. That doesn't mean they don't know how to stop and have fun, it is just that their definition of fun will usually involve juicy discussions about much deeper issues. Nor, incidentally, does that mean that those driven to Authenticate don't have deep and meaningful conversations—it's just that they are more likely to be grounded in practical, real and current life issues.

Those driven to Avoid Authenticate will find that they are motivated by all the intangibles—like passion, determination and attitude. The intention is what is important to Avoid Authenticates—not necessarily the outcome. They need to be 'given the benefit of the doubt in all that they do.

The *Instinctive Drive to Complete*™

It's 6 am. The alarm goes off and you get up and jump in the shower. You know what you'll wear for the day because you probably decided last night; your outfit's ironed and hanging ready for you. After getting ready you go to the kitchen and make yourself two slices of strawberry jam on toast and a coffee. This is your morning ritual, your quiet time—and you need the peace and harmony it gives you before the family rises and the day begins. You know from past experience that if something or someone upsets your routine, it can upset your whole day. You don't like being interrupted.

By 7.15 am your husband and kids are up—fighting for the bathroom, racing around, ironing clothes, deciding which pair of shoes to wear, trying to find socks or underwear—and it's absolute chaos! You chuckle to yourself as you head out the door to leave them all to it. (Your husband often tells you to chill out and go with the flow, but he sure doesn't look very chilled out right now!)

You do not see the fun in last-minute, spur-of-the-moment action. As you have tried to tell them all so many times before, if they would only think a little bit ahead and have a plan and put a system in place, then things would not be so fraught and life would be efficient and, therefore, harmonious. But they never listen!

Two key motivators for people driven by the *Instinct to Complete*™ are to have things running like clockwork—which provides a sense of order, structure, harmony and integration—and to get things back to normal, or whatever 'normal' is for them.

Of all the *Instinctive Drives*™, the drive to Complete is the one that people most jump to conclusions about. People assume that the *Instinctive Drive to Complete*™ means that the person always completes tasks. Although that can be a characteristic of those with the Complete drive, that type of behaviour does not sum up people with this drive. It is true that completing things is part of the *Instinct to Complete*™, but, again, it's not just something that they do every now and again—it is a drive—a raging river inside their mind that flows all the time. Life demands that we all complete projects—and all *I.Ds*™ can do that if they learn to tap into their deeper motivation—but those driven by the *Instinct to Complete*™ need to have everything complete. The *Instinct to Complete*™ is about achieving harmony and integration. Unfinished projects are untidy and it's that sense of disorder that is so stressful for Complete-driven people.

Although everyone is hugely influenced by his or her upbringing and conditioning, those people driven to Complete are especially susceptible to it. Those with the Complete drive use the formative years as benchmarks for 'normality' that can run the course of their life. This is because people who are driven to Complete establish their sense of normality when they do something for the first time. So their experiences in the family define what a 'normal' family life, or what 'normal' relationships are, and time spent with their first friends defines what a normal friendship is.

Using first experiences — in which there are no precedents and no instructions — as a point of reference can become extremely awkward and quite stressful for them. For example, first-time mothers who are driven by the *Instinct to Complete*™, will often find subsequent pregnancies less stressful because the pregnancies will be imbued with a sense of predictability, structure and routine. At other times, Complete-driven people may be lucky enough to be in a role where everything is structured and predictable, but this can be difficult when — for many of us — life is about change. Therefore, Complete-driven people are forever burdened with the need to get everything 'back on track' or 'back to normal'. Because the world is always changing, they often struggle to find true peace and can live life with a comparatively high level of stress

Driven to avoid the *Instinct to Complete*™

You're halfway through the report and the phone rings — you jump to pick it up. As far as you're concerned, any interruption is a good interruption. You love the unpredictable nature of life because it offers the opportunity for new experiences. The call is from a client confirming an order — fantastic! You hang up and completely forget about going back to the report; you've got something new and different to think about now.

You really love your role because it offers you variety, which you find very motivating. You were even offered a promotion recently and it would have meant more money and more responsibility; however, it would also have meant that you would know today exactly what you would be doing tomorrow — and that is your definition of hell. You know, after years of experience, that you are at your best in the middle of uncertainty. You are a natural fire fighter — loving the possibility that everything could change in a heartbeat, and when it does you come alive.

Someone who is driven to avoid Complete rarely stays with the plan and randomly changes his or her mind during a process. When Avoid Complete people get up in the morning, they prefer not to have their clothes already chosen, or if they have they will have prepared at least several options because they won't know what to wear until it's time to get dressed. If Avoid Complete people don't know about I.D. and cave in to stereotypes about being prepared, they may, for example, organise an outfit for an event on the following day only to find in the morning that what they had prepared is the last thing they want to wear. Even if they just change a tie or shirt, they will rarely do it exactly as planned. It can appear fickle, but they just need flexibility—and too much planning demotivates them. Although Avoid Complete people don't have a particular routine, they will still get things done.

Their propensity to move between things can appear flighty to others, and they are often accused of leaving things half finished. For Avoid Complete people there is usually a litany of projects that were started with a flurry of enthusiasm, only to be cast aside shortly after as something new comes along. That could be the half-finished shelf unit in the garage, partially knitted jumpers or the correspondence writing course that they sit their computer monitor on! Those driven to Avoid Complete always mean to get back to projects, but they rarely do—it's now or never. That is not to say that people driven to Avoid Complete can't finish things—they will—but the route to the finish post may change as they take a few detours and become sidetracked with subprojects before they cross the line. This can look very inefficient and chaotic from the outside!

To someone with the Complete drive, rules are there to be followed so that harmony and order can be maintained. To someone driven to Avoid Complete, rules are nothing more than guidelines designed to set the scene, who knows where it will go from there. If someone driven to Avoid Complete is told, 'This is how you do it and this is the path to follow', that will be the way they choose not to go! It's not that they won't follow the path; they are driven not to follow it. As Ralph Waldo Emerson said, 'Do not go where the path may lead, go instead where there is no path and create a trail'.

Those driven to Avoid Complete need a start date and an end goal but not the plan of how it has to be achieved. They are flexible, adaptable and creative, and are demotivated by predictability and routine. They can appear flippant because they are so changeable, but that changeability is their strength. They bend and weave with the moment and are incredibly adaptable, which makes them a valuable asset in a crisis.

Those driven to Avoid Complete are the initiators, and those driven to Complete are the implementers. Get the two confused in a workgroup and there will be trouble! But in their right place the two drives create a very powerful combination.

The *Instinctive Drive to Improvise*™

It's Friday morning and you have to give a presentation at 3.30 that afternoon. You've known about it for about a week, and although you've thought about it intermittently in that time, you haven't really dedicated any time to it.

Your logical mind, as usual, has been whispering at you for a few days now, saying that you should get on with it. But experience has proven to you too many times that if you want to give a great presentation today, you can't start thinking about it until after lunch.

You could have started last week — and a number of your colleagues with similar tasks certainly did — but somehow the energy just wasn't there for you. The build-up of work and pressure empowers you and moves you into action. Once the deadline is critical the lights go on and you plunge into the madness. For you it's all about the energy. You love that a looming deadline is like a power source that charges your batteries and creates moments of brilliance — even if you do say so yourself!

As discussed earlier, if I could have used names for the *Instinctive Drives*™ that were not so loaded I would have. Most people want to be able to improvise — and believe that they can — because it is rarely seen as a negative. However, just like the other *Instinctive Drives*™ I'm not describing an occasional ability to improvise — which most people have — but instead a compulsion to improvise.

Those with the *Instinctive Drive to Improvise*™ need energy and are decimated by negativity, which can take many forms. People have standard understandings of certain words, and negativity is one of them. Most assume that negativity means complaining about something, but for someone who is energised by positivity — such as a person driven to Improvise — negativity is much more than just grumpy behaviour. People with the *Instinctive Drive to Improvise*™ may find the following situations negative:

⮞ *silence and delays.* Silence and delays without explanation are seen as negatives by an Improvise person. On the other hand, if someone was to say to an Improvise person, 'I'm going to think this through for twenty minutes and I'll get back to you', that would be okay for the Improvise drive because he or she would know what's going on.

⚕ *closed doors and closed blinds.* They can find these constraining and dark; Improvise-driven people require freedom and light.

⚕ *not knowing what's going on.* When this happens they will fill in the gaps of their knowledge and will often make assumptions that turn out to be inaccurate.

⚕ *doing things slowly.* They thrive in fast, high-energy environments where there is plenty of interaction, buzz and noise. They can feel utterly isolated and drained when things are too quiet.

⚕ *no deadlines.* They simply won't do the work without deadlines because they thrive on the pressure deadlines entail. Deadlines pump up their adrenalin, providing a certain buzz that fires up the passion of Improve people. It's not the deadline that energises them, but the adrenalin that deadlines bring.

⚕ *longwinded instructions or communications.* Monotone, whiney or downbeat language is seen as a negative to them. They are highly susceptible to tone and will often pay more attention to that than the actual words spoken. They need punchy, exciting and animated language—and it always needs to be brief. So expecting them to remember long-winded instructions is unrealistic – they just want the highlights.

⚕ *neutral colours.* They need colours that they see as exciting because it gives them energy—and those colours may not necessarily be the bright ones, like yellow and red.

One thing that can be said of those with the Improvise drive is that they can be guilty of having 'just enough knowledge to be dangerous'. Their interest is highest when their energy for a topic is at it's peak, which is invariably at the start of discussions and projects. It means they can be tempted to think they have the crux of the matter within minutes. So those driven to Improvise who are reading this book for example will already have decided that they understand the concepts by the second chapter—in fact if they've made it this far it's probably a miracle! Chances are they have been tempted to put the book down a number of times because they are confident they understand the theory!

This type of behaviour—accentuated by their drive towards the positive—means that Improvise people are often more than happy to commit to things without really knowing the full extent of the situation. They get a little bit of the puzzle and assume they know what the complete picture is, but invariably they don't, and this requires those with the Improvise drive to stretch and innovate to find a solution. Working in this way is their most productive mode of operation. So a person with the Improvise drive will make their commitments without even knowing if he or she has the time, energy or even the skill to successfully carry them out! Often it is something that is virtually impossible and right outside their existing knowledge or skill—yet they say, 'Yes!', and ask questions later.

Then they discover the true extent of the project and can be a little cranky about it, even to the point of feeling betrayed that others didn't let them in on all the details. The truth is, however, that the person driven to Improvise came across so optimistic, enthusiastic and confident that the other person just assumed they knew what they were doing!

Although, to their credit, once the person driven to Improvise has said, 'Yes', they will engage their formidable powers of innovation and persuasion to achieve the outcomes. It's a steep curve for many of these individuals, but they need the challenge. This is how they learn to expand their definition of what's possible—and nothing gives them greater pleasure than pulling it off! Those with the Improvise drive will usually rise to the challenge—and even surprise themselves sometimes!

Friends and fellow workers look at Improvise people as if they are slightly demented at times, often fearing for their health as what looks like pressure and stress increases. Little do they realise that it is precisely these situations of extreme pressure that invigorate those driven to Improvise, pushing them towards their inspirational best.

The flip side, however, is that because those driven to Improvise have elevated 'winging it' to an art form and are so full of energy and enthusiasm, they can give the impression to others of being more competent than they really are. So although they have no problem getting into situations, they often have to negotiate themselves out of them. They can appear incongruent, insincere and unreliable; it's vital that they learn to manage expectations and deliver on their promises.

Driven to avoid the *Instinct to Improvise*™

The team is due to have an annual conference meeting in a few minutes, but you're a bit sceptical about the agenda. It gets underway, and under the section of potential keynote speakers the chair mentions the name of the intended opening keynote speaker. There is great excitement in the meeting but all you feel in concern. Because you immediately see the risks, it often feels like you have missed something because surely everyone else realises the suggestion is impossible. As the other team members start to rant and rave about how good the speaker will be, you feel torn. If you don't share your fears, you feel like you'll be guilty by association if your concerns materialise, but if you do speak up you risk being seen (yet again) as the wet blanket! Eventually your silence and withdrawal speak louder than any words so you are asked for your opinion. You are not deliberately being moody; you are genuinely weighing up the pros and cons of speaking up.

When you point out your concern about the potential conflict of interest for this speaker given his relationship with a key competitor (an angle no-one else considered for a second even though it was blindingly obvious to you!), the energy in the room comes to a sudden stop. Bang! You've done it again. Thankfully they're amazed at how you think of these things — especially when everyone else was just running with it. It doesn't mean you still don't feel bad for being a wet blanket, yet this feeling is at least helped by their sincere gratitude to you for speaking up.

Your preferred working environment is peaceful and quiet, somewhere you can immerse yourself in the task at hand. Open-plan offices were one of the worst inventions of the twenty-first century as far as you're concerned. While at work you don't enjoy hearing about Sally's Saturday-night exploits, and, frankly, you couldn't care less whether John's son was picked for the rugby team or not. That conversation belongs at lunch or after work — where you enjoy getting caught up with the news — but when at work you want to work. You have a natural diligence and your formidable focus means you really apply yourself to the task at hand.

Work and fun are two very separate things for you. You don't expect or necessarily want to have fun at work, nor do you appreciate it when work interferes with your fun time.

While those driven to Improvise need to express their passion and animation, the reverse applies to people who are driven to avoid Improvise — they need to keep things on an even keel. They are unable to understand why their Improvise drive colleague can't just slow down and be calm about things. They don't want to be in the middle of all the interaction, noise, buzz and energy — they prefer low-key situations. Those driven to Avoid Improvise don't like chaos in their working environment, and chaos to them includes noise. They are able to sit on their own and focus on the task at hand and cannot comprehend why the person driven to Improvise insists on flipping between stations on the radio and creating unnecessary commotion wherever possible!

Those driven to Avoid Improvise are very diligent, and their work quality and quantity usually speaks for itself. They don't appreciate being pushed to complete projects with unreasonable deadlines that cause them to rush — when they are more likely to make mistakes or not enjoy the process of doing the work. When feeling pushed and pressured, many Avoid Improvise people are more likely to mistakes; ironically, the reverse is true for those with the Improvise drive. Where a person driven to Avoid Improvise will make errors of judgement when pressured and deliver quality results when given plenty of time, someone with the Improvise drive is the opposite — he or she will make quality decisions when pressured and mistakes when given too much time!

Just watching someone driven to Improvise can make someone driven to Avoid Improvise feel pressured and exhausted! Any excessive noise can cause a person driven to Avoid Improvise to feel under fire. They prefer a calm, quiet environment and will often spring their colleagues with comments like, 'I can tell by the amount of laughter that there isn't much work getting done!'

For Avoid Improvise people logic always outweighs emotions. As a result, others — especially those with the Improvise drive — misunderstand those driven to avoid Improvise and label them as party poopers who are always trying to puncture everyone's excitement and enthusiasm. When others observe those driven to Avoid Improvise being conscientious and diligent, they may label them as boring, assuming that they never have any fun. But people driven to Avoid Improvise love fun — just after five o'clock! In fact they have probably been called a dark horse a few times — being the type to let their hair down at the staff Christmas party by jumping up on the pool table and dancing! Those driven to Avoid Improvise easily separate work and fun — if they're at work they're seriously working and if they're at play they're seriously having fun!

Their conscientious nature means they are very talented at seeing the challenges in future plans. Although people driven to Improvise may see this as being defeatist or negative, neither conclusion is accurate. This ability to seek and eliminate risk is one of the many valuable assets of those driven to avoid Improvise.

Myths and stereotypes

In the course of researching the *I.D. System*™, I was able to break down some of the common stereotypes and myths that people have about behaviour. My research shows that:

▷ Men aren't more 'hands on' than women. In fact many girls labelled as tomboys are probably just driven to Authenticate—wanting to get out there among the real work or action in order to be productive and useful.

▷ Women don't change their minds more than men—there are just as many men driven this way.

▷ Some men can't read maps either! And some men will even ask for directions! It's all about the drive—not the gender.

▷ There are just as many male 'born organisers' as there are female, though many men suppress this ability (even though they may find disorganisation frustrating) in order to be seen as messy and 'cool'. Many of these types of men make a remarkable change back to orderliness once they move out of home and have responsibility for their own space.

▷ There are just as many women naturally suited to problem solving and crisis management as there are men—but there are still many male-dominated cultures that don't give women the chance to show it.

How to get the most from this book

Each *Instinctive Drive*™ has specific needs that must be met for individuals to feel 'in stride' and validated, happy and fulfilled. Each drive and direction also has innate talents and vulnerabilities, and they often play out according to certain characteristics. Appendix A includes a reference chart of those needs, talents and vulnerabilities. As you read the book refer to the chart and you will no doubt recognise yourself or your partner, friends or colleagues in these pages.

Even the way you read this book will provide clues to what *Instinctive Drives*™ motivate you. If you are driven to Verify you will be trying to determine if this is 'right' for you. You may want to see proof or you may want to know more about how the *I.D. System*™ was developed; in that case, the University of Western Sydney's validated research on the *I.D. System*™ will be important to you. All the information about development of the *I.D. System*™ is presented in appendix B—feel free to flick forward and read it if it will enable you to put your doubts to rest and get the best out the book.

Readers who are driven to Authenticate, on the other hand, may just want the book to be real and relevant. So they're after examples that will help them link *I.D.*™ to their own life—in order to see the practical applications as well as the results. They may also be fascinated to understand how it all works, how it was developed and how I discovered it. Of more importance to Authenticate-driven people, however, is that that the book be useful. Their need for relevance and usefulness might also compel them to miss certain chapters and go straight to an area of their life in which they're interested in. So if they are currently happy with their career, they may skip chapter 3 and go to chapter 5 because they are interested in relationships. Or because their health is a priority, they may flick forward to chapter 8.

By contrast, people who are driven to Complete will likely get the most out of this book if they take note of the contents page and then read it from front to back, preferably without interruptions. They typically learn best when they feel like they are putting the pieces of the puzzle together; so depending on what that puzzle is for them, they may actually need to read the book in a non-sequential order so they can obtain the answer they're looking for first—thereby filling in any knowledge gaps—and then go back and read the book cover to cover!

People who are driven to Improvise, on the other hand, will love the personal stories and the bits that challenge them personally. The key lies in keeping them energised. They'll probably need to read all the bits about the *Instinct to Improvise*™ first—asking, what about me?—so that they can be constantly challenged by what I'm, in effect, saying about them. When it comes to reading about the other instincts, Improvise people should remember that doing so will help them to better understand others, and most importantly, to also learn how others *really* see them. I've made a point of being particularly direct about each instinct in this regard so that learning about their 'shadow side' and how others perceive their differences is of great stimulus and value to them.

True to form though, they'll now probably do the exact opposite, just to be defiant! And I have no problem with that! Those driven to Improvise have even been known to read the endings of fiction novels after the third chapter! People driven to Improvise want to get to the bits that mean something to them because it's the fastest way to see results. If they are inspired by what they read—and it's new and exciting for them—then they will keep reading. So I've tried to do that for them!

Before you begin the next chapter, remember that:

▷ Each instinct is equal in value—none is more useful or desirable than the other.

▷ The drive to use or avoid an instinct is equal in value—neither direction is better than the other.

▷ Research shows there are just as many people who use an instinct as there are people who avoid that instinct.

▷ There are just as many women driven to use or avoid an instinct, as there are men—and sometimes in contrast to stereotyping and social expectations.

▷ The various drives that make up *I.D.*™ are equally distributed across all walks of society regardless of nationality, culture and socioeconomic status.

By understanding *I.D.*™ and specifically your *I.D.*™, you will develop insight into any and all areas of your life. Once you understand your innate nature, can recognise when others in your life are irritating you and can see when you are going against your grain, you can then change your approach so that it better suits your *Instinctive Drive*™. And the great news is that although those changes can be subtle shifts, they can instantly resolve internal tension and stress.

Knowing your *I.D.*™ will have huge implications for your life—in terms of happiness, fulfilment, success, health, wealth and productivity. It will even enable you to create and maintain wonderful relationships—be that with your colleague, partner, friend or child.

Chapter 3

In stride with your career choice

If you are particularly interested in this chapter, chances are that at least one of the following scenarios applies to you:

➤ You are at the start of your career and looking for some direction.

➤ You are a parent of a child faced with a similar situation.

➤ You are at a crossroads in your career and seeking some guidance on whether you are in the right profession.

➤ You are looking to fast-track your career.

➤ You want to gain more purpose and meaning from your career.

➤ You are looking to avoid the consequences of the Peter principle — being promoted out of your comfort zone or ability.

➤ You are happy in your role most of the time, but you are curious to see whether there are other career paths that may be even more fulfilling and rewarding for you.

Although the *I.D. System*™ is much more comprehensive than most profiling tools, it is nonetheless essentially a profiling tool. The strategy behind profiling has traditionally been employed by businesses wanting to find the right person for the right job and minimise costly recruiting mistakes.

Profiling as a strategy has a lot of merit; a survey conducted by the Institute of Chartered Accountants in Australia (ICAA) some ten years ago identified that staff turnover costs are equivalent to the annual salary of each person that leaves — and that's at a minimum! Imagine that you're running a business. Add up the number of people who might've left the business in a year; multiply that number by their annual salary and you'll quickly have some idea of the minimum amount that can evaporate from the bottom line. How scary is that number? It's precious profit going straight down the drain. I once had a client in an accounting firm monitor the change in profit the year after the firm had zero staff turnover, and that little equation did indeed play out.

Of course staff turnover is not the only place from which your profit may evaporate; poor customer service, wastage, low productivity due to conflict and inefficiencies, missed sales opportunities and poorly motivated staff can all affect profit margins. Some companies have most of these ailments and yet still produce handsome profits often in the billions. Talk about succeeding in spite of yourself!

Now that's the business world itself, but the same principles and issues apply to the performance of individuals in the workplace:

- ☞ Staff turnover indicates that people are changing tasks or roles and not staying with them long enough to reap the fruits of their effort.

- ☞ Poor customer service demonstrates that some people in the workplace have poor relationship and communication skills.

- ☞ Wastage indicates that some employees are inefficient, poorly focused and lacking in discipline.

- ☞ Missed sales opportunities indicate that some employees may be becoming distracted by others things or under stress.

No wonder it makes sense to find a career that you can approach with passion and fulfilment. People want to lead a meaningful life in which they feel like their existence on this planet matters. The last thing we want is to meander through life 'existing' and 'surviving' until our number is up—reminding me of a verse I once received via email:

> Life should not be a journey to the grave with the intention of arriving safely in an attractive well-preserved body, but [something] to skid into sideways, cigar in one hand, champagne in the other, body thoroughly used and worn out, [with you] screaming, 'Whoo hoo! What a ride!'

Traditionally profiling has been used to identify the traits of employees in order to determine those features that ensure success in a given position over another. This supposedly enables an employer to ensure that he or she only hires candidates possessing those 'successful' traits—ultimately making the business more successful. Although that makes sense, it doesn't typically work. Just when you think you have a profile that you can use to accurately predict someone's behaviour, another person with that profile will demonstrate the opposite predicted behaviour and wreck your theory. This reality of profiling is indeed my experience.

For example, in my research I have found that 85 per cent of accountants have a specific I.D.™; however, I have also found very successful accountants who do not fit that typical mould and accountants in the 85 per cent who would not be considered as successful. So to stereotype people in terms of their career is much too limited.

In my opinion profiling for selection purposes almost shouldn't work because it takes much more than hiring right for a candidate to work out successfully. Some other key ingredients include the ability of the person's superior to manage him or her effectively and a candidate's degree of 'fit' within the team. Therefore it's actually possible to have someone join who has all the raw ingredients, but because that employee doesn't quite gel with the boss or team, he or she won't succeed. That's why moving someone to a different team can be very successful. It also explains why low-performing individuals can blossom when the boss is replaced by someone with a completely different leadership style.

This chapter looks at whether there are certain careers that are more suited to certain I.Ds™ than others.

Choosing your career

The great thing about not having a designated career for your I.D.™ is that you can choose your career based on your passion, and then adjust how you pursue your passion and career so that your approach matches your I.D.™. Pursuing your passion and purpose—while being true to your I.D.™—is the key!

For some lucky people their I.D.™ and passion seem to align, pointing them in a direction of what I'd call a 'natural fit' with their I.D.™ However, people are commonly directed towards their career based on their grades in school subjects. Enter the advice of the old 'vocational guidance' experts at school—if you're good with numbers, try accounting, or if you're great at debating, try law.

To delve deeper into the influences that shaped your current career choice, ask yourself the following questions:

- How did you choose the career you have today?

- Was your motivation for choosing your career based on your passion?

- Did school grades determine your direction?

- Did an influential teacher point the way?

- Was your career choice influenced by your parents and their expectations—whether you followed in their footsteps or rebelled against them?

- Did peer pressure play a part in your career choice?

- Perhaps you just chose the shortest queue at university?

- Did you simply seize opportunities as they arose?

- Do you have no idea how you ended up where you are today?

Your answers will indicate that there is much more to determining a career that will lead to ongoing fulfilment and lasting success than being guided by external influences; passion should always be your starting point.

My passion is passion—and what motivates it. I love understanding what drives passion in different people and in different situations. I also thrive on delving beneath the surface to understand the actual moment in time when a decision is made—especially an emotional one, like choosing to get married, stay married or divorce. I'm also committed to looking for a possible formula behind these decisions that can be used as a tool for turning confusing and seemingly unpredictable situations into simple, manageable ones—thus giving people more control over their lives and destinies.

Finding your passion

I mention in the introduction that finding your passion is often touted as the answer to all of life's problems. Yet few people naturally stumble on their passion, let alone pursue it as a career—but with some conscious thought it can be easier to detect.

When I am asked about career choice I always advise people to take the following steps:

1   Identify your passions.

2   Identify your particular aptitudes and skills.

3   Look at your I.D.™

4   Look at the culture in which you are looking to work to ensure it aligns with your values and your I.D.™ needs.

How do you identify your passion? To help you find it, just jot down your instinctive answers to the questions below. This exercise should take only a few minutes to do. Don't think about the answers—just write down your initial responses. Don't censor or try to make sense of them. Don't dress them up or play them down—simply write down the first thoughts that spring to mind. The clue to discovering your passion isn't in the actual answers you jot down, but in the patterns that connect all your answers together somehow. There are likely to be common factors in your answers that will illuminate a possible avenue for exploration.

So look for the common characteristics within your answers. It can help to do the exercise with someone and share your answers with them because it is often easier to see the patterns in someone else's situation than it is to see them in your own.

▷   What would you do if there were no limitations, no restricting responsibilities and no lack of resources? In other words, what would you do if you were completely free to do anything?

53

⌦ What would you do if money was no object?

⌦ What would you do if you knew you couldn't fail at it?

⌦ What would you do if you knew no-one would laugh at you for it?

⌦ What do you get excited about?

⌦ What sort of conversations and topics inspire you?

⌦ What can't you help talking about — even at dinner parties?

⌦ What subjects on the TV grab your attention, stopping you from flicking between the channels?

⌦ What topics make you really animated in conversation?

⌦ What do you hate with a passion? (It may hold some clues!)

Hopefully you now have some idea of your passion in life, but how can you be sure that you have it right? The following questions should help. Ask yourself:

⌦ Would you do it regardless of whether you were being paid for it or not?

⌦ Do you get emotional about it?

⌦ Do you gravitate towards it whenever time permits?

Identifying your passion is primary. It typically includes the things you love to do in your spare time — things that you would do whether you were being paid for it or not. They are most likely activities that come easily to you — when hours pass like minutes. Pay attention to your passions and head in that direction first. If you don't see yourself as a passionate person, think of passion in terms of what you are interested in — what fascinates you. And remember that your passion may not be a niche or specific area; it may just point you in a direction of how you want to live. We all want to live passionately — it is how that path takes form that differentiates us.

Next identify your aptitudes and skills; bear them in mind as you look for roles within your area of interest that will work with your nature and not against it. Note down why you find them interesting. The answer is often not connected to what but to why or how; for example, if you love word puzzles in which you have to crack codes to solve them — and if you instinctively see the patterns — then perhaps you should consider working in cryptology. The specific roles within the field of cryptology could be very different; for instance, some roles in the area may require working for long periods on your own, whereas others may involve working in a team or dealing with numbers and words. Some positions may even require you to become a specialist in a particular algorithm, but others may require more general skills. In addition, there may also be administration and management roles in those areas too.

Your preferred workplace culture should also play a part in your career choice. Is it a bottom-line, results-oriented, internally competitive environment that motivates you? Or are you drawn to a more team- and relationship-oriented atmosphere in which people are focused on helping each other succeed? Are they sincere about their stated values and vision? How do they align with you?

So by knowing your *I.D.*™ — and therefore your essential nature and instinctive motivational drives — you can diminish the element of chance in your career decisions and move towards a profession that will best fit your nature. Once you add in consideration of your intelligence and aptitude, you'll be even closer to the mark.

What career or job will best match my *I.D.*™?

Before I tackle this question I need to highlight a very important point. One of the reasons I went searching for a better alternative to the profiling systems available was because I saw the wrong people being passed over for jobs or being given jobs based on their profile. Although there may be a higher density of specific *I.Ds*™ in a particular field, I have found enough exceptions to know that any *I.D.*™ can do any role. To demonstrate it this section uses architecture, nursing and photography as examples of career paths that suit different *I.Ds*™ in different ways.

Architecture

Architecture is a wide and varied field, yet it would suit all *I.Ds*™ in some way. For example, an architect driven to Verify would thrive in the scientific side of architecture because of its precision and the accuracy required for designing buildings. Conversely, an architect driven to Avoid Verify would be attracted to the creativity of architecture, which has resulted in magnificent buildings such as the Sydney Opera House.

An architect driven to Authenticate is driven to see the building take shape. He or she would build the three-dimensional scale model of the building to see what it would look like in real life, and then take pleasure in seeing the model become reality and as a durable reminder of his or her work. By comparison, an architect driven to Avoid Authenticate would be drawn to the ideology of architecture and what it has meant down the centuries — for example, how a building can represent a philosophy or how a building like the Sydney Opera House can symbolise Australia's spirit.

An architect driven to Complete would thrive in the process of architecture — working out the plans, budgets and schedule. Complete people are driven towards harmony — and where better to develop it than in the creation of homes. On the other hand, an architect driven to Avoid Complete may thrive in a specialist architectural company in which the design of one-off buildings is paramount. For Avoid Complete people innovation and a flexible approach are important.

An architect driven to Improvise may revel in the world of architecture because it provides opportunities to make a stunning impression and to solve problems by brainstorming with colleagues in an environment that encourages experimental design. An architect driven to Avoid Improvise, however, may be drawn to architecture because of the solitude that its work environment offers — a calm, quiet atmosphere in which time is allocated and the work process requires diligence and logic. These architects will take pride in creating strong solid buildings that will last for years to come.

Nursing

Nursing can take many forms and attract many types of people to the field. A nurse with the Verify drive would be attracted to the accuracy of diagnosis, whereby there is a specific problem that requires a specific solution. Verify nurses would investigate situations thoroughly and persevere until the desired result is achieved. A nurse driven to Avoid Verify, however, would thrive in the environment of support and camaraderie that can exist in nursing. He or she would need patient interaction that includes giving unconditional encouragement and acceptance. (An Avoid Verify drive nurse may thrive in a children's burn unit, for example.) They would also appreciate an environment that deems all patients to be worthy of and entitled to the same level of care, irrespective of wealth, position or success.

A nurse with the Authenticate drive would need to be personally involved with patients. They are motivated by the actual 'doing' of nursing—such as bathing, feeding and administering drugs—and the more gruelling the environment, the better. They also flourish if they can see that their contribution is helpful and useful—especially when they are able to help people who are unable to help someone themselves.

If you want to know what is really going on with your health, ask a nurse driven to Authenticate because he or she will stick to the facts. A nurse who is driven to Avoid Authenticate would enjoy the human side of nursing; Avoid Authenticate nurses are naturally empathetic and perceptive so are great at reading between the lines and teasing out additional information from patients that could be very important. They can also often be very intuitive in their approach to healing.

A nurse with the Complete drive would love the process of nursing because it contains a start, middle and end and is all about restoring things to normal. Nursing requires dedication and adherence to procedure and rules—which is both natural and compelling for them. Nurses who are driven to Complete are the cornerstone of the health profession—not only for their attention to process but also for their drive to bring harmony to their environment and get people 'back on track'. A nurse who is driven to Avoid Complete has the potential to be an outstanding nurse in a chaotic environment. Accident and Emergency would provide the variety and spontaneity these types of nurses crave. If you were in a real emergency—especially if you were presenting with unusual symptoms that require a quick-fix solution—you'd want a nurse who is driven to Avoid Complete because he or she would find innovative, fast ways to help you.

A nurse with the Improvise drive would also be great in an emergency; Improvise nurses can be wonderful in extreme situations. These nurses are the type of people who will go into war-torn countries and assist refugees. For them no challenge is too big; they thrive in 'fly-by-the-seat-of-your-pants' environments that would have many other people in a cold sweat. Nurses who are driven to Improvise would love an almost impossible challenge in which resources are tight because they like to pull off miracles.

Nurses driven to Avoid Improvise are very assured; they can seem unemotional to an outsider but their steadiness is an excellent fit, as they can quietly and competently deliver medical care to their patients.

They thrive in the medical environment because it gives them an opportunity to remove risk—and their natural composure in stressful situations brings a calming influence to distressed individuals.

Photography

Photography is generally regarded as a creative profession, yet any *I.D.*™ will suit the profession because different facets of the job would appeal to different *I.Ds*™. A photographer driven to Verify, for example, would be motivated to capture the perfect shot. These people are inspired by the precision and technique of photography—such as the effects and subtleties of light and different lenses. A photographer driven to Avoid Verify is likely to enjoy photographing people and the interaction he or she can have with them. Much more intuitive than other *I.Ds*™, photographers driven to Avoid Verify can breeze in, take a couple of shots and leave because they know they got the perfect shot first time!

Photographers with the Authenticate drive would enjoy the practical processing of the photographs perhaps more than taking them. They cherish time spent in the dark room—where they can see their work come to life—and enjoy choosing or making the right frame. It's important to Authenticate photographers that the photo gives a true likeness of reality and captures the truth. Conversely, a photographer driven to Avoid Authenticate would be more interested in the mood of photography; he or she would want to capture the feelings of the moment to keep it alive forever. These photographers are attracted to photography because a picture paints a thousand feelings, and they are able to illustrate that depth of emotion in their work.

Photographers with the Complete drive would appreciate the process of photography—the steps required prior to taking the picture—and the checks and balances that can determine the outcome. They are also interested in the sentimentality that portraits bring out in people, so can, for example, be attracted to taking photos of a family as they grow up so there is a record for them took look back at and recall various events.

A photographer driven to Avoid Complete would be most attracted to individualising their photographs—to airbrushing, cropping and tailoring them, for example. But while a wedding photographer with the Complete drive would have a list of what shots are to be taken and when, a wedding photographer driven to Avoid Complete would not have a routine in place. Avoid Complete photographers are more likely to go with the flow and work with the subjects more intimately, capturing special impromptu shots as they occur.

A photographer with the Improvise drive would be more likely to enjoy photojournalism because of the unpredictable nature of the business. War photography — with its high risks and rapidly changing situations — allows Improvise people to use their ability to think on their feet, making them feel creative and alive.

Photographers driven to Avoid Improvise, on the other hand, are likely to be very thorough in their preparations and will remove every conceivable risk from the shoot. They may be attracted to studio photography; whereby they can minimise the variables and increase the reliability and certainty of the outcome — thereby minimising the risk. They are driven to produce quality shots, so the photographs usually speak for themselves — without the photographer needing to 'sell' the pictures. They are also interested in photography from the standpoint that it prolongs experiences, giving longevity to special events.

So to say that only those driven to Verify are suited to the profession of architecture, that only those with the Improvise drive are suited to photography or that only people with the Complete drive make good nurses is simply not true. It may be that more of the inherent activities or attributes required to do a job match more closely with one I.D.™ than another — as is the case with accountancy — but no I.D.™ is excluded from any profession. You may need to search out a particular role in which the culture and environment naturally aligns with your Instinctive Drive™, but there are no closed doors or free rides.

So although there may be careers in which your I.D.™ predisposes you to success ahead of a different I.D.™, you must understand your own strengths and vulnerabilities so that you can work within your chosen profession in a way that you find easy, natural and rewarding. If you learn to work in stride with your I.D.™, what you choose to do for a living becomes far less important.

Remember, as the song title goes, it's not what you do but the way that you do it — that's what gets results!

The *Instinctive Drive to Verify*™

Verify people are commonly driven by the following characteristics:

⇨ comparisons

⇨ priorities and lists

⇨ evaluations

⇨ scepticism

⇨ critical thinking.

Bearing in mind these characteristics it is easy to see that people with the Verify drive would do well in scientific, engineering, medical, veterinary or accountancy fields. They also suit careers as school teachers—although they are more likely to be high school teachers than primary school teachers. (Those driven by the *Instinctive Drive to Verify*™ need intellectual stimulation and precision, and it is more likely that older children will provide that for them.)

Those driven to Verify can't resist trying to solve problems—and the way they tackle it will be influenced by their other drives. If someone was driven to Verify and also Authenticate, he or she would probably enjoy practical problems, such as how to assemble a flat-pack computer desk! People with a strong Verify drive like practical, real-world solutions that require them to get their hands dirty. I, on the other hand, am driven to Verify and to Avoid Authenticate, so I hate flat-pack furniture, but have used my problem-solving capacity and my passion for ideas and philosophy to discover the *I.D. System*™.

This problem-solving capability can be seen with both doctors and accountants. According to my research, for both professions there was a high per centage (over 85 per cent) of people who had the Verify drive and were driven to Avoid Improvise. The link in both professions is quite obvious—both doctors and accountants are always evaluating and looking for solutions to problems their patients and clients present to them. They also tend to be quiet, serious, risk averse and even-keeled, which are traits more commonly associated with people who are driven to Avoid Improvise.

People often say that doctors can sometimes lack bedside manner. I remember being asked to go into a local hospital because its management wanted me to look at the Accident and Emergency department to see if there was anything I could do to improve its customer service. In terms of capability of the medical staff the results were very good, but there were complaints about the communication style of staff members. The specialist in charge, for example, was really cranky and became even more so when I arrived! His response to me was, 'We don't need to be doing any of this stuff. Have a look at our stats; we have the best success rate in the business'. I asked how he measured success and he abruptly replied:

> Take a look at how many people don't die here. People carry on about this 'bedside manner' stuff, but what do they want? Do they want us to be nice? Or do they want the patients to live?

I never realised the two were mutually exclusive! Now obviously the specialist has a point, but there is no reason why the results can't still be achieved with a more compassionate approach. For those with the *Instinctive Drive to Verify*™ everything is often seen as an either/or decision. Combine that with the naturally serious nature of doctors who are also driven to Avoid Improvise and you're left with people who can appear uncompassionate. But it doesn't have to be that way. Take Patch Adams, the doctor made famous by Robin Williams in a movie about his life, for example. I have never tested his *I.D.*™, but I would guess that he probably isn't the standard *I.D.*™ for a doctor (Verify and Avoid Improvise). My sense is he probably has more of the Improvise drive than most of his colleagues—he is certainly quite radical, and was especially so back in his heyday. He also loves to make his patients laugh—not just because he knows the healing power of laughter, but also because he is a fun person. He probably needs laughter as much as his patients do! Although he enjoys the interaction with his patients and is animated, it doesn't make him any less competent as a doctor. In fact, as history will attest, it made him a truly extraordinary doctor—and his patients loved him. Indeed even many of his medical adversaries have come to respect him—and I'm sure many have come to love him too.

Society expects doctors to be serious because medicine is serious—doctors deal with people's lives. It is almost as though the more serious and unapproachable doctors are, the better they are seen to be! But this doesn't mean doctors can't smile or have some fun.

For those driven to Verify, purpose is essential; it's important to them to connect to why they became involved in a situation in the first place. It is easy to just go through the motions and forget the reason why you wanted to be a doctor, dentist, lawyer or teacher. Usually someone driven to Verify will be drawn to a career because of a higher purpose — to make a difference and help others — but then once that person's in that role he or she can get bogged down with the day-to-day and lose sight of that higher purpose.

Now let's say you are driven to Avoid Verify and driven to Improvise, and you want to be an accountant. You may start as a junior in an accountancy practice and work hard until you reach the top and become a partner. Or you may take on more subjects than others because you enjoy the challenge, try to acquire more client-oriented roles so that you can utilise your people skills or create tight deadlines to maintain the challenge and your interest. What's important is that what makes a good partner is often very different to what makes a good junior accountant. The currency that is valued at the different stages of a career are more suited to some I.Ds™ than others, but as long as people deliver consistent results everyone will have his or her time in the sun — eventually!

So junior accountants may be valued for their precision — a characteristic of people driven to Avoid Improvise — whereas accountancy firm partners may be valued for their understanding of business and relationship development, which is a characteristic of the Improvise drive. A good accountant crunches numbers, minimises risk, follows procedures, and dots the i's and crosses the t's. A good partner, on the other hand, is much more of a people person — being required to meet clients at a high level. Interactive networking and social skills become a far bigger part of the role at this level. Yet to make it as a partner and to reach the level at which you can perhaps express more of your natural personality you need to have 'done your time' in the traditional accountancy roles. The question is, can young accountants make it through the period in which they are working against their grain in the initial years and do the job well enough — despite that — to be promoted to a position that is natural to them? All I.Ds™ can make it to the top of any profession, it's just that the enjoyable elements of that role may change depending on I.D.™

One of my earliest clients, Wayne Pearson, a senior partner with executive roles at Howarth (a major international chartered accounting firm), first learned about I.D.™ in his mid twenties, during the early part of his accounting career. As a partner he still needs to understand the technicalities of accounting, but he now spends the vast majority of his time and energy on business development and strategy. He said:

> I could see why I was feeling like a square peg in a round hole but because I knew my I.D.™ and knew that was normal for me considering my I.D.™—and most importantly that it wouldn't always be like that—I stuck with it and now I love my job. But if I didn't know that and I thought that my future was going to be like my past then I would have left long ago.

Another example like this involves one of Australia's leading paediatricians, whom my wife and I were lucky enough to have caring for our fourth child, Sam, after he was born. It was a particularly challenging time, and the doctor placed as much emphasis on his relationship with us as he did the technical aspects of looking after Sam. He ultimately changed what was a very serious and potentially upsetting experience into one that was fun and pleasantly memorable! His gift with people sees him now regularly appearing on daytime TV shows as their resident medical expert. Knowing that he is strongly driven to Improvise, I asked him how on earth he got through university. He explained that it was a hard slog, but also something he saw as a 'game'—and a great social occasion! He had a lot of fun and put as much emphasis on that side of his university days as he did the academic side. Interestingly, if people driven to Improvise bend to pressure and study diligently, they can often do worse than if they had just stayed in stride, had lots of fun and crammed at the last minute.

All I.Ds™ can make it to the top of any profession

He is clearly very well suited to medicine even though he doesn't have the same I.D.™ as many other doctors. He loves the fact that he never knows what new challenges the day will bring. Some of these challenges may be tough but there are also magical moments that he will never forget. Because of his positive outlook, he is also able to relay bad news in a positive light that is full of hope and promise. He understood early on in his career the power of the mind and the importance of hope in the healing process—a critical point that has now become a growing body of knowledge supported by proven research.

Because those driven to Verify see what's wrong, they also make excellent proofreaders and auditors. Any job that involves finding where something isn't right and fixing it is natural for someone with the Verify drive.

Driven to avoid the *Instinct to Verify*™

People who are driven to avoid the *Instinct to Verify*™ are also driven to be:

⇨ unassuming

⇨ accepting

⇨ non-confrontational

⇨ agreeable

⇨ non-discriminating

⇨ natural team players.

Those driven to Avoid Verify are the creative freewheelers who thrive in areas in which there is no definition of right and wrong—in which self-expression is a fluid, creative energy. These people are often musicians, artists, creative designers or some other profession in which it's important to 'get it right' the first time. Avoid Verify people can also be found in business—and in this environment they respond well to less formal structures.

Although the world is divided equally between those that use an *Instinctive Drive*™ and those that avoid it, society has a certain bias for certain drives. All four drives and two directions have a valid and necessary role in creating the variety we see in society. Yet certainly for western societies the behaviour common in those driven to Verify is seen as more valuable than the behaviour typified by those driven to Avoid Verify. So if as a child you announced that you wanted to be an artist, you probably would have been patronised or, worse, ignored in the hope that you would grow out of it and 'get a real job'. Even if you did insist on being an artist, your parents would have added, 'Maybe you should just get that Marine Biology degree anyway—just to fall back on'. Given the choice between soap opera star or marine biologist—the fish get it every time! Verify-type professions—such as an accountant or lawyer—often infer a sense of substance or solidity, whereas careers in the creative arts are seen as flaky, inconsistent and certainly not stable enough to raise a family on.

However, those driven to Avoid Verify can do some amazing things, and for them it's all about getting it right the first time. Doctors who are driven to Avoid Verify, for example, can be incredibly efficient in their initial diagnosis—often without needing the test results to back it up—if they trust and listen to their sense of knowing. Those driven to Avoid Verify hate being questioned and may not be able to articulate why they have done something a certain way or chosen a certain option over another. They avoid confrontation and can lose composure if asked to justify their actions. To avoid these situations many people driven to Avoid Verify go into precise areas such as science, becoming highly educated in the field, perhaps to the point of gaining a doctor of philosophy, (PhD) so they won't be questioned on their actions as much. This way they can use society's stereotypes to their advantage; by studying for a PhD they can rise above question because society tends to assume those with a PhD are highly intelligent experts in their field, and therefore above reproach.

Those driven to avoid the *Instinct to Verify*™ want to be loaded with the answers so that they can locate them in their heads at short notice rather than think new thoughts. All their study loads them up with those answers, enabling them to feel completely comfortable about knowing their subject. An Avoid Verify photographer, for example, needs to be able to capture the right shot, and it's the photographer driven to Avoid Verify who will 'know' the exact moment to take the perfect photograph. But if someone asks that person how it was accomplished, he or she may appear unsure, and would-be clients may then lose confidence in the person's capability. Yet if the photographer had studied photography inside out, although it may not actually have made the person a better photographer, the study would enable the photographer to prove his or her abilities, providing him or her with confidence in the role.

This sense of knowing is a unique gift, and something I discovered my son Mitchell had when he was about ten years old and the two of us were going go-cart racing. Mitchell is driven to Avoid Verify, and driven by the *Instinct to Authenticate*™, so he always wants to be involved and do things. He jumped in the car and drove like a demon—never checking for other go-carts—even when overtaking he just seemed to sense the right time to move. He wants to be a

65

motorcar driver when he grows up, and I can see him on a race track because he has a really strong sense of physical space.

The *Instinctive Drive to Authenticate*™

People driven by the *Instinct to Authenticate*™ are naturally:

➪ hands on

➪ literal

➪ direct

➪ visual

➪ honest

➪ focused on tangible results.

Those driven to Authenticate need to do things, so they are often drawn to physical work such as that found in the professional trades or farming — roles in which they can see something tangible for their efforts. So a builder driven to Authenticate will be aware of a house taking shape, brick by brick. He or she will see a hole in the ground transform into a finished structure and take great pride in that evolution. Likewise, a mechanic driven to Authenticate will enjoy seeing a car in bits and then putting those components back together.

Needless to say, Authenticate-driven people hate meetings and are generally not good at delegation. They need to be personally involved, delivering outcomes that are practical, durable and of a high standard. Because so many people with the Authenticate drive can be found in trades and other physical professions, it is often very difficult for them to cross the line between a one-person operation to running their own business. If builders show talent, they are often encouraged to employ more builders. Eventually they become so busy managing other builders that they don't build anymore and wonder why they are so miserable! This is especially hard for people driven to Authenticate because they attach so much of their identity to what they do. Their physical effort is a reflection of who they are; all of their 'raw materials' — including their skills, attitude, experience, personal values and people skills — are combined to produce a tangible result. Because builders driven to Authenticate see their profession as part of their identity, they can be fanatical about quality. Conversely, for me—who is driven to Avoid Authenticate—the *I.D. System*™ is something I discovered, but it does not define who I am.

Despite their predilection for work of a physical nature, those with the Authenticate drive are still successful in white-collar work. There are accountants driven to Authenticate, for example, who are able to perform well in that role because they can look through the lens of their *I.D.*™ and see how accounting is relevant and how their skill can make a real difference for others—thinking such things as 'I'm saving people real money'. But for many in white-collar work the only thing real about the work they do is the money they earn. That income allows them to do what they enjoy—such as going surfing on weekends or rebuilding their vintage car. Authenticate-driven people need to physically exert themselves. If their job allows them the financial freedom and time to pursue that out of work—either in the form of a hobby or sport—then they can be quite content and deliver consistent, high-quality work in their professional role even if the position itself is not as physically demanding as they would like.

Driven to avoid the *Instinct to Authenticate*™

Those people who are driven to avoid the *Instinct to Authenticate*™ are often:

⚑ diplomatic

⚑ discreet

⚑ philosophical

⚑ idealistic

⚑ intuitive.

Those driven to Avoid Authenticate are into depth—what's happening under the surface; hidden meanings, feelings and emotions, the 'gist' of things, ideology and philosophy are what matter to them. They are suited to roles in which thinking (in terms of pondering), talking and understanding the nuances are king. Those with this drive are naturally suited to working with people, especially if it involves supervising or counselling them. They can also gain real value from being actively involved with other people, particularly when it relates to helping someone feel better.

I can picture an ambulance officer, doctor or even a financial planner with this *I.D.*™ feeling quite in stride—as long as his or her motivation stems from helping a patient or client feel better. Yet there are other not-so-obvious roles that would suit someone driven to Avoid Authenticate. In a place like Disneyland, for example, there are thousands of workers busy 'doing' their jobs all day so that visitors have an extraordinary experience. However, for those Avoid Authenticates among Disneyland staff, it is not the 'doing' that is important to them, but their ability to help others; they see themselves as helping to take people's feelings to a new level, as giving visitors the experience of a lifetime and demonstrating excellence—a philosophy you can follow for the rest of your life! As a visitor driven to Avoid Authenticate I can assure you that these priorities also influenced me as the customer.

At Disneyland you walk through that front gate in the morning as one person, and having experienced the atmosphere, the rides and the familiar characters you leave transformed after a day of fun and laughter. Knowing that their work is attributing to that holistic experience is probably a very fulfilling outcome for Disneyland workers driven to Avoid Authenticate. As for good old Walt Disney himself—God bless that amazing man! Imagine what his *I.D.*™ would have been. He was a dreamer and a visionary with an ability to believe in magic and fantasies; he was also courageous, perseverant and brilliant. It's impossible to guess a person's *I.D.*™, but I can't help thinking that Walt might've been driven to avoid the *Instinct to Authenticate*™.

Avoid Authenticate people's sensitivity and intuition can also see them do well in fields such as life coaching or consulting, which is why those driven to Avoid Authenticate make good therapists or psychologists. Helping clients to access the heart of their feelings and really connect to their passion, or to uproot some past destructive conditioning would be very rewarding for someone driven to Avoid Authenticate.

You are also likely to find these types of people in academia and in theoretical and strategic positions rather that at the tactical end of business operations. Those driven to Avoid Authenticate still accomplish tasks well but they tend to delegate or find ways to leverage their effort so that the same action can have multiple applications or outcomes.

The *Instinctive Drive to Complete*™

People who are driven by the *Instinct to Complete*™ are also naturals at:

➻ planning and design

⌦ anticipating outcomes

⌦ predictions

⌦ handling structured environments and situations

⌦ focusing on the task at hand.

You will find those with the Complete drive anywhere they can apply their formidable operational mind to either assist people or processes, which may include:

⌦ Preventing people from veering offcourse.

⌦ Maintaining equilibrium.

⌦ Assisting people or processes to return to 'normal' (or that sense of equilibrium).

⌦ Making progress towards whatever their particular goals or 'next steps' are.

Those motivated by the *Instinctive Drive to Complete*™ are driven to get things 'back on track'. Getting back to normal is a major driver for them — and normal is whatever they perceive it to be. Therefore, you will often find these people in fields such as health care (indeed nursing is the personification of this drive), in which they can assist people to recover and get back to 'normal'. Similarly, teaching and training attracts many people with the *Instinct to Complete*™, as does financial planning.

I've also found that many people driven by the *Instinct to Complete*™ are attracted to franchising over starting their own independent business because of the structure, training and support it provides. This is also why many Complete-driven people become particularly frustrated when franchisors and employers fail to deliver on those expectations and promises. As structure, training and support are vital for them to perform at their best, the confusion, fog and hopelessness they feel when these essentials aren't forthcoming often — unless they have some prior experience or a sound contingency plan — pulls them so out of stride they can fail.

Those driven to Complete can also thrive in maintenance roles, rescue services and environmental and animal protection. People in national parks, for example, work with wildlife to ensure that there are enough birds and animals that the ecosystem can be maintained and sustained in harmony. It is the long-term perspective that is natural for them rather than a short-term or bandaid solution, which won't have continuity.

People with the *Instinctive Drive to Complete*™ have a respect for rules and appreciate the value of good administration. They may not necessarily enjoy administration, but they will do it well because they recognise the necessity and value of good systems when it comes to delivering consistent, quality outcomes. They are reliable and dependable; when a job must be done in a way that is already set out clearly and systematically, then no-one will do it better than the person with the *Instinctive Drive to Complete*™. The strong regiment and order of the military aligns with those driven by the *Instinct to Complete*™ for that reason. If you ensure that these people can work without constant interruptions, they'll build up a momentum that makes them incredibly productive. In fact, when it comes to producing volume, this is the instinct that will propel people to do it naturally and repeatedly. You know the saying 'When you want something done, ask a busy person', well that person is the type who is driven to Complete. Just make sure you ask them questions before they start or when they are having a break!

Those with the Complete drive are energised by the detail and intricacies of pulling something together and then seeing it run like clockwork—and the busier they are, the better they perform. Events management or wedding planning are common fields for those individuals to work in. In fact in the busyness and high-paced atmosphere of an event they can often feel like they're not actually there—almost like an out-of-body experience. When it's all humming like clockwork and progressing exactly as they planned it is heaven for them—a real 'in-the-zone' experience! But really any career or role that accommodates their needs and values will allow those with the Complete drive to shine.

People with the Complete drive also have an ability to anticipate future events, so they can see the potential hiccups that may prevent continuity of effort or restrict efficient momentum as a project unfolds. Hence, not only do they have 'plan B' but they also probably have a plan C, D and E too! Furthermore, the hiccups that they see aren't just the obvious problems, but also the small, indirect consequences of problems—things that are likely to impact on the harmony of the bigger picture. Those driven to Avoid Complete may see the obvious problems, but they are less likely to formulate the jigsaw puzzle of potential outcomes apparent to those with the Complete drive.

For Complete-driven people, obstacles, surprises and negative impacts equate to anti-harmony and allow projects to become blocked—which can be a major source of stress because that situation represents the antithesis of their *I.D.*™. So they need to know all the possible things that could go wrong and allow for them before they can even begin. This same talent also gives them a gift for accurately predicting timelines and durations because they can foresee the curve balls that those driven to Avoid Complete don't see.

I know many teachers driven by the *Instinct to Complete*™. Complete-driven people are natural teachers and nurturers because they are driven by the legacy that excellent teaching can have on a child. Leaving a legacy may be important to all drives, but it is compelling to someone driven to Complete. Take an example of a Complete driven primary school student, Julia, who has been taught by a teacher who is motivated by the *Instinctive Drive to Complete*™. If Julia's teacher, Mrs Jones, had told her something that shaped Julia's life in a positive way, then Julia too might have been motivated to dedicate her life to teaching so that she can positively influence other children and leave a legacy—just as Mrs Jones had done.

Even those with this instinct who choose a different career or profession often end up teaching in some capacity. Teaching is such a natural fit it's almost like a magnet for them! Verify people might have the expertise and enjoy sharing it, but it can often be a one-way teaching style—whereas teachers driven to Complete nurture people through the learning process in a logical and sequential manner—which is especially important in a school context because each year is a building block to the next.

Driven to avoid the *Instinct to Complete*™

People who are driven to avoid the *Instinct to Complete*™ are often motivated by:

▷ variety

▷ exceptions

▷ a focus on the short term

▷ opportunities to experiment or pioneer something.

Those driven to Avoid Complete respond to projects in which they can see the start, middle and end—and if they can't see that it can feel like a prison sentence. As a consequence they excel at managing projects. Someone driven to Avoid Complete may thrive in an advertising agency, for example, where they can have many different projects for many different clients usually with a three month lifespan or less.

Although they enjoy different projects and variety, don't expect them to remember long 'to-do' lists. Their instinct is to deviate, so if you give them instructions they might get there eventually, but they will probably do half-a-dozen things in between and veer from your instructions. This is often misinterpreted as forgetfulness or laziness and can be plain irritating. But this behaviour is not deliberate and is actually one of their greatest strengths because they discover new things by working this way. They thrive on tackling problems and tasks for themselves, so they will rarely write instructions down—and if they forget them they will welcome the buzz of working out a solution all over again!

I remember saying to my son Jace—who is driven to Avoid Complete and has an *I.D.*™ of 3728—when he was about four years old, 'Jace, go upstairs, get ready for bed, clean your teeth, bring your dirty clothes down to the laundry and give mum and I a kiss goodnight before you go to bed.' He replied, 'Okay Dad', but he didn't even get halfway up the stairs before he became distracted by one of the other kids or the TV. It often happened that he would totally forget what he had been asked to do or appear to just duck off and do something else. At times I honestly thought he was being disobedient—and sometimes it drove me nuts. Once I realised that it was just his instinct to deviate I actually saw it as quite humorous. My point is that he just wasn't taking in several instructions at the same time.

Now I've learned to break down my instructions to him. So in this example I would say, 'Jace, go upstairs and get ready for bed', and then when he was up there and I could hear him rummaging about in his room, I'd shout, 'Jace, clean your teeth'. Then I'd hear the tap turning off and I'd shout, 'Mate, bring your dirty clothes to the laundry and then come and kiss your Mum and I goodnight'. If you want someone who is driven to Avoid Complete to do something, break the task into steps and don't give them more than two instructions at a time!

Jobs that are suited to those driven to Avoid Complete are those that require almost a 'consultant' mindset because these employees can solve one-off problems really fast. They are interested in short-term projects or problems that can be fixed fast using experimentation, innovation and clever short cuts. However, this can also include following the rules if that's the shortest way to the desired result.

My research shows that approximately 70 per cent of senior executives are driven to Avoid Complete and relish the constant change and unpredictability of business at the strategic or senior level. They continually pioneer new solutions, keep their options open and maintain a flexibility that is imperative at a high level. I have even worked with organisations in which all the senior management team members were driven to Avoid Complete. As dynamic and capable as they were—and for all the success they were bringing to their organisation and demonstrating throughout the world—they caused major challenges down the chain of command. Their constant changing of direction—which was also perceived as a lack of accountability and inconsistent communication made it difficult for their subordinates to interpret what was required of them. You never know what's around the corner when you are working with someone driven to Avoid Complete.

Those driven to Avoid Complete will try anything. They may not have thought it through, considered the ramifications or be trained in it, but that won't stop someone driven to Avoid Complete. This spontaneous, gung-ho attitude can appear vague and half-hearted, but these individuals don't make commitments easily and prefer to keep their options open. Let them figure out their way—after all it is what they're best at. When dealing with an Avoid Complete person be sure to help them see the ramifications of their actions both in terms of outcomes and people as they are not often immediately apparent to them. If you do that in a non-critical, non-limiting way, and let them make the choice, they'll really appreciate your input—and you'll probably get what you want as well. Whereas if you tell them what to do, I'll almost guarantee you they'll defy you!

On the plus side, Avoid Complete people can stay with roles and relationships forever if their needs—constant variety, short-term wins, experimentation, unpredictable issues to deal with—are met. But they change employers and possibly careers several times along the way. They are also the type of people who end up having their own business in order to have the freedom, autonomy and independence they need. If an employer, however, can provide the variety they need, the Avoid Complete people will stay in a role and reward the business with their loyalty for many years.

So can those driven to Avoid Complete be fulfilled as teachers, nurses or financial planners? Can they also be successful doctors, lawyers or candlestick makers? And can they stay with something long enough to make a successful career out of it? You bet they can. But they'll need strategies to deal with the components that are routine, structured and predictable. For everyone driven to Avoid Complete, variety is definitely the spice of life!

The *Instinctive Drive to Improvise*™

People with the *Instinctive Drive to Improvise*™ will be the best they can be when they can:

⇨ say yes first and ask questions later

⇨ be interactive

⇨ thrive on urgency

⇨ be animated

⇨ be persuasive

⇨ be passionate.

Those motivated by the *Instinctive Drive to Improvise*™ thrive in fun, high-energy situations. Even in serious situations these individuals don't see why things can't still be fun. They love having an audience and they enjoy interaction with others. Those driven to Improvise are usually pretty easy to spot — they are the entertainers among us.

There are many professions that allow these individuals to exhibit that flair for performance and interaction with an audience. Individuals with the Improvise drive can often be found in schools in front of an audience of thirty kids every morning! Teachers driven to Improvise are often drawn to primary and preschool teaching because it is a lot less regimented; the scope for interaction, fun and interesting activities is more evident in primary school than in high school — in which curriculums must be stringently followed and essays reviewed and marked for detail.

Those with the Improvise drive can breathe life into just about any profession with their high energy and persuasive personality. They are often natural public speakers and love nothing better than getting up and talking about their passion. You will find them in training companies, and many seminar presenters are driven by the *Instinctive Drive to Improvise*™.

Tour guides are often driven to Improvise — as demonstrated by their enviable ability to meet and greet a party from the airport with a beaming smile at 4.00 am. They need a fun and dynamic atmosphere in which they can be the centre of attention and make a wonderful first impression.

Those with the Improvise drive are great with people and can do well in a variety of professions as a result. This is a distinct natural advantage for them, and it explains why they will often find themselves in leadership roles. They have a natural flair for persuasion and can often have far-reaching influence across an organisation. This ability coupled with their highly sought-after, creative problem-solving skills can take them far in business. Their instinctive answer is always 'Yes', which can make them exceptionally good in customer service and sales roles because they will bend over backwards to please the customer.

Not everyone with the Improvise drive is extroverted, but each thrives in high-energy, high-pressure situations in which they are called upon to think on their feet.

Driven to avoid the *Instinct to Improvise*™

People who are driven to avoid the *Instinct to Improvise*™ are often also driven to be:

➷ quiet or serious

➷ non-interactive

➷ anti-risk

➷ people who work at their own pace

➷ even keeled

➷ quality driven.

Those driven to Avoid Improvise are suited to jobs in which success is measured by accountability and clearly defined responsibilities. That way they can just get on with their job in the knowledge that the results will speak for themselves. They will then consistently deliver high-quality output. They are less interactive than those driven to Improvise and need to go at their own pace. Their quiet, serious demeanor is the epitome of the stereotypical accountant or lawyer.

Those who are driven to avoid the Instinct to Improvise™ are driven to eliminate risk rather than acting despite risk—a talent that is extremely valuable in financial planning, construction, car-safety engineering and similar professions. Those driven to Avoid Improvise do not self-promote so they are often the unsung heroes in a workplace often overshadowed by loud and boisterous individuals driven to Improvise. While people with the Improvise drive can get excited about something as commonplace as the opening of an envelope, the individual who is driven to Avoid Improvise is much more level-headed. Finding ways to eliminate risk and deliver a quality result that speaks for itself is exciting for Avoid Improvise people. They are happy to leave the trumpet-blowing to those with the Improvise drive, knowing that once they have delivered their output it will not need any hype or hyperbole but will instead be recognised for its quality. They thrive in environments in which their results can speak for themselves and they don't have to 'sell' their contribution.

People driven to avoid the *Instinct to Improvise*™ are very dependable and diligent and will meet obligations even if they are not that enthusiastic or if a deadline doesn't exist. Where those driven to Improvise don't differentiate between work and fun, those driven to Avoid Improvise are serious people who clearly separate fun from work. But when they have fun they have serious fun. When out for a night on the town it is those driven to Avoid Improvise who will be the last ones standing! Once colleagues have witnessed the transformation they may ask, 'Why can't you be like this all the time?' It's a question Avoid Improvise people themselves will have pondered before, but it's just not in their nature. The best word to describe these people is diligent, which for them means applying themselves to the task at hand and completing it to a consistently high standard. So when a project just has to be done, these are the people you want on your team.

You may also find those driven to Avoid Improvise in unusual jobs and obscure professions that you may not even have considered such as crime-scene cleaning. Their ability to just get the job done without fuss or fanfare or indeed emotional involvement is perfect for such a career.

Job interviews

I am often asked how various *I.Ds*™ perform in a job interview; I've found the main discrepancy between the drives is with the *Instinctive Drive to Improvise*™.

Normally in a job interview you either want the role or you don't care. (Perhaps you are already happy in your current role and may just be going along out of curiosity.) If, on the other hand, you have been out of work for a year or hate your current job then you will want that job badly!

When people driven to Avoid Improvise are required to think on their feet they freeze; their mind goes blank and they can't process information. As a consequence they often interview very poorly. The minute they leave the interview, however, perfect, witty, insightful and intelligent answers will come flooding into their mind because they will no longer feel the pressure.

This freezing in pressure situations can be seen in sports too. Since 1996 I have worked with some of Australia's Olympic-level swimmers, and occasionally they will make a false start — such as the one Ian Thorpe famously performed in a qualifying round. After a false start swimmers will then berate themselves for it because they know it never happens in training, and they can't understand that. I think most Australians will remember the heartbreak when cyclist Shane Kelly's foot slipped of his pedal in his 1000-metre time trial at the 1996 Atlanta Olympics.

What I've found is that 90 per cent of elite athletes I have worked with are driven to Avoid the *Instinct to Improvise*™; they have to be to maintain the discipline and dedication of training. I remember hearing the coach give the pre-race speech to one of his swimmers, whom I'll call Scott for this example. The coach began:

> Now Scott, for eight years you have trained for this moment. Your mum and dad are up in the stand. There are thousands of people at home cheering for you right now and all your relatives are here from interstate to support you. Every morning and every night you have trained when others were out having fun and it all comes down to this moment.

No wonder Scott later choked during his race—talk about the coach adding to the pressure. Once the coach knew about *I.D.*™ he changed his pre-race speech to the following:

> Now Scott, this is just the same as the hundreds of times you've done it in practice. It doesn't matter if you win or lose—there is always another race. What's important is that you feel good about yourself and you give it your best shot.

As soon as the coach softened his approach with Scott, the boy started winning.

For those who are driven to Improvise, on the other hand, high-pressure environments such as interview situations are a walk in the park. They thrive on the sort of pressure that requires a quick-fire response. Interviews offer them the perfect place to make a magnificent first impression, which they invariably do. Consequently, they are very often offered every job they go for.

Back in the early 1990s, due to the countrywide recession there was a high rate of unemployment. I was doing some work with various 'job clubs' in Victoria in 1994 to assist the long-term unemployed to get back to work. In one particular job club there were ninety-one people who had been unemployed for longer than twelve months. One of my company's consultants did a project with them to see what would happen if they knew their *I.D.*™ and employed strategies that worked with it rather than against it. Out of the ninety-one, seventy-six were driven to Avoid Improvise, yet once I'd finished working with them (a process that took eight weeks) all but three had found work within three months.

So if you are in a job interview and driven to Avoid Improvise, pretend you don't want the job and do whatever you need to do to relax. Just pretend you are having a conversation or that you are interviewing them because it will take the pressure off. Those driven to Avoid Improvise often change jobs after being head hunted because they perform well in a role that they know well and are comfortable with. So although they are often noticed and recommended, they just don't excel in interviews.

Those with the Improvise drive, on the other hand, usually make a spectacular impression at the interview but can fall short of expectations once they are in the role. But because they are personable and fun, they can get away with much more than those more serious individuals who are driven to Avoid Improvise.

So if you want to interview people who are driven to Avoid Improvise and really obtain a sense of what they will be like, invite them for a pre-interview chat and a cup of coffee. They won't be so stressed and you will get a far more accurate idea of their ability and suitability for the job.

I hope that I have illustrated throughout this chapter that there is no such thing as a perfect I.D.™ for a specific role. What I recommend is that you choose a profession or job based on your passion. If you love numbers and excel at maths, then accountancy is an obvious choice, or if you watch all the law programs and never miss an episode of *Law & Order* then perhaps you should consider a career in law. Go first towards your interests and passions and then specialise based on your I.D.™. So for example, if you love those law programs and are driven by the *Instinct to Improvise*™, you could be great as an expert witness because you'd need to think on your feet at a million miles an hour and be great under pressure. On the other hand, someone driven by the *Instinct to Verify*™ may be excellent as a judge as he or she can see both sides of the story. Individuals driven by the *Instinct to Authenticate*™, though, may make outstanding prosecutors because everything is so black and white to them — they won't take their eyes off the relevant issue, no matter what level of emotion, explanation or context is introduced.

So if people understood the broad range of options that exist within a certain profession, they might be more willing to tweak their role to find something that suits them better — rather than, for example, spending years to train as a doctor only to drop out and become a beekeeper in Tasmania! So a doctor who is driven by the *Instinct to Complete*™ and driven to Avoid Improvise is probably going to be more stressed in Accident and Emergency than a doctor with the opposite I.D.™! The uncertainty and chaos works against their grain — they will likely be quite out of stride. General practice may be much more suited to someone like that.

Remember that there is more than one way to be a doctor, a builder or lawyer! I have found all I.Ds™ in all professions; however, I have also often found a dominant I.D.™ 'style' in particular fields.

This skew towards certain drives in particular fields does not preclude you if you seem to have less suitable drives; it just means you need to use your uniqueness to your advantage with strategies that ensure

Chapter 4

In stride with career development

The fundamental point of this book is that you must be true to your I.D.™ if you want to enjoy a career that delivers genuine fulfilment and success. The degree to which your I.D.™ needs are met in the workplace determines the level of your actual success and fulfilment, and therefore job tenure.

Now that I've established that there is not an automatic 'best career' fit for your I.D.™, you need to understand how to use your I.D.™ to navigate your working life in a way that meets your needs—thereby maximising your enjoyment, fulfilment and success.

When you have found an area that you are interested in or an area that inspires you, the next stage is to learn how to work with your natural advantages while being aware of your vulnerabilities so that you can compensate for them when necessary. This chapter is still on the topic of career but looks more at optimal operating styles for each I.D.™ and provides strategies you can employ to assist career progression. But remember that it's important to stress the balance between nature and nurture. Anyone can be good at each stage with the right knowledge and skills. The power of I.D.™ lies in its understanding of your innate strengths, enabling you to be in stride more often and optimise your success. It also helps you with knowledge about your natural vulnerabilities so that you can either avoid those areas or seek training to minimise their impact.

Fast-track your career

This section provides each drive and direction with suitable strategies for the workplace that can be used to aid and even accelerate career advancement.

Driven by the *Instinct to Verify*™

People who are driven by the *Instinct to Verify*™ must ensure they are in an environment that gives constant, specific feedback. They respond to this type of feedback because it allows them to refine their approach and improve, which will fast-track career progression. In addition, they should make sure they work for someone they respect and that the company they work for is at the top of its field. When negotiating remuneration it is important to Verify people that the pay seems fair. If they feel they are being paid more than they deserve, they will strive to rectify that imbalance and improve as a result. (For Verify people a pay rise is an incentive to raise their game.) Conversely, if they are being paid less than they think is reasonable, they will instinctively—and even subconsciously—lower their efforts to 'match' that remuneration, which will not move them in the right direction. Finally, people driven by the *Instinct to Verify*™ are more suited to specialist roles than general roles.

Driven to avoid the *Instinct to Verify*™

Those who are driven to avoid the *Instinct to Verify*™ are natural team players because they are naturally collaborative and accepting of the differences and nuances others bring to the table. They automatically reach out to others for answers and solutions and are encouraging and non-critical of their responses. This can also bring out the best in a team because it encourages the team members to work with each other, avoiding each person being precious about their territories; this binds the group together in a positive way. The best way for

Avoid Verify people to fast-track their career is for them to work with people whom they like and respect and to adopt a synergistic, symbiotic approach.

Driven by the *Instinct to Authenticate*™

Working in an environment in which they can be real and honest and make a real contribution is essential for those driven by the *Instinct to Authenticate*™. They need to really matter. Congruency and transparency are real ingredients for their success, so political play, innuendo, sarcasm and corridor talk are all guaranteed to poison their enthusiasm. They should make sure they are also receiving real and honest feedback—preferably in the moment because that is when it is most relevant to them. (Being told three weeks after an event that their contribution wasn't up to scratch lacks relevance and therefore usefulness for them.) They need to bear in mind that as their

The power of I.D.™ *lies in its understanding of your innate strengths*

career develops, their ongoing success will probably have as much to do with the quality of their relationships as it will with the quality of the actual tasks they perform. Workers driven to Authenticate may well need to find a way to redefine their notions of 'useful' and 'constructive' so that they can moderate their literal sense of honesty and better accommodate the apparent incongruence of others—which to people around Authenticate workers is nothing more than harmless 'shades of grey'.

These people will thrive in an environment in which they can 'do' and in which they can receive on-the-job training. When these things are possible they can very quickly prove their worth.

Driven to avoid the *Instinct to Authenticate*™

Because people driven to avoid the *Instinct to Authenticate*™ are motivated by the way others perceive them, they can fast-track their career by listening and reacting to the perceptions that relevant stakeholders feed back to them. They also have a knack for reading between the lines and picking up on innuendo and behind-the-scenes comments. Due to their strong sense of others' feelings, these people have a talent for bringing difficult or divisive issues to the table in a sensitive and constructive way. They naturally pay attention to the vibes from others and tune into their feelings—leading colleagues around them to feel respected, appreciated, motivated and comfortable. This 'people factor' is their natural playing field; the more they're able to act intuitively, the better they'll perform. Avoid Authenticate people need to trust that important talent—and they should help others trust that part of them as well.

Avoid Authenticate people also have an innate skill for leveraging opportunities and making one action add value to a product or service in many other often unexpected ways, which is vital for their productivity. But they'll probably need to point this out to others because the things that seem obvious to them are not necessarily as obvious to other people—as they won't read many of the Avoid Authenticate person's often subtle 'signals'.

Driven by the *Instinct to Complete*™

People who are driven to Complete learn best when they are given structured, formal training so that they know exactly what is expected of them. They thrive when there is constant feedback because it lets them know they are on track. But unlike those driven by the *Instinct to Verify*™—who need feedback to be specific so they can finetune their approach depending on it—these individuals need more general confirmation to know they're meeting standards and heading in the right direction. For them it's not about being precise, but about meeting expectations. They thrive if they can feel 'settled' before actually starting work in the morning—which means having uninterrupted time to review their emails and voicemails and get themselves organised for the day. But it's imperative they tell their colleagues they'll be unavailable at certain times so that their fellow workers know to leave them alone for those first twenty to thirty minutes. And the busier they are, the better they'll perform. People always say that 'if you want something done ask a busy person'—well that person is usually the one in the office who's driven by the *Instinct to Complete*™!

Those driven by this instinct tend to build momentum in their efficiency when they don't have constant interruptions, so they should make sure to factor 'focus times' of at least two hours, twice a week, into their schedules. They should also tell their colleagues so that they know to leave them alone at those times if possible.

Driven to avoid the *Instinct to Complete*™

People with a strong drive to avoid the *Instinct to Complete*™ can fast-track their career in a project-based environment, in which the variety of work keeps them stimulated and productive. These individuals have an innovative and pioneering spirit, which can see them flourish in creative positions in which they are free to tailor an ideal solution and then deliver it in a different way. Given that their energy and focus are best at the start of a task or process, they excel at troubleshooting rather than longer term implementation or maintenance.

Driven by the *Instinct to Improvise*™

Improvise people thrive when others believe in them and feel inspired and energised when there are constant challenges. They prefer sink-or-swim situations because they activate their creative impulses — and their talent at creatively 'winging it' in certain settings can produce some really extraordinary outcomes for them. Impossible deadlines and pressure-cooker environments bring out their best, acting like a light switch for them.

They need to make sure they work in an environment in which tight deadlines are commonplace. If they are not, their manager should know that they respond well to tough deadlines and instil them in their working life. Self-imposed deadlines with no real consequences don't really work because they don't evoke the adrenalin rush and energy these individuals need to lift to their best.

Driven to avoid the *Instinct to Improvise*™

Individuals who are driven to avoid the *Instinct to Improvise*™ are outstanding in areas in which diligence and substance are the order of the day; they are the proverbial quiet achievers. They need a job that isn't glamorous but is still fundamental to the success of the team. They'll happily accept tasks that simply need to be done — with no fanfare, real buzz or excitement, or major rewards.

Avoid Improvise people also see risks that others miss. If they are allowed to present these potential challenges along with positive solutions, their contribution can be considerable.

They also prefer that the quality of their work speaks for itself, but it is also wise for these individuals to learn to share their achievements.

After all, in a working environment everyone is busy; sometimes if people don't make a point of ensuring their colleagues know they're doing a good job, they simply will not be noticed.

Blind spots

Just as there are strategies that work for certain *I.Ds*™ in the workplace, there are also I.D.-specific vulnerabilities that can restrict career advancement for some people.

Driven by the *Instinct to Verify*™

Those who are driven by the *Instinct to Verify*™ should be wary of focusing too intently on technical accuracy and being 'right' to the detriment of the people they work with. They can become so caught up in rectifying problems that they start getting involved in fixing other people's, sometimes railroading others into their viewpoint. To prevent this they need to ask themselves what they want the outcome to be, and then change their thinking so that they're focused on that result. Sometimes being right isn't conducive to a successful outcome; allowing others to be right can be a much better tactic.

Driven to avoid the *Instinct to Verify*™

People who are driven to avoid the *Instinct to Verify*™ can let projects run away from them because they don't prioritise their time; they can therefore be indiscriminate with time and people, which leads to conflict and inefficiency. They can also allow difficult situations to fester for far too long; instead of dealing with a small issue they can ignore it until it becomes a big one.

Driven by the *Instinct to Authenticate*™

Because they're so focused on the 'doing' and don't evaluate their productivity, people who are driven by the *Instinct to Authenticate*™ have trouble seeing the contribution of their tasks to the bigger picture. In addition, they don't pick up on the signals from people about how they are feeling and can miss crucial yet subtle pieces of information as a result. They can also appear blunt and insensitive, and this can cause tension with others. They would sometimes do well to remember that they can catch more bees with honey than vinegar.

Driven to avoid the *Instinct to Authenticate*™

These individuals, out of all the types of *I.D.*™, are perhaps the most vulnerable to misunderstandings because they expect other people to glean more from their conversations and instructions than they actually articulate. In addition, they can compromise their credibility through excessive hyperbole and 'rainbow chasing', and their philosophical nature can sometimes appear too detached from reality.

Driven by the *Instinct to Complete*™

People who are driven by the *Instinct to Complete*™ can be caught out if they don't fulfil their need to feel settled in the morning. Therefore, agreeing to meetings first thing can be unproductive for them, and it can have a significant detrimental effect on their day. If they allow themselves to be interrupted constantly, it can also diminish their productivity. However, they also need to find a balance so that they don't appear unapproachable and defensive as a result of being sidetracked. In addition, they can be too rigid about sticking to schedules and routines, and also tend not to allow for change—a necessary part of business life.

Driven to avoid the *Instinct to Complete*™

Avoid Complete people can find themselves in hot water when they don't anticipate all the contingencies. Their drive to move from project to project can result in things being missed, so they need to allow for that if they want to succeed. Projects can run over time and over budget because they don't see the details and are easily sidetracked on tangents.

Driven by the *Instinct to Improvise*™

These individuals can encounter problems in the workplace because they think they can talk their way out of things all the time. Due to this, people around them can lose faith in their word, and this can be detrimental to performance and team harmony. They need to follow through on tasks or delegate them to ensure things are accomplished and to maintain their fabulous first impression. It is therefore important that they temper their initial desire to say yes to everything and instead practise saying, 'Let me get back to you on that'.

Driven to avoid the *Instinct to Improvise*™

People who are driven to avoid the *Instinct to Improvise*™ can miss opportunities because they are too busy assessing risk — and becoming paralysed by it. They can appear negative and dismissive of new ideas so should be careful to couch their feedback in more positive terms. Instead of always pointing out the flaws in a plan, for example, they could appreciate and articulate the positives in it too. It will enable them to be seen more as the valuable asset they are, rather than as the colleagues who always give reasons why something can't be done. They are also prone to missing opportunities because they steadfastly refuse to blow their own trumpet.

Career-development phases

Over the years I have met countless people who have been in their particular profession for ten or twenty years. For some of them, when they started in the role they loved it because they found it energising and enjoyed the challenge, but then — many years down the track — they began dreading Monday mornings. Imagine a doctor who's been a general practitioner for twenty years — and who loved every minute of the job when she began. In the beginning she enjoyed interacting and connecting with patients, and she took pleasure in watching the children grow up and be part of a community. But twenty years later she hates it because it offers no challenge for her anymore, and she is sick of hearing about little Johnny's sore throat!

At forty-five years old her logical solution to this problem is to change professions, but all her friends and family think she's crazy. People begin telling her that she couldn't possibly start again because she's too old to go back to school! Although I don't agree with that — I think that anyone can do whatever they want at any age — I was curious as to why someone could love something for so long and then seem to hate it with a passion. What changed?

Well each career has different stages, and just as there are certain I.Ds that gravitate towards certain professions, so too are there I.Ds that are more comfortable in particular stages of the career-development process. In any career — be it farmer, fire-fighter or psychiatrist — there are six stages of development:

1   learning

2   applying

3   mastering

4   supervising and teaching

5   leading

6   coaching and transition.

Although each phase is more suited to some I.Ds than others, all I.Ds can navigate each career-development stage if they're aware of their strengths and weaknesses at each one. When I explain this idea to people it usually facilitates an 'Ah hah!' experience—a light bulb moment. They are often stunned by the simplicity of the strategy, and it usually makes a huge difference to their ability to pilot their working life. For example, the dissatisfied doctor I spoke about earlier in this chapter was able to see which phase she was in—enabling her to understand why she had lost her passion for the

Some people are more suited to typical learning modes than others

job—and employ strategies that could turn that around. Often when we are dissatisfied with something—whether a job, relationship or friendship—we decide to discard it rather than looking at what is causing the problem and addressing it with effective strategies.

By understanding your I.D.™ and the natural motivations that underpin that I.D.™, you can better ensure that your needs are met.

Learning

Part of any new job is learning how to do it. Whether that involves on-the-job training or classroom training, learning is the first step for us all. But we all learn according to our I.Ds™—meaning that some people are more suited to typical learning modes than others. If you don't realise this, your natural predisposition for learning can be misinterpreted as a wrong choice or as confirmation of a right choice. So say you love kids and want to be a primary school teacher. You are outgoing and fun to be around, and kids love being with you and seem to really thrive in your company. You start learning to be a teacher but discover that you dislike the learning process. You may then easily misinterpret that as a symptom of a bad career choice. In actual fact you may be driven by the *Instinct to Improvise*™, and as such not naturally inclined towards learning step by step. If you know that you can employ strategies that will help you persevere, you may well become an outstanding primary school teacher once you're actually in the role. Conversely, you may be driven by the *Instinct to Verify*™ and love the step-by-step learning and training; you therefore may be lulled into a false sense of security. You may believe that you have indeed made the right career choice, only to find that a classroom of six-year-olds is not for you. You discover that the mental challenge you found in teacher training has gone because there are rarely problems to solve in the classroom, leaving you bored. It doesn't necessarily mean you made the wrong decision, but you'll certainly need to manage the role with appropriate strategies in order to sustain your enjoyment and success.

That every job will have boring bits to it is a very important point. What those tedious aspects are will be different for different people, but if you know your *I.D.*™ you can pre-empt the boring bits and work around them.

Driven by the *Instinct to Verify*™

Those driven to Verify thrive on learning because they need to know why things occur. They thrive on thinking things through and seeing the empirical deduction that leads to the final correct outcome. They are also driven by the feedback of the learning stage and the reassurance that comes from clarifying their understanding. They are energised by evaluating problems and determining solutions and strategies. Classroom training is particularly enjoyable for most people with the Verify drive because they receive specific information in writing, which can be studied and digested. Of all the drives it is those driven by the *Instinct to Verify*™ that respond best to the traditional classroom environment.

Driven to avoid the *Instinct to Verify*™

Those driven to Avoid Verify can find the traditional ideas of learning quite difficult. They don't necessarily see things as right or wrong, so 'all roads lead to Rome' for an individual driven to Avoid Verify. If Avoid Verify students are given unconditional encouragement and acceptance within an environment in which everyone's contribution is regarded as vital and equal, then they can learn well. But if that's not provided — making them feel as though they are being judged all the time — then they can struggle with learning. However, they are fast learners because they are driven to do it the correct way first time.

These people typically thrive in preschool because there they are constantly encouraged by teachers who praise everything they do — who see all their work as good. However, in more senior school years students are assessed and judged on their ability to reach correct outcomes by following prescribed methods — and Avoid Verify students can find that hard to take, making it more difficult for them to excel.

Driven by the *Instinct to Authenticate*™

Those driven to Authenticate need and like to see how things work. The kid that insists on taking things apart to see how it works is probably driven to Authenticate! Therefore, the individual with the Authenticate drive especially likes the learning stage if he or she can learn by doing; they enjoy practical demonstrations and being able to learn on the job.

Those driven to Authenticate do not necessarily thrive in a classroom or theoretical environment because they can get confused when they take the teachers and other students literally. To a large extent their success as a student can have much to do with the ability of the teacher to understand their literal and hands-on approach. They are best suited to practical learning, whereby they can test their theory and do what is being taught. Practical application and relevance are vital ingredients for optimising their learning!

Driven to avoid the *Instinct to Authenticate*™

Those driven to Avoid Authenticate learn best when they can see how the knowledge they've learned can be leveraged. If what they are learning has two or three benefits outside of training then they are driven to learn. They enjoy conceptualising and theorising, so classroom study can be inspiring for them — as long as they don't actually have to do anything about it! The learning stage is not a natural place for these people, and they can find it hard to engage.

Driven by the *Instinct to Complete*™

Those driven to Complete enjoy the learning stage when they have time to finish the lessons, when the learning is structured and when there is a logical progression and process to the training. Individuals with the Complete drive thrive when they undertake formal, structured training — and even if the formal training is not that good, they will feel comfortable knowing they received it. Conversely, if they can do a certain task that they weren't formally trained in, they will invariably feel compromised until that formal-training gap is filled. Even if they don't learn anything new they'll benefit from knowing with certainty that they are doing things properly.

Complete-driven people will fast-track their career when they receive structured induction training from their role. Theoretically those driven to Complete can do well in a classroom environment if it is very structured and the teaching has a logical flow to it. They also need time to rehearse and practise. The person who first said, 'Repetition is the mother of skill', was probably driven by the *Instinct to Complete*™.

Driven to avoid the *Instinct to Complete*™

Those driven to avoid the *Instinct to Complete*™ enjoy variety and spontaneity, which is not usually the domain of learning. Whether they receive what they need depends to a large extent on the skill of the teacher and the degree to which he or she is able to accommodate a variety of approaches. If an Avoid Complete student is told what the desired outcome should be, given the parameters by which he or she can get there and allowed to independently pioneer a way from A to B, the student can learn well and thrive on the challenge. If, on the other hand, Avoid Complete pupils are being spoonfed and given step-by-step directions, they will be bored out of their minds. They need different scenarios, examples and stories to stay engaged. If the learning stage offers some flexibility and encourages innovation and the finding of new solutions then they can do well — otherwise it can be a struggle. Certainly traditional classroom environments with a set curriculum can be tedious beyond words for these individuals.

Driven by the *Instinct to Improvise*™

Those driven to Improvise don't find learning so easy — unless its fun! At the very beginning of the subject they can be quite focused because it's novel — and therefore interesting and something different to think about — but their attention soon drifts, and they do not have the perseverance that the other drives have. For Improvise people learning needs to be exciting, fun and experimental; that requires a very specific learning style from the teacher. If it's not fun they can find it very hard—and as a consequence they can find the learning stage tedious and be seen by others as fickle. These are the people who have beautiful black acoustic guitars gathering dust in the corner of the living room after four lessons! These are the students who want to go from nil to Jimi Hendrix in two lessons, but become disenchanted when they can't!

Driven to avoid the *Instinct to Improvise*™

Those driven to Avoid Improvise can learn well because they just do what needs to be done. If learning is a part of the job then they will diligently apply themselves to it. They prefer a quiet, calm environment in which everyone takes the learning seriously. As such, they respond well to traditional classroom teaching. They are also keen to know if what they've learned will assist them to eliminate risk in the future. So these are life's paper traders—they will practise how on a dummy system long before ever going live.

Applying

So you've learned what you need to learn and it's now time to start doing the job and applying what you've learned. Some drives are better suited than others to the applying stage of the career-development process.

Driven by the *Instinct to Verify*™

Individuals with the Verify drive are happy applying themselves because it gives them a chance to test their theories and then improve. They are motivated to find ways to become better—even to be the best—so application allows them to finetune what they've learned and systematically improve. It also provides them with an opportunity to test theory against practice and see if what they learned is true. It provides them with evidence to support their theory. When doing the job they work through their priorities accordingly, while always seeking to develop and share their expertise.

Driven to avoid the *Instinct to Verify*™

Those driven to Avoid Verify can apply themselves as long as they know exactly what they are doing and don't have to think about it. They will also apply themselves if they feel safe in their environment and feel they are not going to be judged—especially when applying a new skill. If the work is a 'no brainer', they will happily apply themselves; if not, it can be more difficult for them.

Driven by the *Instinct to Authenticate*™

As long as they can see the relevance of the task at hand, those driven to Authenticate are energised by the applying stage because it's the 'doing' stage. People with the Authenticate drive need to see physical results for their effort and thrive on being able to see progress made on a daily basis. In that respect, those driven to Authenticate can often be found in blue-collar work because it's much more physical—and lends itself more to tangible results—than white-collar work. Although if white-collar workers driven to Authenticate see the pile in their in-tray going down, they will achieve that same sense of fulfilment from what they are doing. As long as they can see the results of their day's work, Authenticate workers will feel fulfilled.

Driven to avoid the *Instinct to Authenticate*™

Those driven to Avoid Authenticate are not natural doers. They are much happier in the ruminating stage, loving concepts and ideas. They can apply themselves if everything happens according to their particular ideals. They are also more motivated to apply what they have learned if the result of that application meets a number of different objectives. That way they can obtain leverage from their learning—if they can't gain that, applying themselves consistently to a given task can be a struggle.

Driven by the *Instinct to Complete*™

People driven by the *Instinct to Complete*™ are happy working because it means they are busy and productive, which they find fulfilling. They are more than happy in the applying phase if there is a system to follow and if they are given the time to finish the work without interruption so that they can gather momentum. They also need plenty of advance notice about what is required of them so that they can keep everything organised.

Driven to avoid the *Instinct to Complete*™

People driven to Avoid Complete can have difficulty with the applying phase if it is too regimented, repetitive or long. If it involves different projects and there is variety and spontaneity in the work, they are more than capable of applying what they have learnt and doing it well. They need to pioneer ways of doing things better and require the flexibility to keep their options open—otherwise they can shut down. Monotony can lead to hostility and negativity for Avoid Complete people.

Driven by the *Instinct to Improvise*™

Those driven to Improvise are okay at this stage, but only if it's fun and they feel like they are getting somewhere. People with the Improvise drive thrive on positive energy, so if they are fast-tracking their career and can see that the work is going to propel them to where they want to be, they'll work more quickly. They are not motivated by doing the work, but by how that exertion will accelerate their career. It's the results of effort that those with the drive to Improvise are interested in—not the effort itself.

Driven to avoid the *Instinct to Improvise*™

People driven to Avoid Improvise just get the job done, so they have no problem applying what they have learned without the need for fanfare. They don't appreciate being rushed or pressured. If they are able to apply their knowledge calmly and diligently they will be fulfilled.

Mastering

Mastery comes from the ongoing application of your learnt skills. By applying what you know over and over again—while constantly seeking improvement—you will eventually arrive at mastery. This stage is not for everyone. Whether you elevate your application skills to mastery is as dependent on your values and ambition as it is on your I.D.™ However, just as some I.Ds are better suited to learning and application, so too are some I.Ds more suited to achieving mastery easier than others.

Driven by the *Instinct to Verify*™

Those driven to Verify are into mastering because it gives them the opportunity to be the best. Of all the drives the Verify drive is the one most conducive to mastering because those individuals live by constant improvement. The danger with this is that once they have reached mastery, those driven to Verify can become bored and stop enjoying the job because all the challenge has gone. After being in a role for a significant time, they can feel as if there are no more problems to solve because they have come across all the possible scenarios. This can drain all the fulfilment out of a role for someone with the Verify drive. As a master, the person driven to Verify will be called upon to share his or her expertise, and this can offer an opportunity to extend enjoyment of the role.

Driven to avoid the *Instinct to Verify*™

People who are driven to Avoid Verify do not find this stage natural and see the process to achieve mastery as a challenging one. They are more naturally accepting, so they therefore deliver results and move on—rather than dwelling on how they could have done things better. Even when they do review things, they don't necessarily see where things could be improved—making the challenge of mastery rather difficult. However, if they know how to improve things—or what to look for to achieve mastery—and receive genuine encouragement along the way, then they will be much more inclined to pursue mastery. They'll pursue it especially if it means they'll be more capable of producing the results they want first time—thereby avoiding both criticism and the need to re-do things.

Driven by the *Instinct to Authenticate*™

Those driven to Authenticate thrive on mastering because it is an extension of application, which is their forte. 'Doing' energises them, and they have very specific standards and views on how tasks should be approached. Authenticate people are keen to reach mastery as efficiently as possible—particularly if it fits their image of themselves as the 'craftspeople'.

Driven to avoid the *Instinct to Authenticate*™

People who are driven to Avoid Authenticate find this stage difficult because they have no real motivation to master something. You can't really master thought, which is their domain. Mastering a skill or ability involves practice—which means 'doing' something—and people driven to Avoid Authenticate do not feel at home with that. However, whether people possess life skills and mastery of situations is very much dependent on their people skills and how they interact with others—which are strengths of those driven to Avoid Authenticate. Because people driven to Avoid Authenticate are adept at understanding people, they are able to deal with others in a powerful way.

Driven by the *Instinct to Complete*™

People driven to Complete are not naturally suited to mastery because it implies constant improvement and finetuning an approach. The strength of those driven to Complete lies in their ability to maintain a process or system; they will generally not be interested in improving something unless they can see the work is necessary to achieve a goal or fulfil a plan. Having said that, mastery is often gained through relentless repetition and practice; if they can be undertaken according to a distinct process, those driven to Complete can reach mastery.

Driven to avoid the *Instinct to Complete*™

Those driven to Avoid Complete can master things, but it's usually an accident; they may master something but they probably won't really know how they did it. For that reason they are unique and can find it difficult to transfer or duplicate their knowledge. If people driven to Avoid Complete can work in a flexible environment or somewhere where there are shortcuts to mastery available, then they can reach the mastery stage. But they are unlikely to arrive at mastery through diligent application or by following a formula.

Driven by the *Instinct to Improvise*™

People who are driven by the *Instinct to Improvise*™ are not into mastery either because they are all about 'winging it', so where they fall short in technical mastery and know-how they can it make up with their mouths by talking up situations. Mastery to them seems pointless — much better to be good enough to finish the job and then innovate. They can be masters if it assists in their impression; however, often mastery is more illusion than reality with Improvise people. But it doesn't actually matter with Improvise people because they will demonstrate mastery through a combination of self-confidence and innovation. People say that business is all about perception; those with the Improvise drive are masters of perception!

Driven to avoid the *Instinct to Improvise*™

People driven to Avoid Improvise can master things and are motivated to do so if they know it won't involve selling themselves — they hate blowing their own trumpet. They can also diligently apply themselves, which is needed for the practising that mastery involves. Top-level athletes, for example, will always get to training — come rain, hail or shine — because a lot of them are driven to Avoid Improvise.

Supervising and teaching

This stage sees technical knowledge being replaced for the first time by people knowledge. The irony of career development is that it is assumed that in order for you to supervise others completing a certain task, you should be a master of that task—but the reality is often the opposite. All the people with drives that thrive in the learning, applying and mastering phases of career advancement can find it difficult to make the transition into management roles. By contrast, those who struggled with the earlier stages can blossom in this stage because their primary skills lie in the area of people, ideas and concepts—skills traditionally found in management and leadership.

The topic of teaching in this chapter generally refers to the task of teaching rather than to teaching as a career. Teaching—in terms of transferring knowledge to people in a way that they can engage with it—is a skill that is required in all careers and vocations.

Driven by the *Instinct to Verify*™

Those driven to Verify can find the transition from mastery to supervising or teaching hard because they perceive that no-one will ever do the job as well as they did. But they can be good teachers because they have a great deal of knowledge and a strong desire to share it. They can appear critical, however, when students bring back work or demonstrate what they've learned, only to be met by criticism by the person driven to Verify—who is always looking at how things can be improved. The other issue here is that those with the Verify drive are energised by the challenge of solving problems. Once they move into teaching and supervisory roles, they are pulled further away from the challenges and instead have to focus on managing the people who are tackling them—which can be hard for people driven by the *Instinct to Verify*™.

Driven to avoid the *Instinct to Verify*™

People driven to Avoid Verify can thrive in supervisory roles because they are very accepting of others and naturally encouraging, and they value everyone's contribution. People who work for Avoid Verify leaders usually comment on how they blossomed with the constant encouragement and genuine sense of trust bestowed on them. They often say that if they felt a downside, it usually related to the lack of specific feedback given by Avoid Verify leaders.

Driven by the *Instinct to Authenticate*™

People driven by the *Instinct to Authenticate*™ can be excellent teachers because they often assist the learning process by using demonstrations in their teaching, becoming involved with the transfer of knowledge hands-on. However, as supervisors they will be forced to move away from 'doing' tasks—which they love—instead being confined to monitoring others, which can be very hard to take for those driven to Authenticate. The danger with these types of teachers is that they will become too involved with students and end up doing their tasks for them!

Driven to avoid the *Instinct to Authenticate*™

Those driven to Avoid Authenticate are in their element in teaching or supervisory roles. As supervisors and teachers, they can put themselves on their student's wavelength and adjust their style to work for him or her. People driven to Avoid Authenticate live in the world of ideas and concepts—and that trait is conducive to managerial positions. They are also very diplomatic and sensitive to individual differences and can therefore supervise very successfully.

Driven by the *Instinct to Complete*™

Those driven to Complete don't naturally fit into the supervisory stage. However, they can be good teachers and supervisors because they teach from a framework that emphasises processes and holds people to account. The downside is that they can be rigid about procedures; for some *I.Ds* that approach can be boring, even though it has merit as a teaching method. They can often find themselves in supervisory roles because they bring order and efficiency to a team, but Complete-driven people can also find the unpredictable nature of people in the workplace very difficult to deal with.

Driven to avoid the *Instinct to Complete*™

People driven to avoid the *Instinct to Complete*™ are better suited to supervisory positions than those driven to Complete, but their free spirit means they can find managing people constricting. If they are free to experiment and pioneer ways of doing things, they—and their students—can enjoy the process. The downside is that their speed of transaction can mean that students don't see the whole picture and can feel inferior when they can't duplicate something the teacher has made look very simple.

Driven by the *Instinct to Improvise*™

Those driven to Improvise can shine in these types of roles because they thrive on interaction with others and the buzz that comes from helping them grow. They can energise any team and bring fun and laughter to the workplace, which is always a plus—providing, of course, that results are also achieved. Famous studies—such as that in *Influence* by Robert B Ciadini—have proven that people are much more likely to be influenced by someone they like; those driven to Improvise naturally inject a sense of fun and challenge into their environments, making them very likable. They can also inspire their students or team members to stretch beyond their comfort zones—making them very popular teachers with quite a diverse range of students.

Driven to avoid the *Instinct to Improvise*™

Supervising and teaching does not necessarily come easy to people driven to Avoid Improvise. Because they can be more task and process oriented—rather than people oriented—they can lose their edge. They can certainly transfer their knowledge and deliver the results, but they may not necessarily inspire a team to produce their best.

Leadership

In answer to the age-old question about whether a leader is born or made, I believe both to be true. It is true that not everyone is a natural leader, but if the desire to lead is there then anyone can be an effective leader. By understanding your I.D.™, you can appreciate and amplify your natural strengths while also understanding your weaknesses so that you can minimise their impact. Leadership has many currencies for different drives. Essentially, however, leadership comes down to credibility and respect, which enables you to exert influence. Influence requires credibility and credibility is the outcome of congruence. So once you understand what constitutes credibility for each drive, you can tailor your leadership approach to ensure you maintain respect—enabling you to truly lead, regardless of the diversity of drives in your team!

Driven by the *Instinct to Verify*™

People who are driven by the *Instinct to Verify*™ will lead through their sense of control and expertise. Others find it easy to follow leaders with the Verify drive because they are able to demonstrate their skill and experience in the area—to walk the talk. They have a natural ability to organise and prioritise, which is important in any leadership role. The leader driven to Verify is decisive once all the information is in and they can hold their position easily. They also have excellent focus, rarely taking their eye off the ball—another characteristic of a good leader. Their vulnerability, however, is that their 'perfect' standard can be debilitating for people working for them. Because those driven to Verify need to see constant improvement, others can feel that the goal posts are always moving and that their efforts are not being appreciated, which can be very disheartening. The danger here is that people may stop giving their best because they feel that even their best is never good enough.

Driven to avoid the *Instinct to Verify*™

Leaders driven to Avoid Verify can also excel because they are great at reaching out to people and engaging others in their vision. They are naturally collaborative, and that can be very empowering for others because they can often feel part of the team, the decision-making process and the solution. As Warren G Bennis, a world authority in this area, says, 'Good leaders make people feel that they're at the very heart of things, not at the periphery'.

A focus on collaboration is the gift of leaders driven to Avoid Verify. Their vulnerabilities arise, however, when they don't naturally check in with team members, coach others or give feedback once the vision has been set. They assume that everyone knows his or her role and is doing it. Yet for those people driven to Verify, feedback is crucial—and they can perceive their Avoid Verify leader as wishy-washy because he or she won't necessarily resolve problems, but instead simply find ways around them.

> Not everyone is a natural leader, but if the desire to lead is there then anyone can be an effective leader

Those driven to Avoid Verify may not be able to justify their approach because they are guided by their internal compass rather than logic. Those driven to Verify don't understand this because they require proof—and if they don't receive it they can start to lose respect for leaders driven to Avoid Verify.

Driven by the *Instinct to Authenticate*™

Those driven to Authenticate can be excellent in leadership roles that require leading by example. So these types of leaders are perhaps better suited to leadership in smaller organisations, where they can be seen to be hands on and involved. They are crystal clear in their communication of their vision and great at keeping others focused on it. They are also very efficient—running a lean, tight ship with no tolerance for politics and game playing. Conversely, their vulnerability is related to the processes required to realise goals; the job may be completed but doing it may not have been a particularly enjoyable journey. Also, those with the Authenticate drive can be very dismissive of the human element of business, potentially appearing unfeeling and overly harsh or blunt to their subordinates.

Driven to avoid the *Instinct to Authenticate*™

People who are driven to avoid the *Instinct to Authenticate*™ can make good leaders because they inspire a meaningful vision with their strong grasp of concepts and ideas. They have an innate ability to home in on what is important to each individual person in their team and instinctively 'push their buttons' in order to engage their motivation—which is inspiring for others because they feel understood and appreciated. Although they are able to translate their vision well enough that everyone understands it, their vulnerability is that they can be too forgiving of those not rowing the boat in the same direction. The result is—instead of a lean, mean, fighting machine—a sloppy, unfocused rag-tag of employees who are not delivering. The person driven to Avoid Authenticate will simply move underperforming people around in different roles to either minimise their disruptive influence or because they blindly hope that those individuals will find their niche—rather than just showing them the door! Firing unproductive staff is not something the leader driven to Avoid Authenticate can do easily or naturally. They don't like to hurt people's feelings and genuinely want to find the good in people—believing, for example, that if the person could just find the right role, the situation could resolve itself.

Driven by the *Instinct to Complete*™

Those driven to Complete shine in leadership roles that have a crystal-clear path already established—when the goal posts are positioned and all that is required is delivery of an outcome. They suit, for example, monstrous tasks that they need to monitor and see through to completion while also bringing everyone in the project along in the process. Their vulnerabilities show up if they are in an environment with constant change, a lack of direction, volatility or shifting expectations. They also struggle when there are too many unknowns in a task and too many interruptions.

Driven to avoid the *Instinct to Complete*™

Leaders who are driven to Avoid the *Instinct to Complete*™ thrive in leadership roles that require a certain pioneering spirit. They are the trailblazers among us who are supremely suited to making it up as they go along. They are the entrepreneurial leaders who are willing to jump off the cliff and build their wings on the way down. They don't need certainty before taking action and are comfortable in situations in which they don't know what the outcome will be. However, their vulnerability is that they feel the need to keep their options open—so even when they see an approach or project that will work, they find it very hard to commit to it 100 per cent and drive vision. Although good leaders need to be open-minded in order to see new opportunities, they also need to commit to projects—throwing their weight and belief behind a certain course of action. Otherwise, their 'sitting on the fence' can be misinterpreted as hesitation—and it's very hard to follow a hesitant leader! In addition, this approach can drive those driven to Complete to despair because they will fast lose respect for a leader who does not commit to the plan and implement it.

Driven by the *Instinct to Improvise*™

Those driven to Improvise are in their element in leadership roles. Leadership is so often about people and having the ability to inspire them and ignite their drive and motivation—which is the domain of those with the Improvise drive. Improvise-driven leaders love bringing people together to complete a task and creating an environment that is fun and energising for others. Working in a team or business that is led by an Improvise person can be very challenging because people can feel as if they're being thrown in at the deep end. This can result in people growing a great deal from their experience with an Improvise leader because they were challenged to attempt things outside their comfort zone.

Those driven to Improvise also love the fact that they are often no longer responsible for actually doing the tasks—instead being focused on inspiring others to complete them. Their vulnerability is that this 'can do' attitude can seem unrealistic to the people in the team who actually have to make it happen. Their penchant for making the impossible possible is okay when they can pull it off themselves, but when they move into leadership it is unreasonable to expect someone else to meet those expectations.

Driven to avoid the *Instinct to Improvise*™

Leaders driven to Avoid Improvise come into their own when the job isn't necessarily sexy or fun or exciting but needs to be done regardless. They are also skilled at eliminating or identifying risk in order to negotiate the delivery with the minimum fuss. There will be no surprises in a team headed by a leader who is driven to Avoid Improvise—and that is a very valuable trait in leadership because it adds to the leader's congruence and credibility. Their vulnerability, however, is that they are not natural communicators and don't see the need to inspire the team. Their drive to eliminate risk means that it is unlikely that individuals will be asked to perform work outside the specific role they were recruited for.

Coaching and transition

Coaching differs from supervising and teaching because it involves a greater element of transition. When someone is supervising staff, he or she is in a position of authority—and the same is true of a teacher with his or her students. However, in a coaching role the coach is expected to walk alongside his or her student—working with the individual to facilitate the best outcome. Again, all people possess the ability to be good coaches, but only if they know their strengths and vulnerabilities and employ strategies to ensure that their weaknesses are minimised and their talents capitalised on.

Driven by the *Instinct to Verify*™

People who are driven by the *Instinct to Verify*™ are very good coaches when it comes to understanding technique. They thrive when the person they're coaching is already at a certain level of competency because their gift is in being able to pinpoint the 5 per cent that can be improved—potentially elevating a bronze-medal winner to a gold-medal winner. The challenge comes when the person being coached is not already at bronze-medal level—in which case a Verify coach can appear too critical and 'nit picking'. On the athletics track the difference between gold and silver can be a fraction of an inch; a coach driven to Verify excels at finding that margin. But that critical ability can be very demotivating for people who are not at the professional level at which they can handle it.

Driven to avoid the *Instinct to Verify*™

Those people driven to Avoid Verify excel at getting people into positions in which they can contend for the top spot. So when it comes to starting people off in a coaching environment, the best coaches are driven to Avoid Verify because they are full of enthusiasm, acceptance and unconditional encouragement — and that is enormously helpful. Once the student is competent and requires finetuning, it's time for the coach who is driven to Verify to step in. The challenge that coaches driven to Avoid Verify have is that encouragement and enthusiasm can only take people so far before they need streamlined coaching that will take them to the next level; often Avoid Verify coaches' lack of judgement can hinder that process.

Driven by the *Instinct to Authenticate*™

Those driven to Authenticate can make really good coaches because they become deeply involved — often by demonstrating how things are done. They make tasks real and relevant for the people they are coaching — bringing theory to life. Their downside is they can be personally involved in doing tasks for too long — not allowing their students to try and fail a few times without judgement. Coaches driven by the *Instinct to Authenticate*™ always want to ride in and save the day!

Driven to avoid the *Instinct to Authenticate*™

Coaches driven to Avoid Authenticate can be excellent because they are not driven to jump in and do it themselves. They are therefore happy to let the person being coached just get on with the job. However, they can be too theoretical when they are coaching, leaving the person being coached feeling isolated and alone. By contrast, that doesn't tend to happen with coaches that are driven to Authenticate because those coaches are in there with their student. The coach driven to Avoid Authenticate can also have unrealistic timelines in terms of what can be accomplished. Because they are theoretical and idealistic, they can underestimate the time that is necessary to complete the process.

Driven by the *Instinct to Complete*™

Those driven to Complete are excellent coaches because they tend to be systematic and cover everything. They will have a schedule of coaching and will stick to it. But the downside of that is that they don't read situations very well, or if they do read them, they'll ignore them and stick to the schedule. So a coach driven to Complete, for example, may be the coach of a sales team — and he or she will know that week three in the schedule is all about making the close. Even if the team has been out in the field and really wants some coaching on closing the deal, coaches who are driven to Complete will stick to the planned schedule. In other words, their coaching can be less relevant and dynamic because they focus on processes rather than outcomes and requirements. However, coaching is a long-term commitment, and those driven to Complete enjoy watching progress from week to week. They will therefore be more enthusiastic about coaching after working with people for weeks — and that's a useful coaching quality.

Driven to avoid the *Instinct to Complete*™

Those driven to Avoid Complete are dynamic; in the instance above they would have abandoned the week-three lesson in favour of doing what would be needed in the moment. They are much more focused on the present and can read situations and adapt accordingly — and their coaching can feel more dynamic as a consequence. However, once in the coaching process, they can get bored quickly, so they need to make sure they mix it up a bit and use new and interesting elements in their coaching.

Driven by the *Instinct to Improvise*™

Improvise people are great coaches because they are very inspiring and motivating. They are unafraid to take risks — such as putting people in different roles to test out their suitability for them. They are fun and energetic — and that spills over into coaching. The downside is they can focus on the positives without dealing with the negatives — and often that is where the real potential for improvement lies.

Driven to avoid the *Instinct to Improvise*™

Those driven to Avoid Improvise can be good coaches because they will coach diligently and consistently. They are very dependable and reliable but may lack energy or fun, both of which are often needed to push through the difficult times. The tasks of coaching rather than the goals of coaching often distract those driven to Avoid Improvise, to their detriment.

Now take a moment to reflect on where you are in your career-development path. If you are in a stage that is not naturally suited to you, consider what you could do to achieve fulfilment in your role. If you are driven to Authenticate and are supervising others, for example, take some time to 'do' rather than supervise. If you are driven to Verify and have thoroughly mastered your role, on the other hand, you could consider passing on your knowledge by becoming a teacher at the local college. Find ways to re-engage with your profession instead of deciding to jump ship!

By using I.D.™ and this career-development model I have helped many clients recapture the enthusiasm and passion of their profession. By employing the I.D. System™ and career-development model you too will be able to manage your career development and gain a sense of fulfilment and accomplishment from your role more often.

Chapter 5

In stride with your relationship

Let's face it—relationships are a minefield! Being in relationships with others is where much of the joy in life is, yet most people were never taught—formally or explicitly—how to have good relationships. More often than not, everything we know about how to relate to others comes from role modelling and making it up as we go along. We learn from relationships with our family members, colleagues, friends and—the most confrontational relationships of all—partners.

When discussing I.D.™ with clients, their personal relationships frequently come up in converstation as people want to know how they can be the best in their personal life as well as in their career.

Why do people go to fortune tellers and psychics? Because they want to know whether they will meet the love of their life! It's the number-one question men and women want the answer to. Will she meet Mr Tall Dark and Handsome, for example? Is he going to sit next to Miss Gorgeous on the plane and fall madly in love?

Love truly does make the world go round. So if you've ever wondered if you are with the right partner or why on earth you stay with the one you are with, then read on—you may be surprised to know that relationship harmony is not an impossible quest but just a matter of understanding your essential nature and that of your partner. One of the reasons I am so passionate about I.D.™ is because of the positive impact it's had on relationships—not just romantic relationships but all types.

I firmly believe that people are meant to be in romantic relationships—as the saying goes, 'No man is an island'. Yet over the last few decades people have been encouraged to be more and more independent—especially women. Independence is a valid and worthwhile goal—and we should all strive to reach it—but interdependence is a much more rewarding, though challenging, option.

One of the things I love about I.D.™ is that you can never score a nine in all of the drives. It means that we all have certain talents that are simply not transferable—that are special to us. It means that the only way you can access all those gifts or traits is to link up with other people and come together in partnerships (which is, incidentally, why I called my business Link-up International). After all, if you start bringing people with complimentary differences into a team, the team will become exponentially more powerful with each new member—and the sum of the whole is always greater than the sum of its parts.

I believe people are meant to be interdependent. We need to be independent in terms of being able to look after ourselves, but to be the best we can be, we also need to be interdependent, working effectively and living harmoniously with others. In this chapter I will look specifically at romantic relationships. I am often asked:

- ▷ Are there I.Ds™ that are more suited than others to being in relationship?

- ▷ Are there I.Ds™ that are more likely to remain single?

- ▷ Are there I.Ds™ that are more susceptible to divorce?

- ▷ Are there I.Ds™ that are more likely to make a good marriage (or vice versa)?

What if knowing your *I.D.*™ could help you have a wonderful, fulfilling and happy relationship? Whether you want to meet a partner, re-energise your existing relationship or indeed move on from a relationship that no longer supports you, *I.D.*™ can offer you powerful insights that will make a massive difference.

The *Instinct to Verify*™

Because people driven to Verify are always comparing and looking for ways to improve things, they can seem overly critical — always focused on the 5 per cent that isn't right, rather than the 95 per cent that is. Say two couples go out to dinner and one of them is particularly affectionate, for example. Anyone in the group who is driven to Verify will respond to that by becoming affectionate with his or her own partner too. Because Verify people are always comparing, the Verify person in the group will respond to the behaviour of the affectionate couple by subconsciously thinking, 'So and so has just put his arm around his partner. My relationship with my wife is better than his so I will put my arm around my wife too'. If his wife is also driven to Verify, she'll be happy that her husband has put his arm around her. Interestingly, if the husband of the initially affectionate couple is driven to Avoid Verify, he'll see his friend's reaction to his behaviour and subconsciously think, 'He's just put his arm around his wife — isn't that nice?' He would be unperturbed by the behaviour because Avoid Verify people don't compare — they just observe things and accept them as they are. If the Avoid Verify man's wife was driven to Verify, however, she would be silently sceptical at the other couple's responding with their own affectionate behaviour.

Communication strengths of people driven by the *Instinct to Verify*™

⇨ They persevere until an issue is resolved.

⇨ They consider and discuss issues thoroughly.

⇨ They look for win–win situations.

⇨ They justify their actions and opinions.

⇨ They provide examples for clarity.

People who are driven by the *Instinct to Verify*™ are never satisfied with their relationship. They continually ask questions like, 'Do we go out as much as other couples?', 'Are we as happy as other couples?' and 'Are we having sex as much as other couples?'

If you ask a man driven to Verify if he reads women's magazines, he will probably deny it. But if he walks past his wife's *Cosmopolitan* magazine and its cover is emblazoned with, 'Are you having enough sex? Find out if you're getting enough', he will have the magazine disguised behind *Concrete Monthly* in a flash. If the survey revealed that the average couple are having sex three times a week, he would immediately think back on the previous week and count up how many times he and his wife had made love to make sure they 'hit quota'.

When it comes to sex, people who are driven to Verify want to know how everyone else is doing it, so they are the people who ask, 'Was that good for you?' Ideally they want to know that they were the best lover you ever had, so don't be surprised if they ask for a rating! And that isn't limited to men driven to Verify—women driven to Verify will also ask for feedback.

Communication vulnerabilities of people driven by the *Instinct to Verify*™

- ᴆ They can be critical and sceptical.
- ᴆ They can pre-judge.
- ᴆ They always add a 'but' to the end of positive statements.
- ᴆ They need to know the 'right' way to do something.
- ᴆ They are naturally defensive.
- ᴆ They argue about 'reasons'—rather than addressing the underlying issues.

Depending on their other drives, lovers driven to Verify will always be looking to improve. They will also seek reassurance from other sources, so they may check their own results against averages stated in magazine articles with titles such as, 'Are you good in bed?' If they are driven to Verify and also driven to Authenticate, they are likely to just ask their partner what he or she likes. If their partner is the same, then there are the makings of a very honest and open relationship with great sex! If, on the other hand, their partner is driven to Avoid Authenticate, he or she will not want to have a discussion about their sex life—preferring that the other person read between the lines instead. For Verify people who are with an Avoid Verify partner, whatever they do will be seen as good because Avoid Verify people are naturally very accepting (although they may occasionally leave clues—such as highlighted magazine passages—for their partner to indicate how they're feeling). Also, those driven to Avoid Verify may suffer from performance anxiety due to their need to get things right the first time!

When it comes to communication—a big part of any relationship —those driven to Verify need to discuss things thoroughly. They need to know why something is happening; if there is a problem appearing in their relationship, it is the Verify-driven people who will notice. Keen to solve the problem early and find a solution, they are much more likely than those driven to Avoid Verify to raise an issue. Avoid Verify lovers often don't even see the problem until someone with the Verify drive points it out to them.

In an argument, those driven to Verify can be dogmatic and stubborn and will challenge any statement or accusation thrown at them—defying the other person to prove it with examples. For example, say Susie and John are arguing and John is driven by the *Instinct to Verify*™. When Susie accuses John of being arrogant she may say, 'When we were waiting to be seated at the restaurant the other night, you were rude to the waiter'. He will reply, 'Yeah, well he deserved it—he didn't even offer to take your coat!' Those driven to Verify are really good at becoming caught up in examples and defending and justifying their position, rather than hearing what is being said and taking it on board. Susie could give thousands of examples of John's behaviour, but he would justify every one of them in his mind—but it won't alter the fact that he behaved badly. Susie—who is driven to avoid the *Instinct to Verify*™ and driven by the *Instinct to Complete*™—hates scenes and just wants harmony. Avoid Verify people are typically much more accommodating of others than people driven by the *Instinct to Verify*™—so the incident in the restaurant will have completely ruined Susie's night. Before long—as soon as John starts to justify his position—Susie will just stop talking and say, 'Whatever'. He will think he's won the argument, but really she's just disengaged. She is hurt that he is not listening to her and not appreciating how it makes her feel but because she's non-confrontational, she just leaves the issue. He will then think she now understands his point of view and agrees with him, but she doesn't—she still thinks he's an idiot.

Above the surface it looks like Susie and John aren't fighting because she raised the issue, he justified it and then she let it drop. But under the surface—where all the emotions are—Susie is shutting down, so when John asks her, 'What's wrong?', she will either say, 'Nothing', and sulk or 'I don't know'. Often those driven to Avoid Verify truly won't know why they are upset; they just know they feel invalidated and sad. For people driven to Verify, this can be extremely frustrating. If there is something wrong, they believe that they should know what it is. So Susie and John may often have conversations like the following:

SUSIE: 'I feel really sad.'

JOHN: 'What do you mean by sad?'

SUSIE: 'I don't know—just sad.'

JOHN: 'Why?'

SUSIE: 'I don't know—I'm just sad.'

By the end of the conversation John will feel irritated by Susie's inability to explain her feelings and Susie will feel even worse.

....

Communication vulnerabilities of people driven to avoid the *Instinct to Verify*™

- ▷ They can be too brief.
- ▷ Discussion won't change their underlying feelings.
- ▷ They can lose posture when interrogated because they can't explain why they make decisions.
- ▷ They can be one-sided.
- ▷ They don't delve deep—and can therefore appear uninterested.

....

As someone who is driven to Verify, I used to want to just win arguments—and to prove my point was all that mattered. It took me a while to realise that justifying my position in an argument would do more harm than good. But it usually takes a slightly painful journey for people driven to Verify to realise that when they win, they actually ultimately lose. The minute the other person feels like he or she has lost, no-one wins. I always remember someone saying to me, 'Be wrong so that other people can be right'. If you say to someone after an argument, 'Sorry—I was wrong', and the other person turns out to be wrong, you will have gained much more respect and credibility than if you had persisted in justifying your position. It is better to back down sometimes—especially if the argument is not important. For example, I learned to ask myself, 'What is my motive here?' I realised that if my motive is one of truly trying to connect and be closer to the other person, then my communication will almost certainly land for them in a way that is both sensitive and helpful, but if I am angry and hurt and only want to make the other person see what he or she has done is 'wrong', then defending my position will not achieve anything positive.

I have found that you can talk about anything with anyone if your heart is in the right place. But when an element of competition and an emphasis on being 'right' exists between two people, the communication springing from that can be pretty detrimental to the relationship. So if both partners are driven to Verify, they can spend their lives bickering about detail. On the other hand, if both partners are driven to Avoid Verify, they probably won't talk about things, preferring instead to just keep moving along—although this also depends on how their other drives play out. There are a lot of marriages that have just disintegrated—and when you ask both partners why, neither of them can tell you. People often say that their marriage 'just unravelled' or that they just 'grew apart'. There might never have been a stage when they sat down with their wife or husband and said, 'Maybe we should try and talk about this'—instead all the talking will be done at the end of the relationship when it's too late. That's because people who are driven to avoid the *Instinct to Verify*™ are very accepting of others and may not see that there is anything all that wrong with the relationship until it's glaringly obvious and the relationship is almost over.

People who are driven to avoid the *Instinct to Verify*™ usually see their relationship end due to a major breakdown—like one springing from an affair or a family feud, in which the hurt is extreme.

Communication strengths of people driven to avoid the *Instinct to Verify* ™

- ☜ They are accepting and encouraging.
- ☜ They interpret things as innocent until proven otherwise.
- ☜ They are non-discriminatory.
- ☜ They see the underlying issues or feelings.
- ☜ They are brief in conversation.

Those driven to Verify, on the other hand, will leave a relationship when a wrong is committed that can't be rectified. They will probably leave through a trial separation because they want to test it out before committing to it—to compare life with their partner versus life without their partner. People who are driven to Verify also place importance on living together before marrying for the same reason. They will do a list of pros and cons about living with their partner and living without their partner—and if there is one pro and three pages of cons, the relationship will be over in their mind.

Both people driven by the *Instinct to Verify*™ and people driven to avoid the *Instinct to Verify*™ have their strengths and weaknesses in relationships—so it's important for them to understand the potential pitfalls and develop strategies to avoid them.

The *Instinct to Authenticate*™

People driven to *Authenticate*™ can be very blunt with their partner—and it can be especially pronounced if they are also driven to Avoid Improvise. By comparison, people who are driven to Authenticate and also to Improvise may still be blunt, but they can, for example, deliver a hard truth wrapped in humour—which cushions the blow.

Although people driven by the *Instinct to Authenticate*™ need to be real, honest and truthful, if their blunt communication does not also show a consideration of the needs of the other person, it can be quite destructive for the person on the receiving end of it. It is also important for Authenticate-driven people to remember that truth is often their own version of truth. In other words, yes, the truth may be exactly what they saw or heard in a conversation, but there may also have been things that were not seen or shared in the conversation that may be relevant. They don't need to try and guess things going on under the surface, but they will need allowances made for the fact that there may be more going on than they're aware of. Inappropriate honesty can be a vulnerability for those who are driven to Authenticate. They're not nasty about it — and they're certainly not trying to embarrass anyone or score points to be confrontational — they just say it as they see it, which can often leave everyone else speechless! The good thing about Authenticate-driven people in a relationship, however, is that their partner will know exactly where he or she stands.

Communication strengths of people driven by the *Instinct to Authenticate*™

- ⤷ They are literal.
- ⤷ Their feelings don't get in the way of the truth.
- ⤷ They use demonstrations to explain things.
- ⤷ They are brief.
- ⤷ Their verbal agreements are seen by them as the equivalent to verbal contracts.

People driven to Authenticate are also quite 'hands on' in the bedroom (so researchers tell me!) — they are not the types to 'lie back and think of England'. They need to be involved and it has to be real for them. Honesty is critical to their lovemaking. If they feel that something is not quite right — that their partner is a little distant — they will think nothing of stopping the proceedings to find out what is wrong. They won't even resume their lovemaking until the problem is resolved and the connection between them and their partner is restored. Although this can kill the mood, that's not necessarily their focus. The emotion has to be congruent and real — and if the connection isn't there or if they feel something is amiss, they will just stop.

If both partners are driven to Authenticate, the bond can be a very honest and deep one. The sex is likely to be brilliant because both will know what the other likes. Because they talk about things that others shy away from, there is no guesswork involved — which is healthy and refreshing.

Communication vulnerabilities of people driven by the *Instinct to Authenticate*™

▷   They can be blunt and insensitive.

▷   They don't read between the lines.

▷   They don't expect other people to read between their lines.

▷   They are often inappropriate with the timing of their communication.

▷   They share their truth, but there is also often a more complete truth or picture that they don't automatically volunteer.

Partners who are driven to Avoid Authenticate, however, will expect the other person to read their mind and will be very disappointed when they can't or won't. Those driven to Authenticate find this so frustrating because they think, 'Why didn't you just tell me instead of expecting me to guess or somehow read your mind?' But for Avoid Authenticates, if they have to explain what they want their partner to do in order to turn them on, it would take all the magic out of it—and they would feel less understood by their partner as a result. They just want to 'feel the love, baby' and react accordingly. Otherwise, if they had to be explicit, it just wouldn't be the same for them—and they wouldn't want to talk about any problems; they'd want to explore any issues together by reading their partner's unspoken signals. After all, to them making love is supposed to be a little more sacred and soulful than putting together a wardrobe from a flat-pack instruction booklet!

For those driven to Authenticate, not being able to talk about such things indicates a lack of honesty. This is a different definition of honesty to that used by Avoid Authenticates, but it is honesty nonetheless—brutal, literal honesty. They will see the relationship as dissolving when the honesty dissolves. When they feel as though their loyalty has been broken, they'll find it almost impossible to trust their partner the same way ever again. Couples who are driven to Authenticate find it hard to recover from an infidelity, for example. Likewise, if their joint lives become so separate that they don't do anything together and the relationship feels like a fraud, then, to them, it's as if there is no relationship—and they will need to make that become a reality. They will also likely separate if they don't see that they can do anything constructive to rescue the relationship.

Communication strengths of people driven to avoid the *Instinct to Authenticate*™

⇨ They are intuitive.

⇨ They possess a sense of timing and diplomacy.

⇨ They focus on and connect to other people's feelings and perceptions.

⇨ They are sympathetic and tend to give the benefit of the doubt.

⇨ They embellish things, making their communication quite colourful and emotional.

People who are driven to avoid the *Instinct to Authenticate*™, however, will separate when they no longer share that special place of thought and ideas with their partner. If they no longer feel understood by their partner or if their dreams and aspirations change and are no longer shared, it can pull them apart to the point at which they feel as though they don't inhabit the same 'world' as their partner anymore—and that the ideals that were once their dream are no longer possible.

Communication vulnerabilities of people driven to avoid the *Instinct to Authenticate*™

⇨ They seem to talk around an issue rather being direct about it.

⇨ They use incongruent words that don't express exactly what they mean.

⇨ They can exaggerate, which can create a false reality for others.

⇨ They can read too much into things and reach a outcome that was unintended by the other party.

⇨ They can be preoccupied with what others think.

⇨ They react to the emotion they perceive and can therefore take things very personally.

The *Instinct to Complete*™

For people who are driven by the *Instinct to Complete*™, the measure of their relationship comes down to the amount of harmony in the relationship and how much time they spend with their partner. Even in relationships, they have plans, schedules and routines that would put NASA to shame — even when it comes to making love! I know people driven to Complete who will have sex with their partner at a set time.

I knew one Complete-driven person who made love to his wife on Wednesday nights and Saturday mornings, according to his schedule. His wife was strongly driven to Improvise and Avoid Complete, so she was motivated by spontaneity, variety, new experiences and risk. But the only risk she had to look forward to was whether the video would record *CSI* so that she could get back to it afterwards! The couple laughed about it in the end. Once they both understood their I.D.™ and developed some strategies to inject some variety into their love life, all was well. But right before learning about their I.Ds™, it was deathly boring for her and not much better for him!

Couples who are driven to Complete would not only know that they have sex on Wednesday night and Saturday morning, but probably also the position and location too — much like the couple who can dance together by anticipating every move! It's exciting for them to plan their love life because they like the anticipation of looking forward to something they enjoy. But if the lovemaking doesn't happen when or how it's supposed to, they will know there is something wrong with their relationship because their sense of routine acts as a barometer that gauges the health of their relationship.

Communication strengths of people driven by the *Instinct to Complete*™

- ⊃ They can anticipate what they think others will say and how they will likely react and adjust their communication accordingly.

- ⊃ They possess communication that has a sense structure, context and flow to it.

- ⊃ They have a valuable sense of recall.

- ⊃ They like to keep everyone happy because they need harmony.

I have often heard people say to a new couple, 'Enjoy it while it lasts' — referring to the passion so obviously displayed in new relationships, as if passion is guaranteed to disappear with the passage of time. Rubbish! I think God gives people passion for the first six months of any relationship, but after that couples have to make it themselves. And the best way to do that is for people to understand their I.D.™ and that of their partner, so that they can better understand the innate motivations and needs of their partner that will affect all of their relationship—not just their sex life.

Couples who are driven to Complete also won't start something they can't finish. If·they have children, for example, they will not want to make love just before their children arrive home because they need to have plenty of time to finish what they start! Conversely, if one person in the relationship is driven to Avoid Complete, he or she will need variety and spontaneity—and the possibility of getting sprung and having to change course halfway through is half the fun! Those driven to Complete, on the other hand, don't want interruptions, so they will lock the door and close the curtains. Say a Complete-driven husband has just finished getting ready to go out for the night and his Avoid Complete-driven wife thinks he looks fantastic and becomes a little frisky—her husband would be uncomfortable with that. He'd say, 'Stop Honey', 'My shirt will get crushed' or 'We'll be late'. A Complete-driven husband would do anything to stop because being teased and then not following through on or undoing what he thought he had just completed is no fun. He would believe that he's suited up and ready to go out and that if he makes love to his wife he will be late. Now I don't want to sound as if a couple like this can't be spontaneous, but they will certainly be much better with spontaneity if there is time to 'complete' and not be interrupted in the process!

Although most people love the butterflies in their stomach at the start of a relationship, for those driven to avoid the *Instinct to Complete*™, those butterflies are the best thing ever because they mean the relationship is new and that they're discovering things about the other person. They love uncharted territory—predictability and routine are torture for them. So if their relationship is in a rut and the sex becomes predictable, they become devastated. They want their lovemaking to be like the first time every time. If two people in a relationship are both driven to Avoid Complete, they will have a blast keeping the spice in their love life! These are the couples who experiment in the bedroom in an endless quest to keep their love life new and interesting—especially if they are also driven to Improvise.

You often hear people in relationships say, 'He was so different before we were married' or 'She used to love the beach before we were married'. When one person in a relationship feels as though the other partner has changed, it can cause a great deal of angst for them both. People driven to Complete can appear to their partner like they have changed because they may not be as motivated to do certain things as they used to be. But it's the bigger picture that has probably changed for them, rather than them changing as a person. For example, it's usually all about 'time spent' together for them. Maybe the hobby they no longer seem interested in was merely a ticket to spending time together rather than an attraction in itself for them. This isn't always conscious on their part—just instinctive. Or maybe that hobby or special interest served some other purpose that can also include attracting their partner to them. Once that purpose or context changes though, so does their enthusiasm for it.

Communication vulnerabilities of people driven by the *Instinct to Complete*™

➤ They can be inflexible—determined to use what they prepared or rehearsed even if it is no longer appropriate or relevant to others.

➤ They can focus on seemingly irrelevant things.

➤ They can be preoccupied—worried about connected issues rather than the one in question.

➤ They often only see the context they want to see.

➤ They tend to 'make a mountains out of molehills'.

Say two people, John and Gillian, go out on a date. Because John—who is driven to avoid the *Instinct to Complete*™—loves hiking and heading to the mountains for challenging hikes, he may ask Gillian if she wants to come. She'll accept the invite partly because she just wants to spend time with him—and partly because she knows that's what he likes to do and wants to please him. So John will think, 'Fantastic! She likes what I like'. They marry, and John thinks that they will continue to go hiking—but over time it becomes less frequent and soon he finds himself hiking alone. But for Gillian, the whole context may now well be different.

Another context may well relate to society's expectations. If you think about what is considered 'normal' by society ('normal' being a driver for people driven to Complete), it would be a process of going to school, then university or college, finding a job, meeting a partner and then marrying somewhere between about twenty-five and thirty years of age. So if you are driven to Complete and you are thirty years old and still not married, you would be feeling a great deal of pressure—especially if you are female because you'll fear that your biological clock is starting to tick. You'd probably feel the pressure from society to have at least one child by the age of thirty-five and be married for about five years by that time. It's the same with Complete-driven men—if a thirty-year-old single guy meets a nice woman, he may start talking about having kids on the first date because he's feeling societal pressure to conform—and talking about babies on the first date is enough to freak anyone out!

Those driven to Avoid Complete, on the other hand, don't feel the same pressure to conform. They are likely to be flitting about from one crazy new scheme to the next—and this can keep them happily occupied for years! Although they may still be dreaming of meeting a special someone, it won't be a consuming obsession for them.

Communication strengths of people driven to avoid the *Instinct to Complete*™

- ⇨ They are approachable.
- ⇨ They are flexible.
- ⇨ They can tailor their communication and strategies to suit different situations.
- ⇨ They are spontaneous.
- ⇨ They are goal oriented and single minded.

The trap for Complete-driven people over thirty years old is that they can panic and marry the first person they can lay their hands on. I remember going to a company one day to meet with the company's board. Most of the senior executives were driven to Complete—and many of them had married their secretary! This is how they (humorously) explained it:

> We had been so busy concentrating on our careers that the years had sped past; suddenly, we realised we were becoming older and began to feel the presssure to marry—and when we looked up, who did we see? The secretary!

This type of situation is especially common for people who are both driven by the *Instinct to Complete*™ and driven to avoid the *Instinct to Improvise*™ because dating someone they already have some kind of a relationship with is safer than meeting someone cold.

People driven to Complete will throw in the towel when their definition of harmony shifts from being 'in the relationship' to 'out of the relationship'. When they see that it would be easier, more organised and less chaotic to leave a relationship rather than try to keep it together, they will leave their partner. Needless to say, they may stay longer than others because the hassle of moving out would be a very turbulent prospect for them, so the relationship would have to deteriorate into a very bad position for them to actually leave it.

....

Communication vulnerabilities of people driven to avoid the *Instinct to Complete*™

- ☝ They can be easily distracted.
- ☝ They can be inconsistent—they don't say something the same way twice.
- ☝ They can become bored quickly.
- ☝ They can be defiant.
- ☝ They can ramble on when they focus on the point they want to make rather than the outcome they want to achieve.

....

For those driven to Avoid Complete, they will leave their relationship if they feel trapped in a boring relationship. If they realise that their yesterday was the same as today and is going to be the same as their tomorrow, they would break out of the relationship. To use the earlier example of John and Gillian, when Gillian stopped going hiking with John he would have been saddened but he would have adapted; however, if Gillian had insisted he stop going hiking on the weekends, the relationship would have been on a slippery slope to divorce. People of both sexes who are driven to Avoid Complete need freedom to pioneer and explore—but the problem comes when their partner assumes that this need will automatically lead to infidelity. Nothing could be further from the truth. Paradoxically, the surest way to keep an Avoid Complete person faithful and committed is to give them freedom. But the minute they take it, they'll also want their partner there to share in it with them.

The *Instinct to Improvise*™

Those driven by the *Instinct to Improvise*™ need excitement, urgency and high-energy environments. They are also pretty sociable and outgoing and are able to mix with all sorts of people. So to feel fulfilled in a relationship, they need a positive partner, passion, excitement, challenge and fun—routine is not something they thrive on.

Because they need spice and excitement, they can be phenomenal in a relationship for the first six months, but as soon as the passion starts to wane they can become bored. Those driven to Improvise are therefore perhaps more vulnerable to new romantic relationships. They don't plan for them, but they are vulnerable to them if they appear. Everything seems like a good idea at the time for someone with the Improvise drive.

Communication strengths of people driven by the *Instinct to Improvise*™

- ⌦ They respond quickly—with a positive, can-do attitude.
- ⌦ Their style is naturally energising and inspirational.
- ⌦ They can be persuasive and challenging.
- ⌦ They are good at small talk.
- ⌦ Their language is passionate and their syle animated.

In the bedroom, people driven to Improvise can make a stunning first impression. They want sex to wow their partner—and feel bad when it doesn't. Also, if an Improvise-driven couple are often kept apart because of work commitments, it can actually add spice to their relationship—keeping it interesting and unpredictable. However, those driven to Improvise can put unnecessary pressure on themselves to be the life and soul of the party—and that is indeed the role people see them in. If they go out in company, others look to them to be the entertainment, but those expectations can be tiring for

Improvisers—who can occasionally have their own down days just like other people.

....

Communication vulnerabilities of people driven by the Instinct to Improvise™

- ⊅ They are persuasive.
- ⊅ They can be superficial.
- ⊅ They make things up as they go along.
- ⊅ They can be emotional or animated.

....

People driven to Improvise will leave a relationship when they eventually run out of hope for it. No matter what obstacle comes up, they will want to believe in the relationship, hoping it will work out. They will think they can turn it around—and that they'll actually be re-energised by the challenge. But when they run out of hope, it's over. For example, I have a friend driven to Improvise who had been in a twelve-year relationship; her turning point for breaking it off was when she retreated to the spare room to cool down during another argument and started flicking through an old journal. It fell open on a day two years earlier—the entry written there could have been the same day. When she realised that nothing in the relationship had changed in two years, she called it off—it was over in a matter of days.

....

Communication strengths of people driven to avoid the Instinct to Improvise™

- ⊅ They are diligent at delivering on their commitments and responsibilities.
- ⊅ They are composed.
- ⊅ They are logical.
- ⊅ Their natural style is to use an approach that doesn't put pressure on people.
- ⊅ They will go to great lengths to be clear and understood.

....

Those driven to avoid the *Instinct to Improvise*™ are also passionate, but they don't need that passion woven into every part of their relationship the way Improvise people do. They love to kick back on a long weekend and spend time with their partner. They enjoy just being together with their partner; their relationships are not as manic as those of Improvise-driven people! For example, Avoid Improvise couples might have been going to the same cabin in the mountains for a romantic weekend for the last ten years because they know for sure that they have a wonderful time there — there is no risk.

Communication vulnerabilities of people driven to avoid the *Instinct to Improvise*™

ᴆ They can come across as negative.

ᴆ They need to process thoughts before verbalising them (the written word is more comfortable for them than a pressured conversation).

ᴆ They tend to focus on logic and ignore the emotional elements.

ᴆ They threaten with ultimatums.

ᴆ If a conversation is quick and an off-the-cuff one, they may not take it seriously.

Divorce

I am often asked if there is one *I.D.*™ that is more susceptible to divorce than another. Although I haven't done specific separate research into this issue, I do know from my broader research that there seems to be a correlation between divorce and people who are driven to Improvise and Avoid Complete. Although their relationship skills are no better or worse than other people's, their tolerance for staying in a rut is lower and their willingness to take the risk of moving on is higher. They are generally more willing to make the change if the relationship is not good, whereas someone driven to Complete and to Avoid Improvise would stick it out far longer because they see it as a case of, 'Better the devil you know' and because the end of the relationship would be very traumatic for them.

For people who are driven to Improvise and Avoid Complete, nothing is ever final, so even if they do divorce their partner, they are much more likely to remain or even get back together again than people with opposite drives. For these people, even splitting up can be done in a very positive way — depending on the combination of their partner's drives of course. If they split from their partner, they don't need to know where they are going or how they are going to manage — they just go. Those driven to Improvise tend not to think too hard about consequences until they are knee deep in them.

By comparison, people who are driven to Complete will not leave a relationship unless they have a plan and have thought of all the contingencies. To do otherwise — and some do or are forced to do so — makes the stress even greater because that would be way out of stride for them. If they are not the one leaving the relationship, the break-up period can be an especially stressful time for them. For example, say a husband who is driven to Complete married a woman who is driven to Improvise and Avoid Complete. If she comes home one Wednesday evening and announces she is not happy and is leaving, the husband will go into a tailspin. It will feel to him as though his whole world has changed in a heartbeat because all the certainty and harmony he had previously felt is now removed. It is a devastating feeling for Complete-driven people — not just because of the obvious loss of their partner, but also because of their natural instinct for order and routine (which is of course shattered by a break-up).

People who are driven to Improvise and Avoid Complete don't miss each other the same way as people with other I.Ds™ do. Because they are so easily distracted and always off on some new adventure or hair-brained scheme, they don't pine for their partner as soon as they are out the door. In fact, when not in each other's company they seem almost to forget about the other person. It's not a negative thing or about them not loving their partner, it's just that they would rather get on with other things — and once they are back with their partner, they'll be focused on them and probably re-energised. Of course, there is an inherent danger in that if something or someone interesting comes along!

Another interesting thing to note is that people with this I.D.™ combination can have very volatile relationships. Their need for passion and excitement can manifest in destructive patterns of behaviour — such as always picking fights. (After all, what better way to inject some passion into a dull relationship than to have a rip-roaring, china-smashing argument?) Although it satisfies a need for passion and spice, picking fights can be very destructive in the long term. So if you recognise this behaviour in your relationship, try a different approach. Instead of picking a fight, plan a surprise and find interesting, new and fun things to do—rather than deciding which ornament is going to be the next missile!

I know someone who would always be in a fiery, volatile relationship. The relationship would be very passionate, but she and her partner would fight like cats and dogs, and eventually the relationship would break down. After a string of these relationships she ended up with someone very different to her former partners who was actually very good for her. But she always felt that there was something missing in their relationship because they didn't have passionate exchanges. However, once she understood the *I.D. System*™ and could see that her behaviour was actually quite destructive and that fighting didn't equal love, she stopped feeling like something was missing—and they are now happily married.

I'm convinced that the two essential ingredients for a successful marriage or relationship are common values and chemistry. If they exist, any *I.D.*™ combination in a relationship can work. All you need to do is understand each other, respect your natural differences and learn how to manage them so you can navigate your way through your relationship. Remember that human beings are interesting and diverse creatures; the interpretations, judgements and perceptions that people apply to others' behaviour can be completely wrong—and misinterpretation of a partner's behaviour is the cause of most difficulties in relationships.

I.D.™ gives people the framework to navigate the potential minefields of a romantic relationship. It does this by allowing us to see our own innate nature and accept ourselves as we are. Once we've done that we can apply that same recognition and acceptance to people with different *I.Ds*™, so that we can honour each other and develop honest, genuine relationships along the way.

Chapter 6

In stride with dating

Dating is a billion-dollar business. A whole industry has mushroomed around assisting increasing numbers of single people to meet each other. People are now offered many options for meeting a prospective partner—including speed dating, at which you meet eight people for three minutes each; internet dating, which makes dating more like online shopping; dating agencies, for which you can pay several thousand dollars for someone to find you a compatible match; and other dating services from organisations such as Table for Eight, which organises get-togethers over dinner for equal numbers of single men and woman.

Obviously all those single people want to meet someone special —otherwise the industry wouldn't exist. But the flip side of that is escalating divorce rates, which indicate that meeting someone is only half the problem—the real challenge is staying with your partner and remaining happy.

Those heady days in the beginning of a relationship can be fun! But they are also fragile because the special characteristics of one partner's

I.D.™ can easily be misinterpreted by the other partner—and vice versa. Here I will look at how the traits presented by each *I.D.*™ can be perceived. If you are currently dating and find yourself really liking the person, I've included some tips on how to win extra brownie points so that you can make a better impression—you may even end up in a committed relationship as a result.

If, on the other hand, you've been dating and have found yourself sitting opposite your worst nightmare, this chapter includes sure-fire trump cards you can play to ensure it never happens again! These tips are good to read even if you are feeling good about someone you're dating because for each drive and direction there are potential landmines. Obviously I'm having a bit of fun with this—and I wouldn't recommend you do any of these things because they really would upset the other person—but I'm sure you'll laugh out loud as you recognise yourself or your partner!

The *Instinct to Verify*™

People who are driven by the *Instinct to Verify*™ are always comparing. So if two people driven to Verify are dating, they may say things like, 'You are so much smarter than my previous girlfriend'. Those driven to Verify are always looking for reassurance, so a statement like that lets them know that they are better than the previous partner and will prompt them to give big brownie points! People driven to Verify want to be the best and want others to know it.

People who are driven by the Instinct to Verify™ are always comparing

If, however, you are a Verify-driven person who is dating someone driven to avoid the *Instinct to Verify*™, you might not do so well! People give what they most want to receive. So those people driven to Verify give compliments based on comparison and prefer to receive those types of compliments. But people who are driven to avoid the *Instinct to Verify*™, on the other hand, don't compare; they are much more accepting and non-discriminatory—and they respond to unconditional encouragement, so comparing them to your last partner will quickly turn them right off. They'll be squirming, thinking, 'How dare you even think of your ex while you're with me!'

People who are driven by the *Instinct to Verify*™ are also very persistent; they are the people who never give up—even when their target love interest turns them down. Those driven by the *Instinctive Drive to Verify*™ need to solve problems—and the fact that their future boyfriend or girlfriend hasn't worked out that they are Mr or Ms Right yet is seen by Verify people as nothing more than a temporary problem to be solved. If they are rejected the first time, they will vary their approach until their love interest accepts their invitation or is worn down by their persistence!

Those driven to Avoid Verify, on the other hand, would ask someone out once, and if he or she rejected them, they would be more likely to accept it and walk away. They need to make things right the first time, so they may take a while to work out the best approach in order to make a better first impression, but if they are rejected they may not ask again.

Where's the love?

If you want to make a good impression with a date who is driven to Verify, tell him he is the best-looking, cleverest, tallest and funniest person you have ever gone out with! Obviously don't say it unless you mean it, but if your date is funny, then telling him he's the funniest guy you've dated will be seen by him as more flattering and more of a compliment—because of the comparison used—than if you had simply told him that you thought he was funny. Those driven to Verify also need to be right, so if your boyfriend has just offered his opinion on some current affairs issue that you agree with, tell him that you think he is absolutely right.

If your date is driven to Avoid Verify, on the other hand, he will think you're just Christmas if you tell him how wonderful he is. Avoid Verify people need encouragement and unconditional acceptance—the character of Bridget Jones in the film *Bridget Jones's Diary* was most probably driven to Avoid Verify because she was so excited when Mark Darcy said he liked her just as she was.

Where's the exit?

If you want to make sure that your Verify-driven date never wants to see you again, tell her she is wrong, a problem and to blame for a disastrous evening. If that doesn't do the trick, be sure to explain that your work comes first and that she will never be your priority.

If your date is driven to Avoid Verify, however, and is boring you to tears—interrogate her. Ask her question after question and prompt her to explain and justify her answers. Tell her how she can improve herself and what she should have worn or could have done that would have been better! Or compare her to your last partner; even if you say something complimentary like, 'You're so much prettier than my last girlfriend', she'll still hate it because she doesn't compare and doesn't like to be compared.

Will you marry me?

Because those driven to Verify need to be right and do the right thing, by the time they get to the altar they will have assessed their partner for a long time to make sure they are making the right choice. Because those driven by the *Instinct to Verify*™ are into comparison, if it is their first serious relationship they will be especially reluctant to commit because they won't have an anything to compare the relationship to. It would be scary for a Verify-driven groom, for example, if he had only ever been with his bride-to-be. Unable to compare the current partner to anything meaningful, he would never be sure that he had made the best choice.

Many of the traits of the *Instinctive Drives*™ are not conscious. They stem from innate urges, or instincts, that determine how you process information and behave in the world—and they usually remain in the realm of the subconscious mind. The groom would probably not even realise that his inability to compare could be what is making him feel so nervous. He may even start subconsciously comparing his partner with his friend's partner for reassurance. However, this is also fraught with danger—especially if his friend's wife looks like Elle McPherson!

Most people driven to Verify are happier and more comfortable about their choice if they have been out with a few people prior to the big decision because they will be able to compare former partners with their new one. Those people with the Verify drive who are also insecure will go on comparing indefinitely—often until they are given an ultimatum forcing them to compare in a different way: life with their partner or life without their partner!

Once they have made the decision, however, they want to do everything right. So Verify people will want to shop for the right ring at the right price, book the right venue and buy the right dress. They may also enjoy going to other people's weddings so they can compare and find ideas. They would attend bridal expos and read wedding magazines so they can compare ceremonies and make the right choice. They may even visit half-a-dozen reception venues and list the pros and cons of each venue so that they can easily compare on a range of issues and make a final decision based on the right information. Those driven to Complete may do the same thing, but they'd do it to see what everyone else is doing so that they could fit in—whereas an Improviser would use the same experience to see how best to stand out!

Those driven by the *Instinct to Verify*™ want to be involved, but they like to operate from an all-or-nothing perspective. For example, say the groom is driven to Verify. One of the first things the couple will have done together is to make a list of what needs to be organised for the wedding and then allocate priorities to each of the tasks. If the wife-to-be tells her fiancé, 'Mum and I are going to visit the reception place today', he is likely to feel excluded and from that point forward be involved in the wedding planning very little. So she will go off and look at reception places with her mother but still expect him to be involved in other areas—except he won't be. This will cause tension in the relationship because she will then feel as though she is doing everything and he is not contributing enough to the wedding planning. But he won't become involved in the process because he will feel though he had been excluded from it from the start.

People driven to Verify want people to think their wedding was the best—and they will love to be told as much by guests and family members.

For those driven to Avoid Verify, the whole journey from dating to marriage is more instinctive than logical—and they consequently view the process as fairly simple. They either know the answer or they don't! Those people who are driven to avoid the *Instinct to Verify*™ have an inbuilt sense of *knowing* that is incredibly accurate for them. Their gut feel is very black or white; they either get a sense of something or they don't—and that information guides their choices

The challenge arises when they need to explain those choices to others—put simply, words fail them. Words cannot properly articulate their sense of knowing because it's indescribable—it's beyond even feelings. When they know, they know, but they cannot explain necessarily why they know. Plus, when they don't know, no amount of discussion or analysis will bring them any closer to an explanation.

When Avoid Verify people can't adequately explain their decision-making process, they often feel inadequate and silly. This can then cause them to lose confidence in their sense of knowing, resulting in them dismissing it and instead going with a logical explanation — often someone else's. Every time they don't listen to their gut, they invariably make a mistake.

So when it comes to making one of the biggest decisions of their life, there are simply two questions that Avoid Verify people need to ask themselves:

⇨ Do I know this is the right thing to do?

⇨ Do I trust my sense of knowing enough to be true to it?

These are the people who when you ask how they met their partner or how they knew they had the right person, they will just look at you and say, 'I just knew'. They often will have known their partner was right for them within moments of meeting them; just seeing their partner across the room could even have been enough to give them that sense of knowing that is essentially their internal compass. The difficult thing to comprehend for those driven to Verify is that Avoid Verify people's sense of knowing is as strong a compass for them as copious amounts of evidence is for those driven to Verify!

Avoid Verify people often recognise immediately if someone is a potential serious relationship or just a casual one — and they'll act accordingly. If they get a good sense about someone they will allow the relationship to unfold in its own time and are likely to just go with the flow. If they don't have that initial trust, however, they will not go anywhere they do not wish to!

Those driven to Avoid Verify don't apply a list of 'shoulds' to a partner; they have expectations neither about how their partner should behave, nor about what their partner should do for them. For example, an Avoid Verify woman wouldn't become worked up if her boyfriend didn't open the door for her, and an Avoid Verify man wouldn't be disappointed if his girlfriend couldn't cook. People driven to avoid the *Instinct to Verify*™ need to see the real person behind their partner — without airs and graces — and accept their loved one for who he or she is. They would much prefer to see the true individual than someone trying to meet some stereotypical criteria about how to make someone happy! Their accepting nature also means they don't bring too many expectations to the relationship.

The *Instinct to Authenticate*™

When people with the Authenticate drive like you, they will let you know about it fairly quickly and will probably do something to show you—perhaps by making you a gift. Or they may just ask you out or tell you straight up. Authenticate-driven people are also compelled to add their personal touch—they may, for example, choose to make you a homemade card rather than buy you one. If you have ever received a homemade Valentine's Day card, the sender was more than likely driven by the *Instinct to Authenticate*™. Although people with other drives may enjoy making things for various reasons, for those driven by the *Instinct to Authenticate*™ it is their way of letting others know they care. Making something with their own hands is a very tangible expression of their affection. I know of a husband, for example, who removed beautiful curved oak doors from a dilapidated old wardrobe and hinged them together to make a large flower press for his wife. She loved it. Personally, I would never consider doing something like that in a million years! For me it's definitely the thought and the emotions behind the gift that count, rather than the gift itself!

Those driven by the Instinct to Authenticate™ are driven by the need to be 'real'

When it comes to terrible chat-up lines, those driven to Authenticate may be the prime suspects. Because they are honest sometimes to the point of bluntness, they can say some extraordinary things—such as, 'Here's twenty cents. Go call your mother and tell her you won't be home'. This direct approach may work if they look like Brad Pitt or if their target is also driven to Authenticate, but otherwise they risk a slap across the face.

Those driven to Avoid Authenticate are much more diplomatic. They are sensitive and interested in ideas and concepts. You can spot the difference between Avoid Authenticate and Authenticate couples at any bar across the country; the couple driven to Authenticate will be dancing the salsa, while the couple driven to Avoid Authenticate will be huddled in a quiet corner, engaged in a deep and meaningful conversation about quantum string theory. The way to the heart of people driven to Avoid Authenticate is through their philosophies, values and emotions. They need to connect at that deeper level, rather than just at that 'common interests' level. They love a good conversation and need to know their partner shares their love of the deep and meaningful discussions. By comparison, the way to the heart of people driven to Authenticate is through action—if their date shares their passion for activity, the partnership will be on a path to bliss.

Another difference between Avoid Authenticate-driven people and Authenticate-driven people is that those driven to Authenticate actively dislike the dating process because they find it too contrived. They much prefer to know exactly what the rules are and where they stand—to the point that if they like someone they would rather just go and tell the person to find out if it's mutual. For Authenticate-driven people, even the possible rejection is better than not being told upfront—regardless of the outcome. Those driven to Avoid Authenticate, however, are comfortable with uncertainty and are better able to go with the flow in dating situations.

I'd like to give a word of warning regarding these two very different types of people. Imagine a date that was arranged between a man who is driven to Avoid Authenticate and a woman who is driven to Authenticate. If the agreement between them was that he would pick her up at 7.15 pm—that pick-up time will mean exactly 7.15 pm to the Authenticate-driven woman. If he is late he will lose many brownie points and may never recover from the faux pas. It will result in a black mark next to his name straightaway because those driven to Authenticate are very literal—they mean what they say. But for those driven to Avoid Authenticate, 'I'll pick you up at 7.15' means 'I'll pick you up some time between 7.00 and 7.30'! (Incidentally, this situation could also occur between a woman who is driven to Complete and a man who is driven to Avoid Complete, but the Complete-driven woman would be annoyed for a different reason—she'd be annoyed that the timing had affected her schedule or plan.) Always be on time for people who are driven by the *Instinct to Authenticate™* —or at least let them know beforehand if you're going to be late. Never just be late—they see it as a personal insult.

Where's the love?

If you want to make a good impression with someone who is driven to Authenticate, tell him that honesty is the best policy—and make a point of telling stories that demonstrate your honest nature and values. Because Authenticate-driven people like to be out and about doing things, do stuff with him—go bushwalking, kayaking or horse riding, for example. He will be much more relaxed when he is doing things, so you'll get a real chance to connect with him in those environments. Those driven to Authenticate listen best and connect to others more easily when they are doing something as well as listening. Tell him things that others may never have had the courage to; for example, if you're having dinner with him and he is eating with his mouth open, you could say, 'That's really bugging me. Can you stop doing it?' He may not like the content but he will appreciate that you told him and were honest about how you felt.

Those people who are driven to avoid the *Instinct to Authenticate*™ will think you are wonderful if they really connect with you on certain ideals and values. These are the people who say things like, 'It was amazing—we just talked all night'. They need to delve into the juicy conversations—and once there they will fall in love! Something happens to people who are driven to Avoid Authenticate when they are talking to someone and they discover that the other person has similar values.

They aren't bothered by differences of opinion with their partner, but if they feel as though they are uncovering the true you—and if the true you is someone they admire—then your relationship will be heading in the right direction. In other words, they need to know that you really 'get' them. There is also nothing more appealing to someone driven to Avoid Authenticate than an insightful comment or an interesting question.

Where's the exit?

If you are out with someone who is driven to Authenticate and the date is going so badly you're losing the will to live, tell a deliberate lie and make sure you're caught out. People who are driven to Authenticate hate that! Or ask a friend to call and when he or she does, excuse yourself from the table and whisper into the phone while occasionally looking over at your date. She will assume you are talking behind her back and probably won't be at the table when you return! Or tell her she is lazy and unhelpful and hasn't made a positive contribution to the evening.

If your date is driven to Avoid Authenticate, on the other hand, and she continues to want to dissect the universe while your only interest is dissecting your steak, then bring the conversation back to the weather or what the person at the next table is wearing. Or find a value she is really strongly motivated by and trash or dismiss it. I have an Avoid Authenticate friend, for example, who always asks a date what he would do if he found a briefcase with 10 000 dollars in it in a taxi. If he says he would keep it—it's over! My friend will end their association that instant because his answer goes against her values. Also, if you don't give Avoid Authenticate people the benefit of the doubt and question their intention, they will be gone before you can say, 'Bill please!'

Will you marry me?

Those driven by the *Instinct to Authenticate*™ are driven by the need to be 'real', so their wedding needs to represent them as individuals. Those driven by the *Instinct to Authenticate*™ will want to personalise the ceremony and write their own vows—vows that represent how they feel about thier partner and what the marriage means to them. For example, I was at a wedding for two people who were driven to Authenticate, Jake and Tracy, and the ceremony was magical! They were married on the beach with no formality, and they had both written their own vows, speaking from the heart—there wasn't a dry eye on the beach. In the background a school of dolphins frolicked behind them in the ocean. The ceremony was perfect—and a perfect reflection of how they felt about each other.

Congruence is very important to people with the Authenticate drive—they see what they do and how they do it as a representation of who they are. They don't care about tradition or about how things should be done—and part of that stems from their need to be real and honest. When it comes to a couple who are driven to Authenticate—like Jake and Tracy—if tradition is what they both want for their wedding ceremony, then it would be included in the event. But if they don't want tradition highlighted in their ceremony, they would feel no sense of obligation to include it. To a couple who are driven to Authenticate, the wedding is all about them—as it should be. If they had it their way, Great-Aunt Mildred would never be invited to the wedding because they only want to invite people they care about and people who know the real them.

If, however, Authenticate-driven people are forced to conform to a more traditional wedding with hundreds of unfamiliar guests—either by a family member or by a partner who is driven to Complete (Complete-driven people are very big on tradition)—the whole meaning of the day will be lost for them.

Couples who are driven to Authenticate are likely to make their own wedding invitations or wedding cake. They are keen to put their individual mark on the day. Marriage is a big deal for those with the Authenticate drive because they are very loyal to the spoken word. To someone driven to Authenticate, the vows mean a great deal because they will bind the couple together—something that people driven by other instincts may not appreciate as much.

Those driven to Authenticate need to see relevance and like to have a picture of how things will be. To help clients reach their full potential, my company, Link-up International, provides them with a 'journey toward excellence' questionnaire that asks, 'What are you sincerely committed to achieving in the next twelve months—personally and professionally?' A client wrote, 'I want to resolve my personal relationship—whether I'm going to get married to Sarah or not'. My company determined his I.D.™; he was a 4853—strongly driven to Authenticate. His consultant asked me for some feedback on how best to ensure he got his outcome. I told the consultant to go back to him and ask:

> Imagine five years from now. You are away on holidays with your wife. You're on the beach with a couple of young kids playing in the sand and your wife is right beside you. You turn around and look at her. Whose face do you see?

When the consultant asked him, he answered, 'Sarah's!' They got engaged the next day! Those driven to Authenticate need to avoid waste, so as soon as he got the picture in his head of him and Sarah together in the future, he acted on it immediately because he didn't want to waste another day not being married to her.

For people who are driven to Avoid Authenticate, they are still driven to be real, but it's more about an internal reality for them. They are loyal to the sentiment of the marriage and what it represents, but if they had to conform to a traditional wedding to keep people happy, for example, it wouldn't be a big deal—as long as the couple knew how they felt about each other and their bond was a deep one. Couples who are driven to Avoid Authenticate can appear to inhabit a secret world together—and in many respects they do. They live in the realm of ideas and philosophies—and when two people can share that it can be a magical garden. Avoid Authenticate couples need to know their connection is deep and strong—and if the outward display of that needs to bend to accommodate others, they don't mind. However, a couple driven to Avoid Authenticate would not continue in the relationship just for appearance. Once a relationship is over and that magical world has disappeared, they will leave—they are not interested in maintaining the illusion of a happy couple.

The *Instinct to Complete*™

If you have set your sights on someone who is driven by the *Instinct to Complete*™, be ready to spend a lot of time together. For a person driven to Complete, time spent together is a measure of love. They would also be impressed if you went to a lot of effort to plan the date and anticipate every contingency.

> For a person driven to Complete, time spent together is a measure of love

People who are driven to Complete are really organised people; they know what's going on in their life and what's coming up, so they don't always respond well to surprises—they throw out their schedule. The key with Complete-driven people is to share the surprise with them. You don't need to say what you're doing, but if you say to them, 'Pack a bag on Friday night. I'm taking you away for a mystery weekend', as long as you said what sort of clothes to pack they would love it! In fact they'll love the idea even more so because they'll be able to feel the anticipation build up all week—and that really pushes their buttons.

So if you are asking someone driven to Complete out, you'd better know what you are going to do, where you are going to meet and how long you will be out for. People with the Complete drive will probably have a back-up plan, so they may decide to go for a picnic by the river but will also have an alternative location arranged in case it rains.

For a person driven to Avoid Complete, all that planning and scheduling can suck the juice right out of the experience. People who are driven to avoid the *Instinct to Complete*™ thrive on variety and spontaneity. They prefer a date that is a surprise or made up as it goes along—and it may last two hours or twenty years! They need to keep their options open and enjoy the flexibility that brings. So don't box in people who are driven to avoid the *Instinct to Complete*™; it's okay to plan to go somewhere but don't plan everything and be militant about keeping to it or it will drive them nuts! A common mistake that people who are driven to Complete will make is to hear their date say, 'Oh I love Thai food', and then assume that their date's comment is a hint and from then on take them only to Thai restaurants. But if their date is driven to avoid the *Instinct to Complete*™, he or she will be bored with that because Avoid Complete people thrive on new experiences—and eating Thai food 24/7 is not something that's going to thrill!

People who are driven to Complete are naturally sentimental and have an equally natural respect and fondness for tradition. So if you met your Complete-driven partner by the lake while walking your dogs, that location would become your 'special place'. People who are driven by the *Instinct to Complete*™ are likely to say things like, 'Darling, do you know what day it is today?' If their partner happens to be driven to Complete too, he or she will reply, 'Of course I do. It's our eighteen-month anniversary'. If, on the other hand, their partner is driven to Avoid Complete, they may be in for a very frosty afternoon.

Where's the love?

If you want to make a good impression with someone who is driven to Complete, remember the date you met and the restaurant you went to. You'll score extra brownie points if you can remember what you both ate, what song was playing—he or she will probably see it is as 'your song'—and, importantly, what your date was wearing.

Those driven to Avoid Complete need new experiences so don't repeat the date too soon. Even if they said they loved the picnic in the park, don't repeat it for at least a few weeks—and if you do make sure it's at another park with different picnic goodies to try.

Where's the exit?

If your date is driven to Complete and you've agreed to meet but you suddenly get cold feet, the best way to ensure the date never goes anywhere is to set up a time and then call at the last minute to change your plans. If he doesn't pull out by then, make sure you're late to the restaurant, and then ask for something that's not on the menu—it will make him really uncomfortable!

On the other hand, if your date is driven to Avoid Complete and is driving you crazy in all the wrong ways, explain to him in minute detail the itinerary for your next date and tell him that he 'has to stick to the schedule' and 'must get everything done'. If he resists—which he will—say, 'But you said you would', or, even better, become all indignant and say, 'Well, that's what normal people do'. Finally—just so there is no problem with escaping if things go awry on the date—say, 'Well, I told you so!' (I can already feel half the readers of this book squirming at the thought.)

Will you marry me?

If the bride-to-be is driven to Complete, she would have anticipated that her partner was going to propose before he did it—and she would probably have been waiting for it for some time. She may even have been dreaming about her fairytale wedding since she was five years old. The minute their wedding is announced, Complete-driven brides-to-be will move into organisation mode—choosing the date and venue and perhaps even the colour of the bridesmaids' dresses! They will have anticipated all the questions they will be asked and will have answers to all of them. The event would be planned with such precision that the wedding would run like clockwork on the day. Looking for the wedding dress and finding the right venue is heaven for a bride driven to Complete because it's all part of the fairytale. For a groom who is driven to Complete, he will want to be very closely involved in all the decisions too—not due to a need for control, but instead a need to be included. People driven by the *Instinct to Complete*™ would be excited by the anticipation and planning leading up to their wedding, rather than the wedding itself.

They will revel in the details of the day—such as choosing the flowers and making sure that everyone is colour coordinated to within an inch of their life! I know of one couple who were going to be married—he was driven to Improvise and she was driven to Complete. In line with tradition, the groom didn't see his bride until the day of the wedding. But she was so beside herself when she realised she wouldn't be able to see what he looked like on the day that she threatened to call it off unless he told her what he was wearing.

People who are driven by the *Instinct to Complete*™ relish detail; even organising their wedding's seating arrangements—a notorious topic for causing arguments between couples—is fun for those driven to Complete. A wedding organised by someone driven to Complete is often a massive, elaborate and highly orchestrated affair—especially if it's his or her first marriage! Nothing is left to chance; everything—from the petals scattered down the aisle, to the size of cake, to the gift baskets—is overseen. If the wedding goes off without a hitch and there is harmony throughout the day with no family squabbles, then the wedding will be considered a success by those driven to Complete.

People who are driven to avoid the *Instinct to Complete*™ would be tempted to elope because they are impulsive—having a penchant for 'now or never'—and because it would offer an opportunity to break the mould. Even if they don't elope, Avoid Complete people prefer the amount of time passing between the engagement announcement and the wedding day to be much shorter than other people do. They can become bored very fast—and all the details of the big day can drive them nuts. They don't care how many sugared almonds each gift basket should have in it or what the cake should look like. They don't even care whether there is a cake—they just want the day to be exciting, unusual, fun and memorable. Their pioneering spirit may see them having a very unusual ceremony—marrying their loved one while scuba diving off the Great Barrier Reef, for example!

The *Instinct to Improvise*™

If you are about to ask out someone who is driven to Improvise—make it good! People driven by the *Instinct to Improvise*™ are motivated by fun and excitement; they thrive on the buzz of environments that are high in energy and excitement. They need new adventures and impossible challenges—which enable them to make a spectacular first impression. If your date is driven to Improvise and agrees to go out with you, brownie points are on offer if you can come up with something innovative to do. If you suggest dinner, she will say yes, but she would probably have been more excited if you'd suggested taking her skydiving first!

If people who are driven to Improvise tell you they want to take the relationship slowly, it means they are not that interested. Those driven to Improvise are the types of people who meet on Saturday and marry on Sunday—well, almost! Everything is fast with them—if they think something is right they will jump in feet first. Part of that willingness is down to their attitude to risk and their flexibility. It's not that those driven to Improvise necessarily have a high tolerance for risk, it's just that they tend to see things as opportunities rather than risks. For example, somone who's not driven to Improvise may see an Improvise person's attitude and think, 'What if he's the wrong person for you? What if you find out things about him later that you regret?' However, Improvise-driven people wouldn't even think that things could potentially go wrong because it's seen as a negative to them. Instead they would be more likely to think, 'Imagine the fun we could have together. Imagine this much passion for the rest of our lives. What an adventure this could be. If challenges present themselves, surely we'll find a way to deal with them. Let's get on with it then!'

Those driven to Improvise can appear fickle because they seem to change their mind at the drop of a hat. In relationships this can be tricky because if they decide the relationship isn't working out, they will change it either by talking about it with their partner or ultimately—one all hope has evaporated—by leaving the relationship. If they are also driven to avoid the *Instinct to Complete*™, they can be slow to commit. They are the classic commitment-phobes because they like to keep their options open—just in case something better comes along. They need the fun and variety that comes with that—and they love the thrill of the chase. Obviously these traits in a relationship can present challenges for couples.

Avoid Improvise people can find the unpredictability of new relationships stressful. They see them as risky and as having too many unknowns—which makes them uncomfortable. But once they are in the relationship and know that their feelings are reciprocated, they can settle down and be very committed. Their serious nature can be a positive here because their partner can feel very cared for—knowing that the relationship is serious. When they are single, Avoid Improvise people can be more like party animals than those driven to Improvise because when they go out, they go all out—partying like there is no tomorrow. In other words, they can apply their diligence and focus to work and play! Serious work—serious play.

Where's the love?

Imagine that your date is driven to Improvise and you're getting on like a house on fire, but you want to put the icing on the cake. The best thing you can do is relax and genuinely have fun. Surprise him with a mystery treasure hunt around the city, for example. Or find out from his friends if there is something he has always wanted to do—then book it. Be prepared though—that activity could be anything from white-water rafting to learning to tango!

People who are driven to Avoid Improvise will think you are wonderful if you honour your commitments—doing what you say you will do. So if you say you are going to a certain restaurant for dinner, make sure you do. If you can't get a reservation there, ensure your alternative is as good—if not better than—the original choice. Avoid Improvise people respond to this positively because they dislike risk. Change and instability spells risk to them—and they will never relax into a relationship if they feel they can't rely on their partner.

Where's the exit?

The quickest way to sink people who are driven to Improvise is to be negative. Look grumpy and don't smile—no matter what they say, make a snide or sarcastic comment about it. Before your glass is empty, your Improvise-driven date will be clambering over people to escape from you!

To scare off people who are driven to avoid the Instinct to Improvise™, change the plans—tell them you forgot to book the restaurant, for example. Or rave on about yourself and deliberately change a story before telling it again—it will make them very uncertain about you. Constantly do everything at the last minute and don't pay attention to them, or, even better, draw attention to yourselves in a crowded restaurant! Also, if you appear distracted and don't look at them when they are talking or if you cut them off and change the conversation, those driven to Avoid Improvise will go cold on you so fast that you'll need to get your coat it will be that chilly.

Will you marry me?

If you are driven by the *Instinct to Improvise*™, you'll want your wedding to start straight away because you are just so very excited about it. Improvise brides will be so excited about announcing their impending wedding that they won't even care if they haven't set a date or don't have a ring yet—I've seen people who are driven to Improvise use a rubber band or a plastic ring as an engagement ring. If the groom is driven to Complete and so wants to have everything arranged before breaking the news, it would be almost torture for his Improvise-driven bride because she would want to tell everyone straight away. Brides driven to Improvise will tell everyone they know about their engagement within a day of it happening—and they'll be so excited about catching up with people and telling them about their engagement that by the time the buzz dies down and it's time to organise the wedding, they're over it!

People with the Improvise drive need urgency and excitement, so the idea of actually planning an event that may not occur for twelve months is like pulling teeth for them. When it comes down to inviting Great-Aunt Mildred to the wedding, the groom who is driven to Improvise won't care if she comes or not—and he certainly won't give two hoots where she sits! However, Improvise people will pay attention to details like seating arrangements if it will eliminate any possible tension or negativity—which will destroy the day in a heartbeat for Improvise people.

Because Improvise people are not naturally suited to adhering to long-term plans, when they have no choice but to organise their wedding, they need to find a way to enjoy the process—and splitting up the wedding planning into short-term projects will help with this. So they'll see 'buying the rings', 'choosing a venue' and 'buying the dress' as separate exciting tasks, rather than as elements of one giant task—organising the wedding (which will seem more like a death sentence than an exciting adventure to people driven to Improvise).

Too many complications will also kill the enthusiasm of people who are driven by the *Instinct to Improvise*™. For example, if an Improvise-driven bride walks into a dress shop and sees 300 dresses, she'll see the experience as too complicated and zone out. Those with the Improvise drive appreciate simplicity—and because choosing between 300 dresses is not a simple experience, all their excitement will disappear in a heartbeat.

A groom who is driven to Improvise will probably have proposed to his girlfriend on the very afternoon he'd coined the idea. He will probably have walked past a ring shop, seen the perfect ring and bought it, and then proposed to his girlfriend that very night. Those driven to Improvise are driven by passion—he may only have been going out with her for two weeks. Although society and people driven by other instincts may view this passion-based (seemingly spontaneous) decision as rash or crazy, it is the right way for those driven by the *Instinct to Improvise*. 'Saw it, liked it, bought it', is the motto for those driven to Improvise. For example, a close friend of mine whose wife of forty years had passed away was married again within six months. Driven to Authenticate and Improvise, he visited a longstanding family friend a few hours away in Canberra who had recently lost her husband. He said to her, 'What you need is someone to look after you'. When she replied, 'You're right', he said, 'I'm on my own and you're on your own—let's get married'. She agreed. When they announced their engagement it even shocked their kids. They were all very concerned about whether they were doing the right thing—after all, wouldn't both people still be deeply in shock after losing their longstanding partners? But to the couple, it just felt right—and it worked. That was fourteen years ago and they are still very happily married and frankly even more passionate about each other today.

For those driven to Improvise, their wedding may be organised at the last minute, but it will be a blast. For example, even in preparation for fitting into her wedding dress, an Improvise-driven bride will leave it all to the last minute and just not eat for a week before the big day!

Engaged couples who are driven to Avoid Improvise, on the other hand, often prefer to plan the wedding over a reasonably long time frame. They usually don't enjoy the pressure of rushed, last-minute organisation at all. It typically makes them feel like the day is less than perfect. They would normally prefer to give themselves enough time to organise the event without added pressure or stress. They don't feel a sense of mad urgency to marry because they believe that if they're at the wedding stage, then there would obviously be no question about their commitment to each other. Avoid Improvise people are very deliberate and will assess every situation for the possible downside, so once they've said, 'Yes, I'll marry you', that's it—the decision is made and they are in for the long haul. The wedding itself is just for show — it's the commitment behind it that matters to Avoid Improvise lovers.

As you can see, the combination of I.Ds™ in a relationship can result in many different outcomes — whether it comes to escaping a date, making a good impression with a new date or organising a wedding. For example, if an Avoid Complete bride-to-be has a mother who is driven to Complete, the mother will want to follow tradition — which means she'll want Great-Aunt Mildred to be invited and her daughter to wear her great-great-grandmother's wedding veil. However, for the bride, tradition would be the exact reason why she wouldn't want to invite Great-Aunt Mildred or wear the antique veil. Yet this sort of seemingly innocent disagreement can cause enormous stress in an already fraught situation.

Understanding your own I.D.™ and that of your partner will help you navigate romantic relationships and the minefield of marrying and planning a wedding, by fostering in you a greater understanding of your and your partner's quirks.

Chapter 7

In stride with your kids

Although I disagree with traditional profiling, for the sake of argument let's just follow the logic to its natural conclusion for a moment. When you use profiling as it is intended, you would say there is a 'best profile' for a salesperson or a 'best profile' for an accountant. But if that is the case, why wouldn't it follow that there is a 'best profile' for parenting or teaching? When put in those terms it's easier to see the flaws in the profiling argument.

The fact is there is no best profile for anything—whether it applies to accountancy, teaching or parenting—and that's why I'm writing this book.

This chapter outlines I.D.™-specific parenting and learning strategies that can be employed either by teachers who want to better engage with their students or by parents who want to connect with their children on a higher level and bring the best out of them.

Parenting

If you really think there is a top profile for a salesperson and that there is a certain type of person you should be working with, then you could also believe that there is a certain type of child that you should be parenting. Now imagine you have had a child and it is put in your arms for the first time; You wouldn't say, 'Oh dear. Sorry, I think there's been some mistake. I think this child would be better suited to that mother over there!'

I vividly remember the birth of Mitchell, for example. My first child, Laura, was just so easy to have around. Everyone had warned my wife and I prior to Laura's arrival of the impending chaos of having kids, but the chaos never arrived. She was the perfect little child. Looking after her wasn't easy by any stretch — and it was certainly a change — but it wasn't chaos! We were quietly proud of our mutual parenting skills and decided to have another. But when Mitchell arrived he didn't follow the formula — and no matter how much we worked at it, we thought we were never going to be able to control this kid! Of course, my next two children, Jace and Sam, were just as unique.

Knowing your I.D.™ and the I.D.™ of your children can make a radical difference to your family life

Had I not experienced it myself I wouldn't have believed that kids who came from the same parents could be so different. The characteristics that made them so different started showing up within weeks — and those characteristics are just as strong today. It seems that certain features that make up personality are just as evident in two year olds as they are in seventy-two year olds — those components simply don't change!

So wouldn't it make much more sense to cater to those differences between your children when parenting? The fact is you can't change your kids; you can't trade them in for a different model (although the parents reading this may wish they could do so every now and then!). Remember how in chapter 1 I talk about I.D.™ being like your internal dog tag — an essence that can still be identified as you when you remove everything else such as values, beliefs and conditioning. Your child was born with that dog tag hanging around his or her neck—the trouble is it's invisible. But if it were visible, you'd be able to know exactly how to parent that child—and knowing your *I.D.*™ and the *I.D.*™ of your children can make a radical difference to your family life.

Jace, my third child, asked me one day, 'Dad, do you use our *I.Ds*™ in the way that you parent us?'. I replied, 'Mate, every minute of the day'. It's true—it never leaves my mind. I rang him up at 7.30 on the morning of the Melbourne Cup one year to ask him what horses he wanted to back for the race. He has an *I.D.*™ of 3728, so he has two equally strong drives—Avoid Complete (2) and Improvise (8). Jace loves last-minute things; he really thrives under pressure—not that he looks for it, but it certainly doesn't faze him. So, needless to say, he didn't know what horses he wanted—he hadn't looked, even though he knew I'd be calling. So I said, 'Call me back in ten minutes before I go into a meeting'. He called me back in three minutes with his selection.

Sam, on the other hand, has an *I.D.*™ of 4682, so he also has two equally strong drives—Complete (8) and Avoid Improvise (2). Because Sam and Jace have completely opposite scores to each other in those drives, there is no way I would have said to Sam what I said to Jace. If I did, he would have panicked—telling me either to choose for him because he can't decide in such a short time or that he would have just picked the first horse he saw because he needs to maintain harmony and wouldn't want to feel as though he'd let me down or held me up. Those driven to Complete want harmony—and anything that is a threat to that causes stress. Accommodating these differences, I called Sam and said, 'Read through them, make your choices and I'll get them off you at lunchtime'. By giving him that space, it enabled him to choose his horses in stride (a good omen for the face, no doubt!), and I felt better knowing that I had met his needs in the process. And the bets were on in plenty of time for the race!

No-one actually tells people how to parent, yet there is a stereotypical picture of what a 'good parent' is. Twenty years ago you were a good mother if you always had your house tidy and all the washing done, ironed and put away, and if dinner was punctual and everything ran like a well-oiled machine. You know the scenario—hubby comes home at 6.00 and out comes the beautiful meal, the house is clean and the dishes and surfaces are spotless, and the parents can relax by the TV after a delicious family meal. In these versions of family life kids did their homework—and if they needed an outfit for a school play, their mother would whip up a cheeky little number on the sewing machine!

I know things have changed since then, but it certainly must have been easier for women who were driven to Authenticate and to Complete because they are naturally aligned to those expectations—things running to routine as per the DIY aspects of motherhood. But if all I.Ds™ have existed throughout the ages, there must have been some pretty miserable, frustrated mothers back then! So what happened to the mothers who were driven to Improvise and Avoid Complete? People with that I.D.™ need variety, spontaneity and energy, so many of those mothers would have been stressed out by those expectations! Maybe that's why so many of them started to return to work and why the tension ultimately lead to movements like women's liberation gathering momentum To try and find some comfort some might have conformed to the stereotype, but some probably also became the president of a parents' group or began running the school canteen. In those days, as you know, women who had jobs were scorned upon. Growing up in my street—which was less than thirty years ago—the lady across the road had a job and I know other women looked down on her for it. Nowadays it's the opposite—if women don't go out to work they are seen as the odd ones out.

The truth is all I.Ds™ are conducive to excellent parenting—just as all I.Ds™ can exist in wonderful children. You just have to know what you're dealing with!

The *Instinct to Verify*™

Parents who are driven by the *Instinct to Verify*™ can be really picky—as if nothing their kids do is ever good enough. You see them running along the sidelines at school soccer games, shouting extremely 'useful' information like, 'Kick the ball!', 'Run!' and 'Don't kick it there!' Those driven to Verify need to make sure things are 'right', and the best way to make sure they are right is to make sure there is nothing wrong. They are naturally predisposed to see what is wrong so they can fix it—unfortunately sometimes that's all they see. So the fact that little Johnny scored a goal will be quickly forgotten by his Verify parent when he fouls the opposition and gives away a penalty. All the parent will talk about is what he did wrong to give away the penalty.

I went out to play golf with my son Mitchell and a friend of ours who is strongly driven to Verify and his son. Mitchell and I just wanted to go out together and have a laugh (we're obviously not serious golfers—my handicap is playing!), so we were belting the ball in all directions and just enjoying the day together. Meanwhile, my friend was saying, 'Steven, look at your feet. Where are your feet pointing?', and 'Steven, look at your hands. You're never going to hit straight with hands like that'. Of course, poor Steven took the shot and was so worked up about pleasing his dad that he made a complete mess of it. 'Hopeless!' was the response from his father, who whispered but was loud enough for Steven to hear. Because I.D.™ is such a huge part of my life, all my kids know their I.Ds™ and we talk about them a lot. I had told Mitchell that Steven's father was likely to deal with his son in that way, and our eyes spoke a million words to each other that day as we saw Steven's dad do exactly as we predicted. But it was actually really sad—and the worst part was that Steven's father didn't even know he was doing it. I asked him about it later, away from the boys, and he said, 'I'm only trying to help him'. But as we went around the course, I could visibly see Steven's confidence disappear—his dad was not helping him at all.

If Steven had also been driven to Verify, he wouldn't have been so badly affected and would have instead saw his father's comments as constructive criticism because Verify people respond well to being corrected on the details of their technique, especially if it's something they are genuinely wanting to improve. But Steven was driven to Avoid Verify, so for him encouragement needed to be unconditional. What would have worked for him was if his father had said, 'Good shot Steven. Next time when you take the swing, try holding the club like this'. That way Steven would have received the initial encouragement he needs while also obtaining ideas for improvement.

The upside for people driven by the *Instinct to Verify*™ is that they notice problems early. So if, for example, a child starts to put on weight, the child's Verify-driven parent would probably notice it before it becomes a major issue and address it. A parent who is driven to Avoid Verify wouldn't notice at all and the child would get bigger and bigger. Only when the doctor brings her attention to the problem in the annual check-up will she notice and say, 'Mmm. Yeah, I suppose she has put on a bit of weight'. It's not that the Avoid Verify parent doesn't notice the weight gain, it's just that he or she will accept it without judgement because Avoid Verify people treat everyone equally. Although both parents in this example love their child whether she is chubby or not, the parent driven to Verify will take steps to rectify it.

Those driven to Verify will also stand up for their kids—if there is trouble at school it's the parent who is driven to Verify who would go straight down there to sort it out because Verify-driven people don't focus on the potential confrontation, but rather on making the 'wrong' become right. A parent who is driven to Avoid Verify, however, would be more inclined to wait and see if the trouble sorted itself out first. Avoid Verify people raise their children much more passively—talking things through with their children so they can discover the answers for themselves—whereas Verify parents are, by nature, more dictatorial. Avoid Verify parents, however, tend not to correct their children as much as other parents and will appear much gentler. Parents driven by the *Instinct to Verify*™, on the other hand, will correct their children often and are strict disciplinarians. They will ensure that their kids know what the rules are and that they can't break them without consequences.

There is always someone to blame for the parent driven to Verify

People driven to Verify are also good whereas Avoid Verify parents ask questions that will help the child realise things as he or she answers them. For example, if a Verify-driven parent is helping his or her child to learn to ride a bike, he or she may say, 'You took your feet off the ground too slowly. After two steps take them off the ground and you will be able to get your balance quickly and ride the bike'. By saying that, the child will have a strategy to follow to accomplish his or her goal. Someone who is driven to avoid the *Instinct to Verify*™, however, is more likely to say something like, 'You nearly had it that time dear. Try again' or 'What do you think you could try next time?'

Parental guilt

All parents feel guilty about something, but for parents driven to Verify, they are likely to feel it because they worry they harp on at their kids and indicate that nothing they do is ever good enough. They may even hear those sentiments in arguments with their children when they say, 'It doesn't matter what I do Dad. It's never going to be good enough for you is it?' The way for Verify-driven parents to avoid this is for them to consciously make a point of praising the 95 per cent that is right rather than just focusing on the 5 per cent that is not.

Additionally, there is always someone to blame for the parent driven to Verify. Say a parent goes to put on a CD and discover it's missing; he or she will immediately blame someone for taking it. Even if it's not said out loud, the Verify parent's whole demeanour will be accusatory—whereas an Avoid Verify would just notice it wasn't there and think about where it might be.

Parental guilt felt by those springs from them feeling as though they let too much slide. In retrospect, they will often feel they should have been stricter, asked more questions or held their children to account more.

Interacting with your child

Children driven to Verify thrive in an environment in which they can improve and be noticed for it. Because they naturally compare, they like to know they are the best or are at least getting better. Obviously telling one child he or she is better than another isn't very helpful, but telling a child he or she is better than the child was last week will encourage a child driven to Verify to keep on improving. I have a friend who is driven to Avoid Verify and who vividly remembers playing hockey at school—she was good at hockey and was, more often than not, picked for the team. The teacher was probably driven to Verify because he began to compare her performance to her sister's, by making comments like, 'That wasn't as good as your sister'. My friend stopped playing completely as a result. If she had been driven to Verify, however, that comment might have motivated her to try harder—instead it had the opposite effect.

Natural behaviours for children driven to Verify

They are driven to:

- ask questions—'But why?'
- be defensive
- blame others
- be preoccupied with being 'right'
- hold a grudge
- have a need for equality and to be fair
- have a high level of perseverance.

If you have a child driven to Verify and you want her to do something you have to explain why. Children driven to Verify need a purpose—and the process needs to be fair. So if your child comes home and says, 'Can I go to my friend's house tomorrow night?', and for some reason she can't, you will need to provide an explanation. Saying no and just leaving it at that will end in an argument, culminating in those common parenting phrases, 'Because I said so' and 'While you live under this roof you'll do what you're told'. If you say, on the other hand, 'No. Your brother wants to go to David's house but he can't go either. I need you both to help me clean out the garage, so can you please go another night?' Because the Verify-driven child will see that neither she nor her brother could go, she'll see it as fair and also with good reason and will be more likely to be appeased. I've tried this with my own kids—and it works. They just need to know why.

Natural behaviours for children driven to Avoid Verify

They are driven to:

- ⇉ not be spiteful
- ⇉ be accepting
- ⇉ avoid confrontation
- ⇉ go with the flow
- ⇉ ask questions because they are inquisitive and curious—not because they are sceptical
- ⇉ connect easily with animals because they are so accepting
- ⇉ not be obviously competitive
- ⇉ be concise.

If you want children driven to Avoid Verify to do something, just encourage them unconditionally. Don't engage in arguments because they find confrontation stressful and will shut down. Just reason with them and make it logical, but don't raise your voice. Avoid Verify children will be more accepting of your rules and won't feel compelled to question your every decision the way a child driven to Verify does.

The *Instinct to Authenticate*™

Parents who are driven by the *Instinct to Authenticate*™ are naturally involved with their kids. They are the ones who build billy-carts and go swimming with their kids. They like to do things with their children—if they can get away from work that is. One of the risks for people driven to Authenticate is that they can be so busy doing things that they won't spend enough time at home with the family. Even at the weekends, by the time they've finished tinkering with the vintage car their kids will have gone to bed.

But once they are away on holiday together as a family, Authenticate-driven parents will be the fathers at the beach building sand castles with their kids or the mothers rallying the troops for a pushbike ride. For parents driven to Authenticate, the very early stages of a child's life are the hardest because the baby just eats and sleeps—even though there are still plenty of things to do *for* the child. They are usually much more excited though when the child gets older and they can start doing things together.

What parents driven to Authenticate choose to spend time on will depend on their value system—if they feel they are being more useful by being with their family then they will do things with them, but if they feel they are not as needed at home or could be more useful at work, then they will be drawn to work.

Those driven by the *Instinct to Authenticate*™ need to add their personal touch to things that they do. It's the mothers driven to Authenticate who make the mermaid costume for the school play or fairy cakes for the school fair. Productivity, however, is also very important to those driven to Authenticate, so if it is a better use of their time to buy the cake for the fair, they will—even though in their heart of hearts they would have preferred to bake it themselves.

Those driven to Avoid Authenticate are not into the doing as much as the philosophy behind the doing. If given the choice between mountain biking with their kids or sitting in the sun and talking about how they feel and what their favourite subject is at school, there is simply no competition! 'Deep and meaningfuls' will likely always take precedence over doing for those driven to Avoid Authenticate.

Because of this preference, Avoid Authenticates can really struggle to get involved with their kids. One of the best strategies they can employ to counter this is to use their desire for leverage. For example, a father driven to Avoid Authenticate is sitting by the pool with his kids reading the newspaper. His children are badgering him to get in the pool and mess around with them. He's not that interested in the pool because he's happy reading the paper, but eventually he starts to feel guilty so dives into the pool—except now while he's in it, he'll clean it. That way, swimming in the pool keeps his kids happy and is also a good use of his time because he'll be cleaning the pool while he's in it.

The early years for parents driven to Avoid Authenticate can also be hard because they are happiest when they can have a conversation with their child and talk about what's important to them. Plus older kids can do the things that adults enjoy doing anyway—enabling parents of older children to effectively just do what they want to do, but with their kids along with them too. The subtle difference, therefore, is that they're not doing something with their kids (as the main focus); instead, they're doing something for themselves, and their kids just happen to be there.

Parental guilt

Parents driven to Authenticate tend to feel guilty don't feel that they can help their children. Certain childhood situations are quite normal—such as friends being cruel to each other—but it's still hard for Authenticate parents to stand back and watch their child being bullied. I think it's especially hard on Authenticate parents when their child is in physical pain or involved in some accident that causes disability. This is hard on all parents and most would, I'm sure, change places with their kids in a heartbeat if it meant they could take their pain away. But the helplessness felt by Authenticate parents cuts them right to the core because they're blocked from doing the very thing that is their reason for living—helping. Parents driven to Authenticate really come into their own as the children grow up and they can do more with them—such as showing them things and helping them. They can still feel guilty though when they are too busy to do things with their children and can't talk to them enough. But if they combine the talking with an activity, it can really work well—especially if the child is also driven by the *Instinct to Authenticate*™.

Those driven to Avoid Authenticate, on the other hand, will feel guilty because they don't do things with their kids. Other mothers will be teaching their children to swim or bake cakes, but mothers who are driven to Avoid Authenticate will feel very inadequate. But as the children grow—especially into their teenage years—the mothers driven to Avoid Authenticate can flourish because they can connect with their children by talking to them on their wavelength.

Interacting with your child

For Authenticate-driven children, people have to do what they say they are going to do and do it when they say they are going to do it. Children driven to Authenticate are very literal; for example, my son Mitchell is driven to Authenticate—and I knew he was by the time he was three or four years old—but even when he was a baby he hated having his arms tucked in at night. That was my first signal that he was driven to Authenticate because children driven to Authenticate have to be doing something with their hands. As he grew older my suspicions were validated.

....

Natural behaviours for children driven to Authenticate

They will:

➤ be seen as lazy because they only do exactly what is asked of them—and they won't act unless their involvement is required

➤ be literal

➤ be hands on

➤ impersonate

➤ need to know how things work.

....

This is a typical phone conversation between me and Mitchell (although Sam and Jace would probably follow suit given that they share the same *Instinctive Drives™*):

MITCHELL: 'What time will you coming home tonight, Dad?'

ME: 'I'll be home in twenty minutes.'

(Mitchell looks at the clock. It says 3.37 so he will assume I am going to walk in the door at 3.57.)

(I come home at 4.05.)

MITCHELL: 'You're late.'

ME: 'No I'm not.'

MITCHELL: 'Yes you are. You said you'd be here at 3.57.'

ME: 'I did not. I don't even talk like that Mitchell—I would never say 3.57.'

MITCHELL: 'Well you said you'd be home in twenty minutes.'

ME: 'Yeah, I know I said that.'

MITCHELL: 'Well you told me that at 3.37.'

Once I knew about I.D.™ I realised that he wasn't trying to be smart—it's just that his Authenticate-driven nature makes him very literal. I drove to Canberra from Sydney with him one day, and he asked me how long it would take. I replied that it would take about four hours. 'So we'll be there at 7.46 then', announced Mitchell. My need to Improvise kicked in—because I need a challenge—and we ended up driving into the centre of Canberra at exactly 7.46 pm.

If your child is driven to Avoid Authenticate, he is likely to be more sensitive than children who are driven to Authenticate. It is important that you spend time finding out how your child feels and what he thinks about things. If you want to talk to your child and he is driven to Avoid Authenticate, he will listen and be able to engage in the discussion. But if you want to talk to a child who is driven to Authenticate, you'll need to ask him to do something and then talk while he's doing it. When it comes to Authenticate-driven children, it's better to go for a bike ride or a walk with them and talk about things then; the sit-down chat doesn't work best with these kids.

....

Natural behaviours for children driven to Avoid Authenticate

They will:

▷ be aware of things going on under the surface

▷ be preoccupied with what others think of them

▷ exaggerate

▷ be sensitive to their environment and other people's emotions—and they choose the right moment to talk openly and honestly

▷ be interested in the meaning behind things.

....

If you want your Authenticate-driven child to do something, you have to give him a context to make it relevant for him. So if he comes home from school and says, 'Can I go to my friend's house tomorrow night?' and can't go, then you'll need to make your reasons for your decisions relevant to him. Saying no and just leaving it at that will end in an argument, but if you say to him, 'No—because Grandma is coming over for tea and she hasn't seen you for two months and asked specifically if all the kids could be here, can you go another time?' it will provoke a much better response. He may not be overly thrilled at trading playing *Grand Theft Auto* on the PlayStation for an evening with Grandma, but he'll be far less likely to kick up a fuss about it if can see the relevance of your answer and how it applies to him personally.

If parents driven to Authenticate take it upon themselves to organise the family holiday—the whole family should be prepared for activities galore. If those parents happen to be driven to Authenticate and to Complete, then boot camp could be a more accurate description of the family holiday to come. The whole family would be up at the crack of dawn, having breakfast at 0700 hours, horse riding at 0830 hours and rollerblading after that—and lunch would be at 1230 with a two-hour hike to follow. And if family members think they can get out of horse riding if it's raining, they've another thing coming—the schedule will be followed regardless! This kind of environment would be hell for people who are driven to Avoid Authenticate and to Avoid Complete, who would be craving spontaneity.

The *Instinct to Complete*™

Parents who are driven to Complete need routine, harmony and order—so Saturday may be the day for food shopping for some of these parents, and they probably shop at the same supermarket because they know where everything is. Likewise, they will know exactly what they will buy because it won't vary much week to week because they will have a budget they have to meet. They are the types of parents who plan everything for the family. For example, on Monday nights they will have roast lamb for dinner; on Tuesday night, spaghetti, on Wednesday night, fish; on Thursday night, chicken; and on Friday the family will eat out (probably at the same place). Often these families won't even notice that everything is planned out for them—especially if they are all driven to Complete.

However, this strong sense of routine in Complete-driven people is efficient and productive because there will be no time spent wondering what to have for dinner or what to buy at the grocery store.

Everything has its place and purpose for Complete-driven people, so untidy rooms drive parents driven to Complete nuts. They will also become really frustrated if their Avoid Complete children ask every five minutes where things are. The Complete-driven parent will think, 'If they would tidy their room and have places for things they wouldn't have that problem'.

A parent driven to Complete will have everything in the house running like clockwork. There is no scramble in the morning for clothes or to prepare packed lunches — everything will be arranged. The household will run like a well-oiled machine — and those driven to Complete are the archetypal 'good parents' because of it.

The other great thing about parents driven to Complete is that they keep traditions alive. They always know, for example, that they decorate the Christmas tree as a family on the first Saturday of December. Their vulnerability, however, is that they can be too regimented — especially if any of their children are driven to Avoid Complete (or someone like me comes along)! Avoid Complete children need variety and new experiences, so they can feel really frustrated by routine. Most of my siblings — as well as Mum and Dad — are driven to Complete (yes, I'm surrounded!), but I'm driven to Avoid Complete. I vividly remember going to a small rural property for our holidays as a kid. We went every year and it was in the middle of nowhere — although my family liked it, I believed that we could have gone to prison and had more fun! Today I truly cherish the memories, but I didn't really enjoy it when I was young.

Those driven by the *Instinctive Drive to Complete*™ are motivated by order and routine — and they are certainly not words that spring to mind when a new baby makes an appearance. The disruption that is caused to established systems can be really stressful for new parents who are driven to Complete. They may panic if the baby sleeps through a feed time or not go anywhere or do anything else that could disrupt the routine of the baby. If you invited new parents who are driven to Complete to your party, for example, you may very well hear them reply:

> Oh but we can't because by the time we get the baby down it will be
> about three. Then she will need a feed and to settle in again at five

o'clock and then we'd have to get ready at about seven o'clock—when it's almost time to feed her again. So we're not coming.

However, once parents driven to Complete have had one child and had a chance to re-establish some new routines that work for them, they tend to become more relaxed. Parenthood can initially be very hard on Complete-driven parents. But parents driven to Avoid Complete thrive in the unfamiliar so are often not as stressed when they become parents. They are the opposite of what is traditionally considered a good parent. The house is probably chaos—nothing organised—and they probably shop when they need to, often running out of things. For example, the parent driven to Avoid Complete may be halfway through making spaghetti bolognaise and realise there isn't enough tomato paste so will end up using red wine and throwing in some mushrooms instead. People who are driven to Avoid Complete almost never follow a recipe—whereas those driven to Complete always follow the recipe and would never start a dish unless they had checked that they had all the ingredients.

Monday mornings are usually a scramble to find matching socks and pack the lunches for Avoid Complete parents. These are the parents who put strange little surprises—like last night's pizza—in their kid's lunchbox. A house run by Avoid Complete parents probably operates under a 'just-in-time' philosophy—clothes are washed and in the basket but they won't be ironed or put away, for example. This philosophy can be really stressful for some children. If Avoid Complete parents have Complete-driven kids, this sense of disorder can distress their children no end because Complete-driven children will never feel the harmony they need because there is no apparent stability or routine. I remember when I first met my wife, Kim. She is driven to Complete—as are all four of her children (yes, you read right!). They were all so organised. I'd like to think I was a breath of fresh air but I know in reality I was more like a cyclone arriving—doing everything differently to the way they were so used to. Initially they thought it was fun—a novelty—plus I think they thought I wasn't really like that all the time. But as I—and my differences—became more permanent, I could feel the tension build as it became for them a choice between doing things 'our' way or 'his' way. Deep down I appreciated their level of order and the way everything functioned so smoothly—and I know they appreciated my energy, sense of fun and spontaneity—but there have definitely been times where never the two should meet! Both people driven to Complete and people driven to Avoid Complete make excellent parents, but knowing the

I.D.™ dynamic between each family member can be really helpful for everyone.

Those driven to Avoid Complete are more interested in seeing the uniqueness of every child, rather than focusing on treating each one the same. When I grew up I was one of six children. My parents did an awesome job of providing for us in every way—mentally, emotionally and spiritually. Even today I wonder how they did it. They never complained about the effort—they only ever spoke about how proud they were of all six of us. Both my parents are driven to Complete, so if one child received a new pair of socks and a bar of chocolate, all the kids received a new pair of socks and a bar of chocolate. I just accepted it at the time because I didn't really know any different—although deep down I desperately wanted something different. The first time I recall getting something on my own was a haircut at about age thirteen from a real hairdresser—well, a barber back then. No-one else in my family got a haircut from him; I felt so special. The barber saw me so happy and thought it was because he'd done such a great job. But it wasn't the cut—I'm not sure I cared how it looked—I was just so happy that I got something special.

In comparison to my parents, I am driven to Avoid Complete so don't have the same definition of 'fair'. For example, I took my son Jace to see *The Lion King*; I didn't take my other children or even take them to something similar. If something comes up that I think one of them will like I'll take them, but I wouldn't take them all to everything just to be inclusive—and I've talked to them about that. They see each other receiving different things at different times, know I'm driven to be fair (a Verify trait) and can see that my thinking plays out as a 'system' that seems to be working for us.

Parental guilt

Parents who are driven to Complete may feel guilty about being so disciplined or routine oriented. They can be very inflexible if their child wants to do something different—even about little things like putting Vegemite on their sandwiches instead of strawberry jam! If their child is driven to Avoid Complete they can feel boring because they do the same things in the same way and are not spontaneous—something that their child will no doubt have brought to their attention on more than one occasion.

There is, however, probably more guilt felt by Avoid Complete parents because their house is usually a mess, their fridge half-empty and their clothes ironed on a 'need today' basis. There is always a sense of chaos in a home that is run by someone who is driven to avoid the *Instinct to Complete™*. Even though Avoid Complete parents will muster all their willpower to rectify those household problems, they will always feel a little inadequate because of them. Those driven to Avoid Complete are also easily distracted, so they are usually the parents who can be seen speeding down the street toward the nursery because they've forgotten to pick up their child from playgroup!

Interacting with your child

Complete-driven children respond positively to routine; it gives them a sense of stability. There will also be a measure of how important they are to you, and they feel loved according to how much time they spend with you. People say you should always try and have dinner with your kids as a family; it's the child driven to Complete who would especially enjoy that because it is time spent together—an Avoid Complete child, by comparison, doesn't place as much value on time spent with family.

If your children are driven to Complete and you want them to do something, you have to frame the task in the context of harmony. After all, if your children's friend asks them to come over the following night—they may even say no themselves because it isn't

Those driven to Avoid Complete are more interested in seeing the uniqueness of every child, rather than focusing on treating each one the same

enough advanced warning. But if they don't, you will need to show how going out the next night would upset their schedule and disrupt their harmony, so you may say, 'Are you sure you want to do that? You normally have your guitar lesson on Tuesday nights, and you'll be out of step with the rest of the group if you miss the lesson'. Chances are that once they see a broader context, they will prefer to go another night once they can see how it would disrupt their schedule.

Natural behaviours of children driven to Complete

They are driven to:

⋙ finish

⋙ spend time together with the important people in their life

⋙ take turns

⋙ rehearse and prepare through repetition

⋙ work in an orderly fashion and according to a routine

⋙ have high recall

⋙ want to fit in and please others

⋙ be influenced by peer pressure

⋙ need advance notice.

In 1993 I worked with twenty-two kids who had been labelled as having Attention Deficit Disorder (ADD). When I met these children I was struck by how many displayed traits that would indicate they were driven to Complete. I wondered if their behaviour was due to their lifestyle being out of sync with their I.D.™ and was willing to bet many of them had parents who were driven to Avoid Complete. For children driven to Complete, routines are essential, and the more they can be organised, start their day and get on a role, the more successful, self-assured and happy they will be.

To close off any undue concerns or questions around the correlation between ADD and the *Instinct to Complete™*, my work with the children diagnosed with ADD eventually showed that there was no actual or significant correlation with the *Instinct to Complete™* nor any other single instinct. I found that children with any I.D.™ could be diagnosed with ADD. The main correlation being the degree to which they were able to learn and live in a way that matched their I.D.™ Sometimes this connection wasn't so obvious, but it always existed, so once we started to implement startegies to ensure they could learn and live in a way that matched their I.D.™, things always began to improve.

Natural behaviours of children driven to Avoid Complete

Their nature is to:

🠖 not follow through on tasks

🠖 not listen to instructions and be non-compliant and defiant

🠖 not finish everything they start

🠖 respond to reverse psychology

🠖 be defiant

🠖 become bored easily

🠖 need variety.

Using *I.D.*™ as the basis of my assessment I met with the parents of one eleven-year-old boy who had been on medication for several years. I told them about the correlation between ADD and Complete-driven children. As they described their son to me, it sounded like he might've been driven to Complete, so I suggested they instigate some simple changes—one of which was buying an alarm clock. Needless to say, they were sceptical and almost offended at first! As you can imagine, purchasing an alarm clock sounds like a pretty weird strategy to give to anxious parents looking for assistance with their child's behaviour. I convinced them to try it because I felt it might make a huge difference to their son if he could get into a routine right from the time he started his day—that way he would not feel like he was 'chasing his tail' all day. Moreover, if he could start his day well, feeling organise and on time, it would probably give him a totally different demeanor at school and enable him to engage much more effectively with his lessons. I also asked them to build to wake their son up at the same time every morning and build little routines for him so he could begin to know what to expect each day prior to going to school. The result was a much happier, more settled child who eventually came off his medication and continued successfully throughout his school year.

The *Instinct to Improvise*™

Because those driven to Improvise need fun, buzz and energy, logic dictates that they would be the fun parents—but of all the *Instinctive*

Drives™ these are the people who can be really challenged as parents! The reality of parenting is that depending on a variety of things—such as finances, health, personality differences and career stresses—it can be fun for some, but for many it's not fun much of the time. Improvise parents thrive on freedom—and parenting is, for many, quite restricting on their freedom. It's not that those driven to Improvise are incapable of looking after someone else, it's just that the concept of parenting can imply a lack of choice and a necessity to 'get serious'—and people driven by the *Instinct to Improvise*™ hate serious!

Semantics—the meanings behinds words—are an extremely powerful influence on how people act. People with arachnophobia, for example, have been shown to respond with the same physical reaction in the body when they see the word 'spider' as when they see a picture of a spider or an actual spider. It works in the same way with *I.D.*™ We all react instinctively—whether we like it or not—to certain words that are linked to our strongest drives. So the word *mistake* stirs the Verify people, *help* is compelling to Authenticates, *mess* certainly gets the attention of Complete-driven people and the word *can't* provokes every bodily fibre in Improvise people.

So for Improvise people, when parenting—or anything else for that matter—means they 'can't' do something else, then they will feel compromised. Having said that, their instinct is also to find a way to do both anyway, but when the obligation is long term or so restricting that they truly cant do the things that are more energising for them, then the burden of it all will start to take its toll on them.

Those driven to Improvise need to make a good impression, so if their kids are showing them up they would rather leave than give them a telling-off—especially if the parents are also driven to Avoid Verify (they detest confrontation).

Improvise people are driven to have fun in everything they do, but that doesn't mean they like to party all the time—sometimes solving a complex problem can be seen as fun by them because of the challenge involved, for example. The key for them is that they are performing at their best when they feel like they are having fun—whatever that definition is for them. Actually, it was probably their sense of fun that helped them to become parents in the first place! Many Improvise parents have told me—somewhat facetiously, but I know there was a message in it—that they would ideally love to hand their kids over to someone else until they were eighteen, and then take them back so they can go out and have a good time with them.

Parents who are driven to Avoid Improvise, on the other hand, are the epitome of 'responsibility'. The danger for them is taking their parenting role too seriously—for those that do, it can make thier home quite sedate, which may not suit all family members. They need to know what's going on so they can control or eliminate all known risks. So although parents driven to Complete may have fish on a Friday because they are drawn to the routine, parents driven to Complete and also to Avoid Improvise will also always have the same type of fish, but they'll do it because it eliminates risk. Eating strange dishes, meeting new friends and going out to new places and social gatherings is disconcerting to people driven to Avoid Improvise, so their kids may feel overly protected. These types of parents probably holiday in the same place every year—and preferably in the same caravan! If the kids are also driven to Avoid Improvise, then all will be well in the family, but if there are some kids in the family who are driven to Improvise, then they can be quite frustrated by that lack of adventure—and that clash of I.D.™ styles between children and their parents can cause tension.

Those driven to Avoid Improvise do have fun and can be great company, so they do get involved in activities, but more on the basis of 'there's a time and a place for everything'—whereas for the Improvise driven people, it's about fun 'most of the time' and pretty much 'everywhere'! I will say though that when it is the right time and place for fun.

Parental guilt

Many people driven by the *Instinct to Improvise*™ feel guilty about not being 'responsible' enough; they are the zany parents who allow their kids to push the envelope and 'have a go' at things. But when the boundaries are stretched too far and thier kids are hurt as a result, these parents can feel like they weren't responsible or cautious enough. Take the character of Eddy in the TV show *Absolutely Fabulous* as an example, I can't guess her I.D.™ of course, but I can guess that she is probably driven by the *Instinct to Improvise*™ and that her long-suffering daughter in the show, Saffy, is likely to be the opposite (driven to Avoid Improvise). For people driven to Avoid Improvise, they will beat themselves up about not being enough fun. Their lack of animation at times can also cause them to appear uncaring or unenthusiastic if their kids do really well at something. For example, if parents driven by the *Instinct to Improvise*™ were watching their son win an egg-and-spoon race at his primary school sports day, they would be screaming encouragement from the sidelines and having a blast—whereas if they were driven to Avoid Improvise, they would probably not be so animated.

Those driven to Avoid Improvise can also look unappreciative of other people's efforts because they don't immediately become excited and animated in the way that Improvise people do. To pull themselves out of that, they need to redefine 'risk' and make an effort—especially if their kids are driven by the *Instinct to Improvise*™. Similarly, parents who are driven by the *Instinct to Improvise*™ may need to learn to tone it down sometimes so they don't embarrass their kids!

Interacting with your child

If you wanted to prompt your Improvise-driven child to do something, make it into a game. But be warned, a kid driven by the *Instinct to Improvise*™ will have no qualms about instigating an argument or discussions about it.

....

Natural behaviours of children driven to Improvise

Their nature is to:

  ⟫ be natural entertainers or actors because they thrive on attention

  ⟫ be passionate and animated

  ⟫ have huge highs and lows emotionally

  ⟫ do their best at the last minute and under pressure

  ⟫ be daring.

....

If Improvise-driven children want something, they can be very persuasive and will explore options until a solution is found. So when children driven by the *Instinct to Improvise*™ come home from school and ask if they can go to their friend's house the next day, their parents should prepare for a debate. If the parents tell the children, 'No you can't go because your granny is coming to tea', the children will simply do what they do best—improvise. They would be likely to respond with, 'What if we go straight after school for a couple of hours and get Dan's dad to bring us back in time for dinner with Granny?' because an Improvise-driven child would suggest possible solutions until you either put your foot down or gave up. It's not that Improvise-driven children are necessarily confrontational — generally they are not — but they sometimes don't know when to leave things alone. When Improvise-driven children lock onto something they want, they will go after it like a dog with a bone. They are amazingly resourceful when it comes to obtaining what they want — coming up with alternatives that they hope will enable them to acquire their desired outcome.

Natural behaviours of children driven to Avoid Improvise

Their nature is to:

- become flustered under pressure
- be fearful of tackling new things
- do their best work when alone
- be serious when trying their hardest
- be quite diligent.

Pregnancy

Before I leave parenting and look at learning strategies and optimal learning methods for each I.D.™, I should also mention pregnancy. Can you imagine the stress for a first-time mother who is driven to Complete? She would want predictability there can be no guarantees about what will play out — other than that it will. She would be asking herself, 'When is it due? If it comes early what should I do? How much will it hurt? Will I be able to feed the baby myself? Will I suffer from postnatal depression?' When a person's mind is stressed his or her body tenses up. Yet in order for birthing to be as straightforward as possible, the mother needs to be as relaxed as possible. I know of so many Complete-driven women whose second and subsequent pregnancies (and deliveries) were so much smoother and much less stressful than their first one. In fact, its amazing how many of them ended up giving birth the first time via caesarean section compared to mothers with the opposite I.D.™ — who also often have great first-time pregnancies and natural deliveries because they are free of such stress.

On the other hand, those driven by the *Instinct to Improvise*™ usually have the best first-time births because they are new and exciting. I know one Improvise-driven friend who was jumping on the bed just minutes after giving birth! But although Improvise-driven mothers may have an easier birth — after three months they can easily become bored and need to be out and about again because they miss adult interaction. (Incidentally, my anecdotal research shows that Improvise-driven mums can be more prone to postnatal depression due to their vulnerability to the emotional roller-coaster of pregnancy.)

By now your head may be spinning as you wonder what *I.D.*™ you have and what *I.D.*™ your kids may have. It can feel a little overwhelming to think about trying to parent your children differently — but I hope that from reading this book you will already be seeing why you experience different challenges with each of your kids. Don't panic though — just because your children are different it doesn't necessarily mean you will need to take a different approach with each child — often you'll just need to put a different spin on tasks and activities to get the best out of your kids.

Teaching and learning

Just as there is no perfect profile for parents or children, there is also no perfect profile that guarantees a 'straight A' student, but there are strategies and best ways to learn will suit each *I.D.*™ Children of all *I.Ds*™ can either excel or be terrible at school. How well they fare in school is not linked to intelligence, but, significantly, to how the needs of their *I.D.*™ are met.

One of the members of the original *I.D.*™ development team was the principal of the primary school my children went to. Her experience with leadership, education and kids meant that as the *I.D. System*™ was developed, we became very excited about the possibilities it presented for both teachers and students alike.

To test this possibility out, we set up Classroom Action Planning Groups (CAPS), and each group contained six teachers and myself. I met with them every week to map out lessons so that they would appeal to each *I.D.*™ I knew that given the normal distribution of *I.Ds*™ in the general population, all *Instinctive Drives*™ would be represented in every classroom so my goal was to map out lessons that would appeal to all four *Instinctive Drives™* The teachers were evaluated for their *I.Ds™* so they would be aware of their own individual biases and so that they would be better equipped to 'I.D.-ise' their lessons.

One Tuesday I talked to the teachers about the different *I.Ds™* and how they relate to group work. Teachers are taught that group work is crucial to a child's development. I acknowledge that may be the case, but that doesn't mean children should be judged on that basis. One of the teachers, David—who was driven to Complete and to avoid Improvise—said, 'Are you saying that not all kids like group work or are suited to group work?' I replied that he was right and explained that based on the fact that *I.Ds™* are evenly distributed throughout the population, half his class (the children driven to Avoid Improvise) would probably not like group work. David was incensed. He said, 'That's rubbish Paul. It's fun and it's the most exciting time of the week—all my students love group work'. But the next week he apologised because it turned out that he had been teaching the next day and had decided to test my theory. Adamant that I was wrong, he outlined an exercise to his class and then asked for those that wanted to do the exercise in groups to go over to the right side of the room and those that would prefer to do the work on their own to go to the left. He said to me, 'I couldn't believe my eyes—the room was split down the middle!'

Just as there is no perfect profile for parents or children, there is also no perfect profile that guarantees a 'straight A' student

Another teacher, Jenny—who is strongly driven by the *Instinct to Authenticate™*—had seen quite a change in the behaviour and level of engagement of the kids in her class, so she asked to be involved in one of the CAPS groups. She told me about a standard challenge that all teachers face in prompting students to actually start lessons. She said that a quarter of the class will start their work promptly. She thought that perhaps they were the kids who have a similar style or *I.D.™* to her so can relate to what she is asking—but that the rest can really drag it out to the point where some may not even start or feel able to start. For her this was very frustrating. She would explain the lesson to all her students—which to her seemed quite stimulating—yet many of them struggled to engage. Given her *I.D.*™, Jenny took that rather personally but was keen to see if *I.D.*™ could make a difference. So I helped her map out her lessons so that all four instincts were catered for.

The next day she said to her class, 'I am going to write down four ways that you can start this lesson. When you see a way that works for you then I want you to begin the lesson'. She then started to write up the four options on the board and was flabbergasted when she turned to face the class and found that the whole class was working!

As Jenny found, there are natural study talents and vulnerabilities for each *Instinctive Drive*™ when it comes to teaching and learning; the rest of this chapter is dedicated to identifying them. It's not about what society dictates is a 'good student' but about what works for each individual based on his or her essential nature.

The *Instinct to Verify*™

Those driven to Verify need to have a purpose that is meaningful in order for them to engage with tasks. They also need specific feedback—'good work' is not good enough for those driven to Verify. They need to know what it was that was good and how they compared to everyone else; they even need feedback that compares the different ways they've handled a certain task—such as, 'When you used examples to illustrate your point it was more powerful then when you didn't'. Verify students excel where there is a definitive right answer, so Mathematics and Science are examples of subjects they typically enjoy.

People who are driven to Verify learn best when:

- there are specifics
- they can investigate and evaluate
- they can see it is the 'right' way to learn
- teaching is cumulative and based on previous learning
- there is an empirical approach to determining answers and outcomes.

People with the Verify drive can be very studious, and the risk with this is that they won't go out and mix with others enough — especially if they are more introverted. They can just disappear into books — becoming geniuses at seventeen years old, but with no social skills. It's important for parents of these children to enocurage them to play team sports or at least get out and do things. On the other hand, children driven to Avoid Verify are more likely to be drawn to more creative pursuits because with those types of subjects what's 'right' is more subjective. Subjects such as Art or Design may appeal to Aovid Verify-driven children. It's important to remember that they respond well to unconditional encouragement and like to know they're on the right track.

People who are driven to Avoid Verify learn best when:

- ☞ they receive unconditional encouragement

- ☞ they are not pigeon-holed and judged

- ☞ there is an opportunity to 'get it right' first time

- ☞ they are loaded with the information they need in order to feel confident in their abilities to tackle tasks

- ☞ they trust the teacher not to judge them.

The *Instinct to Authenticate*™

The report card of a student driven to Authenticate is likely to say, 'Susan is a lovely girl but she needs to show more initiative and could apply herself more. Never goes beyond what's asked'. But when you look at that assessment through the lens of I.D.™, it's easy to see that those comments simply reflect the need for Authenticate-driven children to take things literally and avoid waste. In other words, it's their essential nature to do just what is asked and no more. When a teacher says, 'I want you to do a 500-word essay on the biology of a rat', the Authenticate-driven children in the class will hear, '500 words' and that is exactly what they'll deliver. For example, I've had teachers say to me that they have had students stop writing mid sentence because they'd just written down word number 500! The teacher will ask what happened and the child will simply reply, 'But you asked for 500 words'. The teacher thinks will the child is being smart, but really it is just a reflection of how his or her mind works. Those driven to Authenticate don't read between the lines or make assumptions about what they think somebody meant.

People who are driven to Authenticate learn best when:

- they can demonstrate, build or display their work
- the work is relevant to them
- they can 'do'—rather than just listen
- they have the right equipment
- they can see how something works or is applied
- they can see something is real by experiencing it or being shown it (excursions are helpful for them for this reason)
- the impact of what they're learning is durable and lasting
- they can speak and be interpreted on a literal basis.

Authenticate-driven children can struggle with school if they don't see the relevance of what they are learning. These are the kids who will become cranky at having to study Latin or Trigonometry, for example! Or the kids who you will hear say things like, 'I'm going to be a builder, so what's the point of learning History?'

Although parents often privately agree with that thinking, rather than explaining the relevance of those subjects, they often just say, 'Keep slogging away Kiddo. I know it's a pain but I had to do it and so do you!' But that kind of encouragement doesn't help Authenticate-driven children. All that happens in that situation is they will attempt to meet that need for relevance some other way—for example, by providing the cigarettes to the other kids at school because it suddenly makes them relevant. When I've worked with kids with ADD, it's obvious to me that they don't see school as relevant. I've asked them, 'Do you know what you want to be when you grow up?' The answer is always no—demonstrating that it's very difficult for school to be relevant to children if they don't have a clue about what they want to do after school.

Kids driven to Authenticate need to see the point of what they're doing. They also respond positively to role modelling because it gives them a picture of how they should operate. For one-parent families with children driven to Authenticate, finding such a role model can obviously be a real challenge. For example, a boy who is driven to Authenticate without access to his father will struggle to know what's expected of him as an adult and father because he won't have a male role model to emulate, so it's important to have an alternative, positive male role model in his life. In the same way, girls driven to Authenticate who live only with their father will also benefit from having access to a positive female role model.

My son Mitchell is driven to Authenticate. He was struggling in school for a while because of this relevance issue. He wanted to be a motor mechanic, so things like History were seen as a waste of time by him — as he said to me, 'Dad, it's history (literally) so why are we wasting time learning about the past?' I found it hard to argue with this straight talk because I wasn't exactly 'Mr History Major' at school myself. But there are reasons people study things like history, and I wanted him to learn how to apply himself to things he didn't like — not just to those things he enjoyed. So I spoke to him about it. I said:

> I know you hate history, but everything you are taught at school has relevance to what you want to do if you just think about it a little differently. Take history — it's important to look at the past so we can work out what's going on in the present. It's important that we ask questions to get some answers and to keep digging until we find the truth. Say you have a customer that wants their brakes fixed and you take their request at face value without asking the proper questions to work out what's happened in the past — what the history of the car is. You may not find the real solution. That customer may then think you did a poor job and not come back. Use history to practise your skill at uncovering the truth and getting to the real issues because that will make you a better mechanic.

As tenuous as that may seem, it worked — he could see a link so he increased his effort and eventually his grades started to improve.

Children driven to Authenticate, if engaged, can be incredibly focused. If they are skateboarding with their friends at the weekend, they will practise a jump until it's perfect because they can see that skateboarding is relevant to their life and know what they are trying to achieve.

For those driven to Avoid Authenticate, the relationships they have with their teachers and friends is critical to their success and happiness—given how motivated they are by the perception that people important to them have of them. As a result, they can be quite challenging children to teach. But those driven to Avoid Authenticate are also motivated by leverage, so if their study serves more than one purpose then they can be very diligent indeed.

People who are driven to Avoid Authenticate learn best when:

 ⇨ they feel liked by the teacher and popular with classmates

 ⇨ they are learning about things that are deeply meaningful to them

 ⇨ the little things they do get noticed and appreciated

 ⇨ there is potential for leverage in the skill being taught

 ⇨ they are free to conceptualise

 ⇨ they can test theories, ideas and concepts to see if they hold up

 ⇨ they feel a connection with the teacher and feel understood by him or her.

The *Instinct to Complete*™

People who are driven to Complete need a step-by-step process to complete tasks. People say that all kids need routine. To some extent that is true, but for children driven to Complete, it's essential. If there isn't structure or routine—and unless they are exceptionally bright and able to work it out for themselves—children driven to Complete will struggle to get in stride.

They also need adequate time to complete a lesson and can seem lazy or inefficient as a result. For example, a teacher may finish her class a little ahead of schedule and suggest to the class that they use the remainder of the lesson to start their homework, but the children in the class driven to Complete will not do it unless they think they can finish it in that time. Interruptions and having to stop and start are really demotivating for those children driven to Complete. Those driven to Avoid Complete, on the other hand, don't mind stopping and starting, so they would dive in and start the homework—and if they couldn't finish it all, it wouldn't bother them because they'd just complete it later.

The report card of children driven to Complete is likely to mention how organised they are. They can be seen as punctual and studious and as demonstrating many of the traits of a so-called model student. Those driven to Complete are also big on effort, so there may be a comment along the lines of, 'John applied himself well in Science'.

....

People who are driven to Complete learn best when:

- ᴆ they have a procedure, plan or pattern
- ᴆ they know they are on the right track
- ᴆ they have the time to finish
- ᴆ they know the rules or parameters of a task
- ᴆ teaching is sequential so they can see where the learning is leading.

....

Children who are driven to Complete also respond well to time spent with their teacher and can greatly benefit from one-on-one tuition. If children driven to Complete don't have access to quality time with their teacher or if the class sizes are too big, they can give up and just stop trying. They are also suckers for peer pressure because they feel a need to fit in. Their desire to be one of the crowd can put enormous pressure on them to be accepted.

....

People who are driven to Avoid Complete learn best when:

- ᴆ there is variety in the teaching methods
- ᴆ they have short projects to complete
- ᴆ they are free to pioneer new ways of doing things and experiment
- ᴆ there is flexibility in the curriculum and some aspect of choice.

....

Those driven to Avoid Complete can find study difficult because they can have a short attention span. But if they are able to work things out for themselves and are encouraged to find solutions and have variety in their learning, then they can tap into a powerful resource. They do well with lots of subjects because it gives them the variety they crave.

The *Instinct to Improvise*™

Students who are driven by the *Instinct to Improvise*™ can go either way in terms of success at school. They enjoy energised, fun and interactive learning environments—which are more commonly associated with preschool and junior primary years than high school. If the students are bright then they will naturally see the connections that fit with the things that motivated them and may stay interested, but if not then they can become really bored with school.

People who are driven to Improvise learn best when:

⇾ there is a chance to change things or add their own ideas

⇾ they can negotiate—especially on deadlines

⇾ there are challenges and pressure

⇾ there is a lot of interaction because it enables them to interact and brainstorm

⇾ they can see the benefit of what they are doing

⇾ they can dramatise, improvise and experiment.

These are the children who tell you on a Friday evening that they don't have any homework—only to remember half-an-hour before bed on Sunday night that they do. Parents of Improvise-driven children will become frustrated by this because they'll think the child is just being awkward or negligent—but it's neither. Those driven to Improvise are naturally focused on what's urgent, so if they receive homework for the weekend, they won't do it on the Friday evening because it won't be urgent then. However, by the time Sunday night comes around the homework will be urgent so they'll remember to do the tasks and complete it under the gun. This is when children who are driven to Improvise produce their best work. They thrive on pressure, so they'll often do their homework at the last minute and breeze through it.

In universities across the country, students who are driven to Improvise are in the pub instead of marketing lectures, enjoying ski fields instead of field trips and — much to the consternation of those more studious and diligent students who are driven to Avoid Improvise — still breezing through their exams with flying colours. That's why those driven by the *Instinct to Improvise*™ buck the stereotype of how people should study — and they cop some serious flack for it. The accepted way to study is to be diligent — putting in time and effort over a consistent period of time. But for those driven by the *Instinct to Improvise*™, that is both torture and unproductive.

Improvise students fly by the seat of their pants — it's almost like they can access their knowledge only when they are under pressure. When they finally do study — probably a week before the exam, or even later — they will break those accepted study rules. There could be a dozen things going on around them while they study — such as the phone, TV or radio — but they will still apply themselves to the task at hand if they feel pressure to complete it. Their parents will be mortified and say, 'For goodness' sake. Go up to your room and concentrate. Turn off all the distractions and you'll do far better'. But the truth is the student driven to Improvise works best when there are distractions (or, more to the point, interactions).

....

People who are driven to Avoid Improvise learn best when:

⇥ the requirements of a task are clearly laid out so that they know exactly what to do

⇥ there is a quiet environment

⇥ they can eliminate uncertainty and risk

⇥ they are assessed on work completed throughout the year — not just on exams.

....

The school report for those driven by the Instinct to Improvise™ would probably mention that they talk too much. They are drawn to a challenge so may miss a few classes here and there — just to add more pressure to the situation. Those driven to Improvise can also succumb to peer pressure because they want everyone to look at them. They are often the class clowns—not because they want to fit in, but because they want to stand out. They're often personable, persuasive and interactive individuals—which stands out in young people—causing them to be voted into school-leadership roles or elected as captains of sports teams.

Those driven by the *Instinct to Improvise*™ can talk their way out of most situations; their natural people skills mean that they get away with more than their more studious and conscientious counterparts—students driven to avoid the *Instinct to Improvise*™. This can be very frustrating for those driven to Avoid Improvise, who usually think that the Improvise students are just show-offs or clowns.

Avoid Improvise students can crumble under exam pressure or become really stressed out by them. They will study diligently—and will often know more than those driven to Improvise—but put them in an exam situation and they can freeze. Those driven to Avoid Improvise therefore prefer to be marked on work completed throughout the year because it is a more accurate reflection of their knowledge.

As you can see from this chapter, people all have a different approach to how they learn and its incumbent on all of us in teaching roles (at school, university, work and at home) to help our students grow and learn at their best by being vigilant about our biases and doing our best to accommodate the respective needs of our students.

Chapter 8

In stride with your health

Having explored how your *I.D.*™ influences the way you are and the way you interact with others, it's time to look at a less obvious impact of *I.D.*™ — your health. Health is another major factor when it comes to living a happy and fulfilled life — it's hard to feel optimistic when your health is compromised. Yet most people don't automatically see a connection between *Instinctive Drives*™ and health — even though there is a significant connection. Some of the case studies you're about to read are amazing. For many people, learning of the connection between *I.D.*™ and health has been liberating, often life changing and frequently life saving.

Your *I.D.*™ is your internal compass. It represents your true north — your innate, natural and optimal way of being. If being true to your *I.D.*™ doesn't match convention or traditional standards and expectations, you may be encouraged or pressured to conform to those other expectations and standards. But compromising yourself will pull you off course and away from your true north — making you incongruent or out of stride with your true self (*I.D.*™).

I called the *I.D. System™* a system because I believe there are two essential ingredients needed to make a system—a 'closed loop' (a set way for something to operate) and an interdependent relationship between all of the system's parts. Each part must do its job effectively in order for the whole thing to function effectively. Take, for example, the ignition system in a car—it works a certain way and requires a certain key and type of fuel or it simply won't work. Even an irrigation system has a set way it needs to function or the water won't flow and the garden won't be watered.

It works the same way with your body. Bodies are made up of a number of systems—including the cardio, respiratory, digestive and lymphatic systems. This is equally true of your mind—it needs to work like a fully functioning system in order for your body to also function as a system. This means that there is a set way for you to operate if you want to honour your 'mind system'—and that little operating manual is available to you now in the form of your *I.D.™*

Your immune system is compromised when you are constantly dealing with low-level stress

When you're pulled out of stride with your *I.D.™*, your incongruence with it may initially show up in your attitude and lack of motivation. Perhaps you now need an alarm clock to wake you—whereas in the early days of your career you didn't. Or your work may be of a lower standard than you know you are capable of. You could be unusually tired, irritable, bad tempered or easily brought to tears. Maybe you are so used to regular headaches you consider it normal, or you struggle to sleep properly and can't really be bothered doing much about it. You require so many chemicals in your body to combat the stress causing those symptoms, that those same chemicals will not be available to you to combat illness and disease. Your immune system is compromised when you are constantly dealing with low-level stress—making you more susceptible to colds and less able to shake them. I call the symptoms mentioned above stage one symptoms because the stress causing them will pull people out of stride with their *I.D.™*

Does this seem a bit over the top? Well, consider this—people weren't designed to be sick, but to be healthy, happy and vibrant. As human beings, we are actually much more capable than we realise — and some people clearly demonstrate that. When you study these people and their success, you often find that they've succeeded not because of any superior level of intelligence, but because they knew their strengths and worked in stride with their gifts. So it turns out Socrates' time-honoured advice, 'Know thyself', is not so well known for nothing!

People have been conditioned to believe that it's acceptable — indeed normal — to be sick at least once a year — to contract whatever cold or flu might be going around. But these are nothing more than adjusted expectations to justify a way of life that is not optimum. Imagine if human beings could always be healthy, full of energy, confident, fulfilled and 'on fire'. Well they can be — some people refer to it as being 'in flow' or 'in the zone'. But they are also conditioned to believe that if they're lucky enough to experience such a state, it will only be temporary. They're told that because luck eventually runs out, it's better to 'make hay while the sun shines' and to be aware that 'Midas touch won't last forever'. But what if it did? I've spent the last fifteen years proving time and time again that it is actually possible to live without sickness. Being in stride with their I.D.™ actually boosts people's immunity to protect them from whatever diseases are floating around. But it's not just about people being in stride with their I.D.™ To honour their 'system', they also need to have sufficient rest, nutrition, regular exercise and play.

Your personal experiences probably align quite perfectly with this concept if you stop and reflect on it. Think about the times you've been sick — particularly the illnesses you just couldn't shake. What else was going on with you at that time? I'll bet that in some way you were also being pulled out of stride. Perhaps you also had other symptoms? When the tension of being out of stride continues and intensifies, you'll start to experience stage two symptoms, such as depleted energy or exhaustion. These are more intense and more chronic because tiredness and a lack of energy can lead to glandular fever or even chronic fatigue syndrome. Your skin can break out into various forms of irritation — including eczema, psoriasis, acne, rashes, cold sores, skin ulcers and mouth ulcers. Your digestive system can begin to malfunction and symptoms can include irritable bowel syndrome (IBS), gastric reflux and duodenal ulcers. Your respiratory system can also begin to break down at this stage — asthma sufferers could find their asthma worsening and experience more severe bouts of bronchitis. Blood pressure can also sky rocket. My experience is that the stage one and two symptoms typically relate to people's skin and energy, and digestive and immune systems—although other areas can be easily affected.

What doesn't make sense to me is the current treatment commonly used for these ailments—medication. I appreciate the value of short-term relief, but when it's addressing the symptom and not the cause, the problem will of course continue—just in a different form. This is certainly not a criticism of the medical profession; after all, some medical professionals are already embracing root-cause analysis rather than simply dealing with symptoms. By taking a much more holistic mind–body approach to health, people are able to banish many of the medical complaints that are often taken for granted. I believe that medicine—whether natural or not—for short-term relief, balanced by a proper root-cause analysis and practical strategies to help people get back in stride, provides people with a healthy balance for life.

So how do I know that? I haven't studied medicine; instead my knowledge is based on extensive anecdotal research with thousands of individuals. My formula is simple—I look for patterns in the results of all that research and then ensure that the formula leads to absolute outcomes.

I didn't plan on developing a health link with the *I.D. System*™ when I created it; I discovered it as I began working with people. At first I was surprised, but I began to see a pattern that aroused my curiosity and suggested a need for further research. The pattern that emerged from my research was that every person I worked with seemed to 'shine' whenever in stride with his or her *I.D.*™ and experience some form of health issue whenever out of stride. At first this just seemed a mere coincidence, but the pattern was too strong to ignore.

Based on what I saw people experiencing, I eventually found that there were eight benefits of being in stride:

1 fulfilment

2 a sense of achievement

3 peak performance

4 increased self-esteem

5 increased self-confidence

6 better self-worth

7   oodles of energy

8   great health.

People who felt that they were somehow out of stride initially commented that they felt compromised in at least one of those eight areas. As I began to group them together, I found that the symptoms were symbiotic, or interdependent. In other words, when people stated that they were lacking in fulfilment, they also said they felt their self-esteem, performance and health were being compromised. They rarely volunteered that information, but once I realised the symbiotic relationship of those eight benefits and asked people how they felt in relation to them, I always received an answer that confirmed this pattern. So when people were being pulled out of stride, two things seemed to be happening:

▷   The eight benefits they could be receiving by being in stride were significantly compromised.

▷   They experienced an increasing array of health problems depending on the degree to which they were out of stride and for how long.

So how did I know all this was connected to I.D.™? I knew because the pattern showing up in my research of thousands of people enabled me to find absolute outcomes—and this was powerful. I suspected that if health problems were connected to people being out of stride with their I.D.™, then surely those symptoms should disappear when those same people were back in stride.

To my great amazement, this was precisely what happened—in every case. Also, in many cases chronic health problems that people had suffered from for years disappeared—either overnight or in just a couple of days. At the time I truly struggled to believe what I saw—even people who seemed beyond help were able to recover from health problems. I've never had the courage to actually guarantee that the I.D. System™ will help people cure their ailments by being true to the way they were designed to be because I always think that there must be an exception—but I haven't found one yet. It certainly makes for curious research—some of which was being undertaken by the University of Western Sydney at the time of writing.

To use an example of how being out of stride with your I.D.™ can generate health problems, I was sitting at a picnic with a close family friend a few years ago. She rolled her sleeves up just slightly and I could see what looked like bad psoriasis. I said to Karen, 'So what's with the stress? I just noticed your arm'. She gave me a puzzled look and said, 'Oh that. That's just my psoriasis. I've had it for years, I'm applying these creams now but nothing seems to get rid of it'. She also said that she'd been on medication, but that it hadn't worked either. So I asked her again: 'What's with the stress?' She burst into tears. I gathered I was onto something!

Through her tears she told me about how torn she felt about her career choices—whether to pursue a career that challenged her or whether to stay at home and be more supportive of her husband and children. As a loving mother and wife, she felt compelled to stay at home, but she also felt terribly guilty that for some strange reason this wasn't as fulfilling for her as she had hoped. She interpreted this negatively and felt guilty—thinking that perhaps she didn't love her family enough or wasn't as dedicated as she should be and that she therefore must be selfish. I knew none of these were true because Karen personifies love, motherhood and selflessness. She told me she felt like she had lost control of her life, yet she loved her husband and kids dearly and didn't know what to do about it.

I explained the basis of the *I.D. System*™ to her and the implications of being out of stride and then invited her to do her *I.D.*™ When she returned the questionnaire two days later, her *I.D.*™ was calculated as 7553, so her strongest drives were Verify and Avoid Improvise. If ever there was an *I.D.*™ that needed to feel on top and in control, this was it. Via phone I explained her *I.D.*™ and could feel her sense of self return immediately. It was as if I had been reminding her of who she really was. It was actually incredibly uplifting for both of us!

We talked about strategies she could employ to take control her life again. As someone driven to Verify, the number one priority for her is to have things organised—which means makings lists—so she can feel in control. I asked her to jot down all the pros and cons of staying at home versus going to work in a part-time or full-time position. Once she did that, she began to feel clarity about what to do. She discussed it with her husband—who was incredibly supportive—and within hours had a game plan for going forward.

Three days later Karen rang. She said, with excitement in her voice, 'Paul, you'll never guess what's happened'. I replied, 'Yes I think I can. I think I know what you're going to tell me. But yes, I am surprised it's happened so soon'. She said, 'The psoriasis has completely—yes completely—disappeared!' She was in tears; I was in tears. I told her I knew it would because the minute I saw her I.D.™, I knew what would work for her. She's been off medication ever since and has no skin condition at all now. I still well up with tears when I tell this story.

There are countless case studies like Karen's for every ailment listed in this chapter—and all them have resulted in great success. I would encourage anyone who is suffering from any ailment to find out his or her I.D.™ and then incorporate the recommended, I.D.™ strategies to be back in stride again.

Beyond stage two symptoms there are stage three symptoms. They include those that are intolerable and usually life threatening if not treated—such as high blood pressure, depression, chronic infection, migraines, anorexia, diabetes and chronic back pain. When presenting with stage three symptoms, people will enter a very dangerous state unless there is medical intervention. At that point, people can present with stage four symptoms—including a physical, nervous or relationship breakdown.

The breakdown that occurs at stage four isn't just a medical one. It can also involve relationships at home and at work. People change jobs and move out of personal relationships because they 'just can't stand it anymore' or don't feel like they can be themselves. Often when they reflect on their moodiness and temper and the way they've been treating people—especially loved ones—they'll conclude with, 'It's just not me to be like this. This isn't who I am. I don't want to go on living like this'. When people make those comments, it indicates that they are not living according to the needs of their I.D.™—their natural operating style.

At a health level—as opposed to a relationship level—stage four includes symptoms that—without strong and complete intervention—can cause death or at least seriously knock on death's door. I know it sounds extreme, but death is what happens when the stress continues and the treatments are ineffective. Stage four symptoms can lead to major health problems—such as heart attacks, strokes, suicide, drug overdoses and dependency, and organ breakdown.

Knowing your I.D.™ and getting back or staying in stride will have major implications for your health.

Peak Performance Indicator™

The *Peak Performance Indicator™* sums up everything I've been saying in this chapter about health. Many people tell me during my seminars that the *Peak Performance Indicator™* changed their life. This model resonated so profoundly and completely with their own life experience that they couldn't ignore it anymore — and nor did they want to. The *Peak Performance Indicator™* gave them hope; it gave them direction.

People want the eight benefits of being in stride — and the *Peak Performance Indicator™* helps them to live true to the way they're meant to be. Figure 8.1 provides a visual representation of the *Peak Performance Indicator™*.

The shaded vertical arrows represent your *I.D.™* — your journey when in stride with your true self (*I.D.™*) and the numbers represent stress levels. Everybody is driven — and I use that word intentionally — to experience the eight benefits at the top of the arrows.

Figure 8.1: *Peak Performance Indicator™* graph

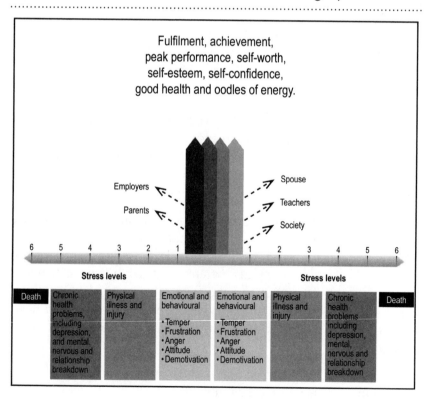

Even though when left to our own devices, we would all travel along the straight road that is true to ourselves, there are forces and people that can inadvertently pull us off track and out of stride — and often for very loving reasons. Parents may try to save their children from making the same mistakes they made, for example, but if they have a different I.D.™ to their children, and most do, then they'll actually be pulling them out of stride — crazy, but true. Or it may be a job or spouse or teacher doing the same thing. The more you are pulled out of stride, the less you'll experience the benefits at the top of the *Peak Performance Indicator*™ and the more you'll start to experience the symptoms along the horizontal axis of the graph.

By knowing your I.D.™ you can know what that vertical axis or pathway is for you, recognise earlier the people and situations that are likely to pull you out of stride and have strategies to help you get back in stride — and stay there. If you are in stride and working with your I.D.™ — working the way that best suits your innate nature — then the benefits are overwhelming.

When you are in stride and working in a role that honours your differences while amplifying your strengths, you feel a sense of achievement on a daily basis. The role becomes fun and almost easy because you are 'running the right software through your hardware' — and you know that you are making a positive contribution to the workplace and to those around you. Athletes call it being 'in the zone', and others call it having the 'Midas touch'.

People know when they are in the wrong job or wrong relationship because they feel dissatisfied — and that affects everything. Yet many people also know when they are productive and in flow. I am proposing that people can live in that state most of the time — and not just in the workplace.

When you know your I.D.™ and the I.Ds™ in your family, you can truly communicate with your family in a way that not only guarantees less arguments but also more harmony and fun. Understanding the innate characteristics of your children can reduce the fighting and result in more cooperation — and every family member will be far more content and peaceful.

The eight benefits of being in stride affect how people feel about themselves and the world around them. When people are content and fulfilled, their self-esteem, self-worth and self-confidence increase — and these all influence health and wellbeing.

The more you are pulled off track—and moved away from your true nature—the more stress and dissatisfaction you will feel. It manifests in your life as emotional and behavioural challenges—such as temper tantrums, lethargy, despondency, anger and a lack of motivation. These are the warning signs that you are offcourse and out of stride, but they don't need to be a normal part of life. The longer you are out of stride the more likely you are to experience physical symptoms—including fatigue, increased colds and flu, skin irritations, allergies, blood pressure problems, migraines and even more serious physical conditions. These symptoms can be related to your energy, your skin or your immune, digestive and respiratory systems.

You do indeed have a best way of operating based on your *I.D*™—and it's as relevant in relationships as it is in parenting, career or health. As you travel through life, however, this best way can be obscured or hidden by myriad influences—including stereotyping, family conditioning and societal expectations. But with knowledge of self from your *I.D.*™ and strategies to help you stay true to it, you can live true to yourself and discover that energy, health and genuine fulfilment no longer elude you.

Being stressed over a long period of time is not conducive to good health. Your body possesses a fight-or-flight mechanism to assist you in times of danger; when you are faced with a stressful situation it kicks in—releasing adrenalin into your blood steam. The pressure of modern society results in people being faced with more stressful situations more often—which means there are many people having to rely on adrenalin to get them through the day. When your body operates on adrenalin for too long, there will be unhealthy repercussions. In other words, worry, stress, dissatisfaction and unhappiness all have a negative influence upon your health.

The answer to life's problems is not contained in a bottle or a packet—as the pharmaceutical, alcohol and tobacco companies might have you believe. Until you get back on track and truly understand your innate nature and honour your own way of being, you will always feel pressured. When your life is inconsistent with your *I.D.*™, your performance and fulfilment is compromised—greatly increasing the possibility of ill health.

The following sections deal with two of the more common health challenges that people face—weight loss and quitting smoking. It's worth remembering that the concepts and strategies suggested here for giving up smoking can easily be applied to anything else you may wish to remove from your life—such as alcohol or chocolate. After all, cold turkey doesn't work for everyone!

Weight loss and fitness

Because everybody is different, there is no universal way that works for everyone, but there is a best way for you—one that is suited to your nature—to eliminate anything that you feel is destructive in your life, including excess weight or below-average fitness. This section provides strategies—tailored to each I.D.™—for tackling these types of health issues.

Driven by the *Instinct to Verify*™

People driven by the *Instinct to Verify*™ can let themselves go because they don't see health as a priority. They know it's important, but when they consider the amount of time in a day and what else needs to be accomplished, they may choose to focus on other things. This especially happens if they assume they'll be able to take care of their health once their other priorities fall away. But as everybody knows, that doesn't happen—other things always come up to distract people from looking after their health. But it's important, as Stephen Covey said in his book *The Seven Habits of Highly Effective People*, 'to put the big rocks in first'.

Until you get back on track and truly understand your innate nature and honour your own way of being, you will always feel pressured

When you are building the foundation of a successful life, you have to put the big issues in place first—those things that will make a massive difference. Health is one of those big rocks; you will never reach your true potential if you are not healthy. Young, healthy people who are driven to Verify may be tempted to skip exercise and live on take-away, but sooner or later they will have to make health a priority.

Those driven to Verify are also tempted to compare themselves with those around them. If their friends are healthy and take time out to go to the gym or be involved in team sports, they are more inclined to do so too. If not then they may feel content to tell themselves that they are not that bad.

Another reason that people with the Verify drive will ignore the issue of health and fitness is that they can't definitively prove anything. For example, if they can prove that a french fry put on a recent lump of cellulite, they may be motivated to change things. But if they can't attribute the weight gain to any one thing, they'll convince themselves that certain foods won't make a difference and become careless as a result.

Turning it around

Those driven to Verify need a sense of purpose to what they are doing, and they need to convert it into a science. Plus, they also need to be able to compare. Verify people will respond to being measured, so before they start any campaign of fitness they need to have all their measurements taken—allowing their progress to be monitored very specifically. They would have their body fat, lung and cardio capacity, flexibility, water content and even cholesterol measured to provide them with a definitive starting point.

Verify people need goals and enjoy intellectual stimulation, so learning what actually happens to the body when they eat certain types of food works well for those driven to Verify—as does being held to account by someone else.

> **If you are driven by the *Instinct to Verify*™ and want to get in shape:**
>
> ▷ Set your sights on a future event that would inspire you to action—a wedding anniversary or birthday, for example.
>
> ▷ Measure yourself so you know where you are, what your ideal is and can see steady progress,
>
> ▷ Be precise about measuring so it's easy and clear when you wish to quantify the change and see the progress you've made
>
> ▷ Ask a friend to hold you accountable.

Driven to avoid the *Instinct to Verify*™

Avoid Verify people may not immediately notice that they are getting bigger or that their fitness level is reducing. Weight gain is usually such a gradual thing that they simply don't notice until, for example, they step in a lift with 360-degree mirrors or run up a flight of stairs and nearly pass out!

Although those driven to Avoid Verify don't judge people by how they look or make assessments about 'fat' or 'skinny', they know that society does. They see magazine covers with stick-thin models on them who have been air brushed to within an inch of their life, but they don't compare themselves with those images the way someone driven to Verify would.

Turning it around

If Avoid Verify people want to turn their situation around, their definition of acceptable needs to change. That can happen after a chance meeting with an old school friend or when a certain weight is reached that has always represented 'fat' in their mind. Loads of unconditional encouragement will do Avoid Verify people the world of good.

....

If you are driven to avoid the *Instinct to Verify*™ and want to get in shape:

⊃ Ask those around you to support you with encouragement, regardless of setbacks you may face.

⊃ Load yourself with information so you know exactly what and when you need to eat—either by following a diet plan or by having food delivered.

⊃ Establish a program of exercise so you know what you are doing and when you need to do it—remove as much thinking from the process as possible.

⊃ Ask a fitness or weight-loss expert to advise what's best for you.

....

They also respond to programs in which they don't have to think—if they are given the solutions and just have to go through the motions. So to lose weight, Avoid Verify people achieve great results from using companies that deliver all the meals ready-made.

Although people shouldn't try to look like the unrealistic ideals portrayed by stick-thin models in magazines, health is important — and those driven to Avoid Verify know that.

Driven by the *Instinct to Authenticate*™

People who are driven by the *Instinct to Authenticate*™ need congruence between their self-image and how others see them. So if they have high self-esteem, they will look after themselves because their physical appearance, health, actions and behaviours must mirror the way they think and feel about themselves. If they don't have good self-esteem and don't feel worthy, then they are almost driven to let themselves go so that their appearance, health, actions and behaviours then mirror that self-image. Congruence between their internal and external self is what drives Authenticate people.

Take Authenticate-driven body builders, for example. It would be very unlikely that Authenticate-driven body builders would ever take steroids because they would see it as fake; they would feel incongruence between their real selves and what others observe. If they did take them, they would feel very empty — especially if it led to any success. Plus, even though they may look fit and healthy externally, Authenticate-driven body builders would be aware of the damage being done internally — and they wouldn't be comfortable with that.

Turning it around

Those driven to Authenticate are motivated by role modelling and self-image, so they respond well to a picture of the sort of body they would like to achieve because it gives them an image to work towards. They would do well to pin up a photograph of themselves when they were happy with their weight and use that for motivation.

They also need to make the connection between health and what they want to achieve in the future — in other words, health has to be relevant to their life in some way. So if, for example, an Authenticate-driven father had put on so much weight that playing football with his twin boys had become too difficult, he could set a goal to kick the football with his sons — thereby making the weight-loss requirement relevant to him.

If you are driven by the Instinct to Authenticate™ and want to get in shape:

⊠ Find a picture of yourself that shows you when you were happy with your weight—or a picture of someone whose shape you admire—and put it up on the fridge and the wall of your bedroom so it's the first thing you see in the morning and the last thing you see at night.

⊠ Learn how your body works. You function best when you understand how things tick because you have an inherent respect for machinery.

⊠ Get real—only buy the food you need to eat. If it isn't in the cupboard, you can't eat it, can you?

⊠ Do something constructive—going to the gym may not be very enticing for you, but learning to tap dance or playing on the local basketball team may be a more practical way to incorporate fitness into your life. Just start with something—anything—you can always adjust the activity once you've started.

⊠ You work best—and even think best—when you're more active.

Driven to avoid the *Instinct to Authenticate*™

There are several possible reasons why Avoid Authenticate people can ignore their health and fitness. Often there's a gap between what they think or believe they're doing, and the actual reality of what they eat or how often they exercise. They can also be so distracted by various theories and philosophies about looking after themselves that they let things slide. In other words, they are better at thinking about exercise or weight loss than actually doing it.

Avoid Authenticate people will let their weight slide if they can't see any leverage in taking action about it. Investing an hour a day, several times a week, for only one purpose—to become fitter or lose weight—isn't compelling for Avoid Authenticate people because it offers no leverage.

Turning it around

Avoid Authenticate people can turn their health around if they build exercise into other activities and other activities into exercise; for example, they can enhance their relationships with their kids or friends by participating in sporting activities with them. Or instead of having a lunch meeting, they could have the meeting on the move—be walking around the local park or having the meeting on a golf course. Rollerblading to work or getting off the bus a few stops early on your way to the office is another option for Avoid Authenticate people because it provides them with leverage. Try running to work; it has several purposes—it helps with fitness and saving money and it is better for the environment.

As an Avoid Authenticate, I used to walk every day—the same route at the same time with the same person for four years. When I reflected on how I was able to do something that for me would normally be so monotonous, I realised that it wasn't about the walk at all. It was all about the conversation—which was dynamic, fun and energising. It helped doing the same route because then we didn't have to think about the walk at all; we could just converse and know we'd be back on time!

I recall when I exercised with my son Mitchell about four to five times a week to help him lose weight. For me, the experience was providing a bunch of benefits—which provided me with leverage. I enjoyed the precious time I could spend with one of my precious kids; the opportunity to influence him during our private chats; the likely life-long memories we were building; the challenge of thinking up different routines each time to keep both of us motivated; the commitment to him to help him lose some significant weight and boost his self-esteem—which he did; and, of course, exercise time for me. As an Avoid Authenticate person, how could I resist all that leverage? Six years later and we still fondly recall that experience.

Another strategy for Avoid Authenticate people is for them to monitor their diet and exercise patterns so that they can see the difference between what they think they do and actual reality. Then they'll see how their current weight-loss theory or diet will play out. When they can see the bigger picture, they'll likely see that exercise or diet adjustments are compelling. For example, I made health important because I wanted to have more energy and feel better when I woke in the morning. The minute I connected exercise and diet to energy,

I was in. I recall even increasing the amount of broccoli I ate, once I learned how rich in vitamins it is.

I also want to be around for my children and grandchildren; my theory is that if I eat and exercise regularly then I'll live to fulfil my dreams. I know other Avoid Authenticate people who finally took action when they began to understand the importance of the mind–body connection. The most brilliant mind in the world will find it impossible to produce results without a healthy and active body.

If you are driven to avoid the *Instinct to Authenticate*™ and want to get in shape:

☞ Obtain leverage—find ways to be fitter that also deliver other outcomes and benefits.

☞ Foster a holistic approach to health and wellbeing—and look at the importance of it in terms of the bigger picture.

Driven by the *Instinct to Complete*™

Those driven to Complete let their health slide if other parts of their life are not going so well either. For people with the Complete drive, everything is connected, so if one part of their life is bad then all parts become bad in their mind in order for them to access a kind of order and harmony. They can't have a great career and a poor home life, for example. It's either all bad or all good with them—and they will sabotage the good things if they have to.

Of course, if one part of their life picks up, then every other part starts to pick up. I have worked with many elite athletes and it's amazing how many of them demonstrate this characteristic. Several of the elite swimmers I worked with were driven by the *Instinct to Complete*™ and they were national swimming champions, held national records in another sport, as well as being the school captains and duxes of their schools. I was stunned that they could achieve at such a high level at so many things, yet through the lens of I.D.™ it made sense. I remember thinking, 'Is this what the potential of all teenagers could be?' When someone driven to Complete is on a roll, everything goes right—and vice versa.

Complete-driven people can also neglect their health and fitness because they think they don't have time to do a fitness routine. If they can't fit it into their schedule, they won't. Exercise is usually the first thing to go when they are busy.

For other Complete-driven people, their level of fitness will have much to do with the friends they keep. They'll want to fit in more than stand out — which is all the more reason for them to hang out with people from the gym. They won't start something if they can't see themselves staying with it. The key is for them is to start doing something about their body and then gather some momentum. Routines will always be interrupted, momentum will always be broken and plans will always change. But if people driven by the *Instinct to Complete*™ have some momentum and feel that they are making some progress, they'll have more chance of continuing and succeeding.

Turning it around

If people driven by the *Instinct to Complete*™ want to get back in shape they need to start small and then build momentum. They need to see progress. Progress for them is achieved exponentially — not linearly. So it's not as if the progress in week one of a ten-week fitness program equates to 10 per cent of their goal. It may only be 3 per cent in week one, but their success will somehow inspire them to achieve 5 per cent in week two, 8 per cent in week three and so on — to the extent that they may well even end up achieving their desired goal ahead of time. Such is the exponential progress of Complete-driven people when they get on a roll. The power of momentum works for them, much like the power of compound interest. Their motivation increases as the momentum increases.

....

If you are driven by the *Instinct to Complete*™ and want to get in shape:

▷ Devise a detailed plan of action. Have a professional assess your health and fitness and put together a program that will fit into your life.

▷ Start small so you have the enjoyment of seeing improvement as you go along.

....

They also thrive in structured, routine-driven environments, so gym classes—as opposed to using gym equipment—can work better for most Complete-driven people because:

⊃⊃ they will have an instructor taking them through the steps

⊃⊃ there is a routine to the classes and a weekly timetable.

⊃⊃ they can quickly observe their progress

⊃⊃ they can go with an experienced friend who knows what he or she is doing so that it's safer

⊃⊃ they can obtain a detailed plan of what they'll be doing to be able to see how they can fit it into their schedule and still find order and harmony in the process.

Driven to avoid the *Instinct to Complete*™

Those driven to Avoid Complete often have the best of intentions, but they can fail to follow them or stay with their plans long term. They start things but don't finish them because the novelty wears off very quickly. Gym filing cabinets all over the world are full of unused gym membership cards—and the majority probably belong to Avoid Complete people. They will be full of optimism about their routine—asking for demonstrations of gym machines and buying their lycra work-out gear—but then never lift a single weight!

If you are driven to avoid the *Instinct to Complete*™ and want to get in shape:

⊃⊃ Ensure there is variety in your approach. You will become bored if there is too much of the same thing, so mix it up a little by choosing different activities.

⊃⊃ Make sure you have a variety of healthy food in your fridge. Don't make your eating too regimented because inflexibility won't work for you.

⊃⊃ Do your exercise first thing in the morning, before you have a chance to be distracted by the rest of your day. But make sure it's a different routine each day.

⊃⊃ Arrange to meet someone else to exercise with so that they can hold you accountable when you don't show up.

If you are driven to avoid the *Instinct to Complete*™ and want to get in shape *(cont'd)*:

⯮ Just start with simple exercise and then push yourself further, using small goals.

⯮ Stay away from predictability in your diet and exercise routine.

Also, if someone driven to avoid the *Instinct to Complete*™ is unfit, he or she will see overcoming that as too big a task to even attempt. Avoid Complete-people need to be see short-term wins from exercise or they won't even start!

Turning it around

The best way to inspire Avoid Complete people to exercise is to focus on variety—such as by swimming one day, rollerblading the next, walking the day after, then Latin dancing on Thursday and yoga on Friday! They need the flexibility to work out any time during their day. They also hate diets because they limit their variety of food, so it's best for them to have lots of healthy options readily available.

Driven by the *Instinct to Improvise*™

One of the main reasons people driven by the *Instinct to Improvise*™ put on weight is their passionate, obsessive nature. They are the people who are more susceptible to binge eating. When they have a craving they well and truly look after it. Plus, many of them love to socialise—which adds fuel to the fire. After all, a quick drink after work that turns into dinner is fine every few weeks, but those people driven to Improvise may do it several times a week!

Another deeper reason for some Improvise-driven people to neglect their health and fitness is that it sets up one hell of a challenge, which, if and when accomplished, looks very impressive.

I often find that Improvise-driven people have a life that resembles a pendulum—swinging from one extreme to the other; they need to go to extremes to muster the motivation they need—it can look very impressive when they lose all that weight in such a short time!

They are also really good at rationalising things to themselves, so they may think, 'Oh, I think I deserve an ice-cream because I've worked hard today'. Or they'll say to themselves, 'Well, that wasn't a great day, but I think I'd feel better if I just chilled out for a while and treated myself to an ice-cream. I'll work hard tomorrow'. Those driven to Improvise are masters of spin and can make anything seem plausible and logical—even pizza!

Interestingly, losing weight is not usually the biggest challenge for people driven to Improvise—keeping their weight off or their fitness up is a bigger one because there is a certain sense of monotony about that. But if they employ the strategies outlined here and frame their challenges in the long term, they can certainly maintain their weight and level of fitness.

Turning it around

Those driven to Improvise need fun, interaction, a challenge and impressive short-term goals. In order to keep with their exercise and diet program, Improvise-driven people need to see results fast—or they will conclude the program hasn't worked and quit. Doing one hour of exercise every few days is going to be useless for them because they have to really immerse themselves in tasks and activities—due to their need to see results fast. Consequently, they respond well to 'fat camps' or health retreats and think nothing of not eating for a week to look good at a special event.

If you are driven by the *Instinct to Improvise*™ and want to get in shape:

▷ Try activities that require high energy and dedication and provide fast results.

▷ Try team sports, dance or exercise classes because the music and people will add energy and fun to your workouts—and the more pumped you feel, the more you'll want to do it.

▷ Impose an important deadline. A 'photo deadline' works well—using the date of an upcoming event at which you are likely to have your photo taken.

▷ Strive to become an instructor—this enables you to lead a class, grow other people and make a real difference. It is something you can become passionate about; helping people grow and making them feel good are motivations for you.

Driven to avoid the *Instinct to Improvise*™

Avoid Improvise people often let themselves go because they don't see the risks associated with ignoring their health and fitness. Or they may see the risks, but not connect them with their life. They need to be certain about something before they commit to it, so unless they truly understand the impact of their lifestyle on their health, they may be reluctant to take action.

At an even deeper level, some people driven to Avoid Improvise may even see 'looking good' as superficial in the overall scheme of things. They may value their intellect, personality, charisma, values and other such qualities more than their weight and energy.

Turning it around

Logic is a key driver for Avoid Improvise people — as is risk aversion — so as soon as a logically compelling argument is presented to them that can make any risks associated with getting fitter or losing weight much smaller than the risks of maintaining the status quo, they'll change. They'll go wherever there is less risk. This is why so many of them don't look after their health until they receive a doctor's ultimatum or a threat from their spouse that they will leave unless their health and fitness improves. No-one likes ultimatums, but Avoid Improvise people respond to them.

If you are driven to avoid the *Instinct to Improvise*™ and want to get in shape:

⇨   Seek professional assistance so that someone can evaluate your health and circumstances and put together a program that makes logical sense — one that you can feel certain will help you achieve results.

⇨   Just find an activity you enjoy and do it. It doesn't have to be exciting or loud. Activities such as yoga or walking may appeal more to you as you don't need to be bouncing off the ceiling to see results. The neat thing about your approach is that you'll typically do the 'slog' regardless of whether anyone is watching or whether it's enjoyable. If that's what it takes, then you'll do it — so long as you're certain it will work.

&#x279E; Consider doing something on your own rather than as part of a team. Martial arts, kayaking, surfing and triathlons all make sense for you because you can then be the master of your own destiny.

Quitting smoking

Smoking is never usually just about the cigarette. It's a habit, but it's usually a cover-up for something else. For example, I know shy people who smoke because it gives them an excuse to escape from conversation with people. I also know busy people who use the cigarette break to access some quiet time. I have one client who disappears from the office at 10.30 every morning for ten minutes. She goes outside with her cup of coffee, smokes a cigarette and has ten minutes without the phone or email pestering her. We talked about this habit and it was obvious to both of us that it was the time away from the office that she craved—not necessarily the cigarette. So she swapped her cigarette break for ten minutes outside reading her magazine. She was able to cut down her smoking dramatically—and later quit—just from this little shift of perspective. It wasn't just the cigarettes she was addicted to, it was the quiet time. By enabling her to see she could access one without the other, she was able to wean herself off the cigarettes.

Driven by the *Instinct to Verify*™

To prompt people driven to Verify to stop smoking you need to give them the facts—such as what it does to their body, how many brain cells die every time they light up and how many years each cigarette will take off their life. They also need a goal to aim toward—perhaps to climb Mount Kilimanjaro for their birthday!

Driven to avoid the *Instinct to Verify*™

People who are driven to avoid the *Instinct to Verify*™ are 'all or nothing' people, so they can go cold turkey and quit. Also, they are prompted to quit if they are being constantly hounded, criticised or interrogated about it—perhaps by their children. Finally they will crack and shout, 'Right. Okay, I'll stop!'—and never smoke another cigarette.

Driven by the *Instinct to Authenticate*™

For those driven to Authenticate, quitting smoking is all about relevance. These are the people who respond to those graphic advertisements in which, for example, a doctor squeezes fatty deposits from the aorta of a smoker. Although those images are quite disgusting and confronting, because people who are driven to Authenticate are motivated by visual references that mean something to them, this approach could prompt them to quit. However, the challenge for them is that once the advertisements are gone, they may lose the desire to quit because the images will be 'out of sight, out of mind'.

Another approach is for them to say the words, 'I am a non-smoker' or 'I have stopped smoking'. The key here is the motivation they gain from saying the words out loud—that will make quitting smoking real for them. Verbalising their thoughts makes them real—and that compels them to action. I would imagine they wouldn't be driven to use nicotine patches because doing that wouldn't seem real enough for them.

Another strategy for Authenticate-driven people to stop smoking is for them to obtain a personal evaluation that specifically identifies their own issues as a smoker. With that evaluation—together with a plan of attack that's tailored to them and that they are held accountable to—they're likely to achieve results.

In addition, they need to focus on what they are going to do—not on what they are not going to do. In other words, they need to concentrate on what they can do to stop smoking or do in place of smoking, rather than concentrating on what they're being denied. (This method actually doubles as a very good teaching and parenting strategy. Parents and teachers often tell children what *not* to do. But a more constructive approach is to help them understand what they should do instead.)

Driven to avoid the *Instinct to Authenticate*™

Those driven to Avoid Authenticate respond to anti-smoking advertisements that are highly emotive. The depth of feeling in those images may distress those driven to Avoid Authenticate enough to take action. But they would need to see the film more than once to keep their motivation up.

Avoid Authenticates are also very motivated by what others think about them, so receiving feedback based on how people close to them perceive them or are affected by them would certainly get their attention.

Driven by the *Instinct to Complete*™

It's probably hardest for people driven to Complete to give up smoking because they live by habits. Their life is scheduled, and smoking fits nicely into a schedule because they can do it without thinking. They're best assisted to stop smoking by finding a replacement for cigarettes that they can incorporate into their routine. They're 'transition' people rather than 'fast-change' people, so they need to see incremental progress. Starting with one less cigarette one day and then reducing their cigarettes each day after that works well for them because it's a gradual process. But prompting them to start that course of action can be a challenge. Say they decide to stop smoking on a Wednesday; they will feel as though they can't start something in the middle of the week, so will put it off until Monday. Then Monday arrives but they'll notice it's the middle of the month, so will put it off until the next month.

Making a New Year's Eve resolution to stop smoking can be powerful for those driven to Complete because it means a new year and a new start—tidy and neat. However, if they fall off the wagon, it's unlikely they'll quit until the next year. Although if a special occasion is looming and they want to quit smoking, they're likely to quit if they think of that date as a deadline.

Driven to avoid the *Instinct to Complete*™

Those driven to Avoid Complete are more likely to be social smokers than pack-a-day smokers because they need variety. Boredom is often the reason they start smoking in the first place. So when Avoid Complete smokers want to quit, keeping busy is a good way to help them stay on track.

Driven by the *Instinct to Improvise*™

Cold turkey is the only way to quit for people driven to Improvise. They can do it that way because it is impressive—and they like making a stunning impression (for themselves as much as for anyone else). Plus, quitting cold turkey is notoriously difficult—and Improvise–driven quitters will enjoy that challenge.

Driven to avoid the *Instinct to Improvise*™

For those driven to Avoid Improvise, stopping is easy when the balance of risk changes. For example, I know of a father who stopped smoking after the birth of his son because he wasn't allowed to smoke in the house anymore. If he wanted to smoke he would have had to go outside and be away from his family; in his mind the decision to quit was an easy one because he simply didn't want to lose time spent with his loved ones. Interestingly, he had tried several times before to stop and had never achieved it, but as soon as his son came along the choice was made in his mind so he stopped for good.

The important thing to remember is that you need to start aligning your actions with your I.D.™ needs. By living more congruently to your I.D.™ you will be in a much better frame of mind to have the strength and energy to tackle challenges such as below-average health and fitness, smoking and weight loss. In addition, over-eating and smoking are often used as substitutes for happiness. By being more in stride with your I.D.™, your dependence on certain things and your need for substitutes will diminish as you find core fulfilment that will open up a whole new experience for you.

Chapter 9

In stride with your wealth

This chapter looks at what each drive values most in life. Human beings often assume that they value the same things—family, success, health, status and fun. Certainly wealth is often thought of in terms of dollars and cents, but money itself is not a driver for everyone. More often than not, if people scratch below the surface, they will discover that people want money for different reasons based on what they value—and what they value is usually driven by their I.D.™, though the connection is not always obvious.

Having money is fundamental if people want to meet the needs and values of their I.D.™. People who are driven to Authenticate, for example, value being useful and productive, so they often need money to buy the tools and equipment that will help them to be even more capable at doing the things they love. They love physical activity and getting out and doing things—and money enables them to do that. They may also want to do the things that match the image they have of their lifestyle—such as sailing or going on skiing trips abroad. If their job enables them to enjoy two adventure trips a year, they may feel incredibly wealthy in their life—regardless of how much money is in the bank.

People who are driven to Avoid Authenticate, however, will enjoy an overseas trip or sailing for different reasons. They love that an overseas holiday will enable them to see some awe-inspiring scenery and enjoy the history of an ancient city. On the other hand, going sailing will appeal to them because they'll enjoy being out on the water—where they can sit and ponder life. Because they also enjoy time spent with friends and family and creating life-long memories, they'll also thrive from activities enabling them to do that. They will only care about a boat's dimensions, power or price if it will affect how they feel. Being free to ponder, discuss and search for answers to the big questions is seen as a measure of wealth by Avoid Authenticate people.

> People driven by the Instinct to Verify™ are driven to know that they are doing the right thing

In others words, knowing what you and those around you value the most—be that in a relationship or at work—enables you to tailor your approach with others so you can have more win–win situations. Take the stressed-out parents, for example, who struggle to keep their head above water because they spoil their kids with too many toys and trips. If they understood their children's I.D.™—and therefore what they inherently value—they would be able to obtain more harmony in their house by doing inexpensive activities with their children that they know they will enjoy.

The same can be said of the business world. In that environment there is always the assumption that when people do well they should be financially rewarded, yet there are non-financial rewards that are appreciated more—and they are much cheaper for businesses to offer. It is much more motivating for individuals to receive something they truly value as an incentive, rather than a one-size-fits-all monetary reward. Besides, studies have repeatedly shown that increases in salary only improve performance for a short time. But if employers show that they understand an employee's needs and want to help the person to meet them, then increased productivity from the employee is much more likely.

This chapter also explores the talents and vulnerabilities that arise for each drive when it comes to money — demonstrating how people can manage their finances and make decisions in a way that is more in stride with their *I.D.*™

Driven by the *Instinct to Verify*™

People driven by the *Instinct to Verify*™ are driven to know that they are doing the right thing, so they tend to fit into western cultural expectations of how someone should make a serious financial decision. For example, people driven to Verify who are looking to buy a house would probably seriously consider their needs and put a checklist together of desired features that would make their perfect home. They would much prefer the more professional and respected agents — and they would probably determine their professionalism by their punctuality, tidiness, treatment of staff and attention to detail.

....

People who are driven by the *Instinct to Verify*™ value:

 ⇨ professionalism

 ⇨ price

 ⇨ respect

 ⇨ status

 ⇨ justice.

....

They would probably need to look at quite a few houses to be able to draw comparisons so that they will be certain they're making the right decision. They would gather information and then compare all the options before proceeding. They'd have the house carefully inspected just to make sure that there won't be any nasty surprises that could make their purchase a bad one. They would also, of course, carefully review any relevant documentation.

Status and image are very important to Verify-driven people. They enjoy the status that money can provide. It is those driven to Verify who are therefore most vulnerable to getting into trouble by trying to 'keep up with the Joneses'. They may consequently have credit card debts that would make most people feel nauseated.

Because those with the Verify drive are motivated by 'the best', they may actually prefer a corner office and a nice company car over an extra $5000 a year. The office and car are measurable in terms of their peers—whereas the money in the bank is not. As discussed earlier, people driven to Verify need to know things are fair and that they deserve what they are being paid. They will react badly if they don't receive a pay increase they feel they deserve.

Reducing financial pressure

When people driven by the *Instinct to Verify*™ find themselves in hot water financially, they should look back at how they ended up in that situation so they can work out a game plan based on that information. If they can see how they can escape their predicament, the pressure will subside. They also don't need to wait until they are out of the mess before the stress reduces—that will occur the moment they feel they've regained control. To help them obtain that control, they should also seek expert advice, which they value.

Investing

Once people driven to Verify are on top of their finances, they may wish to explore ways of increasing their wealth. When it comes to investment options, those with the Verify drive are:

⤷ drawn to investments that enable them to quantify and compare options in order to feel confident that they have made the right decision

⤷ attracted to areas of investment in which they can develop genuine expertise—if they don't feel they have the time to master the subject, they will pay top dollar for that expertise by finding a professional with an exemplary track record they can trust

⤷ are drawn to investments that offer a fair reward and continuous improvement—they are not necessarily looking for massive rewards.

Driven to avoid the *Instinct to Verify*™

Those driven to Avoid Verify may not know if there is more money in the bank this week than last week, but they generally have an overall grasp of their financial situation. They don't attach much significance to money unless it can be used to avoid conflict and interrogation. They would hate to apply for a loan, for example, if it meant they had to justify themselves and explain why they needed it.

....

People who are driven to avoid the *Instinct to Verify*™ value:

⇨ acceptance instead of judgement and interrogation

⇨ feeling valued

⇨ being right the first time

⇨ simplicity

⇨ their sense of knowing.

....

Those driven to Avoid Verify can find themselves in trouble with money because they don't always delve deep, so if there is a scam to be fallen for, it could well be someone driven to Avoid Verify that is duped. Avoid Verifiers also don't read the fine print on contracts — so can find themselves signing a mobile phone contract and paying it off until they're 105!

Reducing financial pressure

People driven to Avoid Verify come up with far better solutions when working with others, so it may help them to speak to an adviser about their money troubles. Once they have a plan and systems in place so they don't have to think about money issues, they will gradually escape from financial pressure. For this reason, they love direct debit because it pays their bills automatically.

Investing

If those driven to Avoid Verify are looking at ways to increase their net worth, they should assess all their investment options because some may suit them more than others. To the outside world their choices can seem rushed or ill considered, but those driven to Avoid Verify are drawn to investment options:

⇨ that feel right — they don't need quantifiable reasons and proof in order to take action

☞ that have the potential to get it right first time

☞ in which there is concise bottom-line information that enables them to make a decision without becoming bogged down in detail.

Driven by the *Instinct to Authenticate*™

People who are driven to Authenticate are motivated by quality and will make practical financial decisions based on long-term considerations.

Those driven to Authenticate hate wasting money — although if there is plenty of it to spread around they can be frivolous with it. Their desire to avoid wasting money is sometimes compromised when a product or service delivers exceptional durability. So they may, for example, be enticed to part with a few extra hundred dollars to tint their car windows because it is guaranteed for twenty-five years — that the car probably won't last twenty-five years isn't going to faze them. Those driven to Authenticate will typically pay more for durability. They are the types of people who buy tools that will last until the next century according to their extended warranty.

....

People who are driven by the *Instinct to Authenticate*™ value:

☞ truth and loyalty

☞ hard work

☞ usefulness

☞ durability

☞ practicality.

....

People with the Authenticate drive would never dream of investing in something they don't understand. They want to know how things work and they want to be involved, so these are the types of people who would be inclined to manage their own superannuation fund or property portfolio.

If you want to sell a car to someone driven to Authenticate, ask him or her to take it for a test drive. People who are driven to Authenticate typically won't want to haggle about the price afterwards though. If they like the car they will probably just buy it because they rarely see the point of haggling. As far as they are concerned, the price is the price—and they expect the price to be the real one rather than a starting one. They can even find negotiation hard to handle because they can interpret it as the negotiator not being genuine with them—and that's enough for them to lose interest in a business deal altogether.

Those driven to Authenticate can find themselves with money troubles because they don't focus as much as other people on preparing for the future. If something unexpected appears, they can hit the financial rocks. Also, because they take people at face value, they can become trapped by the fine print. They can also be left feeling ripped off after signing a deal, but that feeling is often due to a communication breakdown between them and the negotiator.

Reducing financial pressure

When people who are driven to Authenticate feel too much financial pressure, they should do something—anything. Authenticate-driven people are energised by action, so they need to work their way out of a mess. Another strategy is for them to visualise how their life would be without that pressure, so they can see in their mind how they can escape their financial predicament.

Investing

People are attracted to different investment options based on their I.D.™, and those driven to Authenticate like to invest in projects:

- that produce tangible, practical outcomes—anything else doesn't feel real to them

- that enable them to comprehensively understand how they work

- they can be personally involved with

- they have some personal experience of.

Driven to avoid the *Instinct to Authenticate*™

Money is only important to those driven to Avoid Authenticate in terms of how it makes them—or others—feel. They spend money on things that make them feel good—and that usually means things that are very personal to them. For example, they may be offered an apartment for half the price of the value of their existing one, but if it doesn't make them feel good they would probably rather spend the extra money on the existing apartment—even if the other one is in a better suburb. They are not just interested in what others think; it's critical that they percieve that their investments align with their ideals—otherwise they won't commit.

People who are driven to avoid the *Instinct to Authenticate*™ value:

- ⇛ being understood
- ⇛ charisma
- ⇛ philosophy
- ⇛ how they're perceived by others
- ⇛ the meanings behind actions.

They can be concerned about what other people think of them, so although they may like to have nice things, they are much more concerned with how those nice things make them feel. Does the apartment feel warm and homely? Does it inspire them when they walk in or do they want to leave as soon as they arrive? These are the questions they will consider before spending money.

They are generally more interested in relationships and ideas than money. As a result, they can get themselves into trouble because they don't face reality. They are good at sticking their head in the sand. Those driven to Avoid Authenticate can philosophise their way out of anything—often saying, with a shrug of their shoulders, 'Whatever will be, will be'.

What will change things is if they are forced by some external event to face up to their financial problems. After all, an eviction notice can't be ignored forever. This type of external event is often necessary for people driven to Avoid Authenticate to take action and make the changes needed to fix the problem.

Reducing financial pressure

The best way for Avoid Authenticate people to reduce their financial pressure is for them to study their past spending behaviour and look for where they were going wrong. Theorising about their money problems will enable them to obtain a new perspective that will motivate them to action.

Investing

Those driven to avoid the *Instinct to Authenticate*™ often have a different definition of 'real' and are therefore drawn to different wealth-creation options. They are more likely to be attracted by investments:

↦ that offer the opportunity to leverage their effort, time and money

↦ that allow them to use their intuition when making the relevant decisions

↦ that are in line with their ideals, beliefs and values.

Driven by the *Instinct to Complete*™

They like to research every option before they will commit to buying anything. So if they are looking for a property, for example, they will research its area and all the surrounding amenities. These people leave no stone unturned in coming to their 'right' decision.

··

People who are driven by the *Instinct to Complete*™ value:

↦ security

↦ cash flow

↦ harmony

↦ process

↦ tradition.

··

My Complete-driven friends thrive on a budget because it gives them structure, predictability and security, and enables them to plan for the future. Those with the *Instinctive Drive to Complete*™ join things like Christmas clubs because they feel secure knowing they can budget—that they are making provisions for something every week of the year. It also gives them something to look forward to. It's the people driven to Complete who listen to salespeople's spiels about planning for retirement because they are motivated by future security. Also, if they know the salespeople and have a history with them, they are even more likely to buy their product or service.

Those driven to Complete need to know what's happening, so they are often not suited to contract or freelance work because the cash flow can be irregular—making them feel stressed.

Relationships and familiarity are important to those driven to Complete, so they often have a wallet full of store-loyalty cards that they use religiously. Like those driven to Authenticate, they will also take out extended warranties on brand-new equipment because they enjoy having the extra security.

Those driven to Complete can find themselves in money trouble because of their ability to quickly form habits that fit into their routine. So they may, for example, start going to a local club or bar on a Sunday night to play the pokies, but then the next thing they know they'll be popping in after work before going home. The habit could start small but escalate over time—without them really noticing until it is too late.

People driven by the *Instinct to Complete*™ can also run into problems because they like to fit in, but it can have devastating results if they don't have the cash to fund it.

Reducing financial pressure

Complete-driven people need to break their bad spending habits and create a new plan with small steps that they can diligently follow until they reach their long-term goal. They will quickly gather a momentum and make serious progress. If they stick to a budget and can see the progress they're making, they will eventually be able to escape any money concerns.

Investing

Those driven to Complete have specific talents that lend themselves to particular forms of investment. They are more likely to be drawn to investments that:

▷ require them to follow rules consistently and implement a formula—it is this discipline that can make them very successful investors

▷ offer long-term security

▷ allow them to track their progress and make adjustments to meet their expectations.

Driven to avoid the *Instinct to Complete*™

People driven to Avoid Complete are always looking for a quick-fix solution, so they are the ones who populate the get-rich-quick courses that have become so popular. They are invariably disappointed with what is delivered by some investments, yet will continue to lurch from one scheme to the next—ever optimistic of finding a 'king hit' investment. As a consequence, they may find themselves at retirement age with provisions that are totally insufficient.

People who are driven to avoid the *Instinct to Complete*™ value:

▷ new experiences

▷ variety

▷ custom-made solutions that offer short-term wins

▷ flexibility.

They need variety and spontaneity and often have no idea where their money goes because they don't use budgets. Budgets imply a restriction—a lack of freedom. Avoid Complete people struggle with orderly and systematic money management. They can easily forget to pay bills and are liable to pay excesses in interest as a result.

People who are driven to Avoid Complete like short projects; buying a house, renovating it and then reselling it appeals to them. This need for new projects with short time frames can see those driven to Avoid Complete missing out on revenue. Most investments need a reasonable time to mature—compound interest is a powerful thing—yet the investor driven to avoid the *Instinct to Complete*™ will be long gone before the real gains materialise.

Reducing financial pressure

Those driven to Avoid Complete will feel less financial pressure if they set small financial goals and pioneer ways to reach them. They may also need discipline, so consolidating their debt—which enables them to only have to pay one repayment a month—can help them. Making changes to their finances that enable them to see incremental progress, or short-terms wins, will also make them feel more confident about their ability to solve their money problems.

Investing

Those driven to avoid the *Instinct to Complete*™ are not interested in investments that require constant monitoring and attention. They will be more attracted to investments that:

➪ are project based, so they can get in, make their money and get out

➪ offer variety and benefit from investors making and taking action quickly

➪ are unique or creative so that they can pioneer ways to make money off them.

Driven by the *Instinct to Improvise*™

Those driven by the *Instinct to Improvise*™ thrive on excitement—and money creates that. They are often self-employed or entrepreneurial because they are prepared to take big risks for big rewards—although they see risk as an opportunity. They can easily spend money they don't have and are prone to saying yes first and asking later.

People who are driven by the *Instinct to Improvise*™ value:

➪ fun

➪ excitement

➪ recognition

➪ challenge.

Loans appeal to those driven to Improvise because they are into instant gratification. But having to pay the loan repayments also fosters discipline in Improvise people—a good thing for them. Credit cards, on the other hand, can be a little trickier for them. Credit cards also enable them to access instant money, but they are not forced to pay the card off so can continue to simply pay the minimum balance—a road to financial disaster. Those driven to Improvise are greatly influenced by the person they are dealing with because people are so important to them. They will happily pay a little extra for a product because they like the person selling it. Fun is a major driver for people driven by the *Instinct to Improvise*™.

Loans appeal to those driven to Improvise because they are into instant gratification

Those driven to Improvise can also face money problems because they are so impulsive, so if someone says to them, 'Hey, why don't we fly to Paris?', they would say, 'Yeah, why not?' and charge the trip to their credit card. They also need to make a stunning first impression—and that can sometimes cost them dearly. For example, they may take a date to a restaurant they can't actually afford, but they will justify it by spending their Christmas bonus before they're even certain they'll receive one.

The way people driven to Improvise will typically try to rectify their financial problems is by making more money. They are the types of people who gravitate towards sales positions because they offer the chance for people to make a commission on what they sell.

Also, Improvise-driven people will not consider cutting their expenses if it means changing their lifestyle. If their lack of finances becomes critical, however, they are certainly capable of quickly paying off the debt—if only because the negative effect of a heavy debt will spur them into action.

Those driven to Improvise are the entrepreneurs who make a fortune—only to lose it and do it all over again. When the challenge is removed from their business, they can become bored and not pay as much attention as they once did—and the business can flounder as a result.

Reducing financial pressure

The best way for people who are driven by the *Instinct to Improvise*™ to escape their financial problems is for them to just slash their expenses and cut up their credit cards immediately—so that they can see instant positive results. Talking to a close friend about their problems will also help.

Investing

People who are driven to Improvise are likely to be drawn to investments that:

➪ offer big rewards for taking big risks

➪ are simple (because they are irritated by unnecessary complexity)

➪ they can be excited about

➪ they can inspire others to become involved in.

Driven to avoid the *Instinct to Improvise*™

Avoid Improvise people have a natural aversion to risk, so they will usually have looked at every possible investment prior to committing. They also won't borrow money unless they have a cast-iron plan for repaying it. Not get-quick-rich schemers, Avoid Improvise people are disciplined and diligent—which can see them good and consistent returns over the long term.

People who are driven to avoid the *Instinct to Improvise*™ value:

➪ security

➪ quality (such as a quality investment that sells itself)

➪ certainty

➪ substance and longevity

➪ logic

➪ any opportunity that allows them to make up their own minds.

If they do find themselves in the middle of a cash crisis, it is likely to be the consequence of some external event or circumstance that they could not have foreseen. Perhaps the builder they employed to do the extension on their investment property went bust, for example. The logical solution to solving money problems is to cut expenses — and that is always the most obvious course of action for Avoid Improvise people who are under financial pressure. They will look for the biggest expense and slash it — which is why they make such good accountants!

Reducing financial pressure

The best way for Avoid Improvise people to reduce financial pressure is to seek time extensions so they can remove some of the pressure of meeting finance-related deadlines.

Investing

Unlike those driven to Improvise, people driven to avoid the *Instinct to Improvise*™ don't need their investment strategy to be a fun and interesting part of their life. They view wealth creation in the same way as work — something that needs to be done if they are to enjoy the lifestyle they want. As such, they will diligently pursue their investments with consistent and committed effort. People who are driven to avoid the *Instinct to Improvise*™ are much more likely to be drawn to investments that:

ᗌ provide opportunities to diversify their risk

ᗌ should be fully understood before any contract is signed

ᗌ offer a way to eliminate as much risk as possible prior to investment — even if it means lower potential returns.

As discussed, I have found from using *I.D.*™ that people are only motivated by money to the extent that it helps them meet their needs. So because those driven to Complete are motivated by security, for example, having money to pay for their retirement will be important to them. Alternatively, if money is going to enable individuals driven to Improvise to have fun, then financial reward will certainly motivate them.

Conclusion

I hope that as you have journeyed through this book you smiled and chuckled as you recognised yourself, your loved ones, friends and colleagues in its pages. I also hope that a penny dropped for you—whether due to the principles of the I.D.™ model or from the many stories, examples and illustrations in the book. One of the fundamental 'pennies' relates to the I.D. System™ itself—that the key to really understanding people lies in delving beneath their observable behaviour and personality traits to discover their *Instinctive Drives*™ —their true and natural self. That natural operating style may be quite different to the perceptions others have of them—as my dear friend Al Ramos says, 'The I.D.™ taught me that people are not their behaviours'.

My aim with this book is for it to help you grow—no matter how successful you may already be. I want the book to encourage a deeper understanding of yourself and to foster growth in your success and fulfilment and the way you treat others. For society to change the way people treat one another, people need to think differently and act differently. I hope that through the principles and strategies I've shared with you you'll feel abundantly equipped to do both.

So now, I'd like to challenge you. I often wonder why, of all people, I was given the talent and the sense of purpose to uncover such profound and vital information as is canvassed in the *I.D. System*™. Although I feel very blessed, I know that with knowledge comes responsibility. I see that I have a significant responsibility to share this with you—thereby helping you to make the world a better place. Now you too have come to share this wisdom; I hope you feel inspired and challenged to also step up in what you can now expect of yourself, the way you treat others, and the way you can lead and influence others to improve their lives.

For society to be united, people must work together by 'building bridges' and by working in teams and reaching out to others in a spirit of acceptance, understanding and tolerance. When we can do that I believe we can have 'heaven on earth'—a place in which there are no judgements, accusations or unrealistic expectations. I envisage a world in which we are free to be true to ourselves and interact with others in a way that gives them permission to do the same.

You were probably raised—as I was—to 'do unto others as you would have them do unto you'. Although I respect the sentiment, the principle is flawed because people are so different. Of course we should treat each other with respect and compassion, but to assume that we are all the same—that what inspires or motivates one individual will also do the same for another person—is simply not true. I propose we adopt a new, more effective principle—'Do unto others according to what their *I.D.*™ says they need'. People are born as perfect, unique beings with a kernel of truth—or an innate operating system—their *I.D.*™, that lies deep within them. It points them towards their own 'true north'; it guides them every minute of every day, whispering, 'This way or that way'. It's time to stop torturing ourselves by trying to put in what nature left out.

Remember that you as you are is already enough—so find it, accept it, be it and revel in it. Celebrate it and help others do the same!

In your toughest moments, if you just allow yourself to listen to your *I.D.*™, it will always enable you to navigate your way through the ups and downs of life—it will never fail you. Once you've found your best way to operate, you will never be offcourse; you will find peace, fulfilment and happiness around every corner.

Appendix A – Needs, talents and vulnerabilities

Synopsis of the NEEDS of each *Instinctive Drive*™ to ensure action, fulfilment and decision making

(If these needs are not met, there will be procrastination, resistance or resentment.)

VERIFY	AUTHENTICATE	COMPLETE	IMPROVISE
To know why — there must be a purpose for everything. Feedback and reassurance including the opportunity for clarification. A fair reward according to a cost/benefit analysis. To evaluate problems and determine solutions/strategies. To determine the priorities and work accordingly. Evidence to understand, accept and/or agree. Specific information in writing so that it can be studied and digested. To be working with or working towards 'the best'. This includes comparing options to find the right or best one. To develop and share expertise.	A congruent environment where what is promised or proclaimed actually happens. To see how things work, preferably by personally experiencing them. To be constructing things that produce tangible, essential and practical outcomes. Loyalty to the spoken word. To demonstrate skills, knowledge, attitude, etc. Quality tools, equipment and resources. Two-way, upfront literal communication and a candid environment. To know what is essential. To visualise the outcomes.	Time to finish — or else they won't start. Advance notice — so they can keep things organised. Long term solutions and continuity. Harmony. Contingency plans for all the ramifications — even those that are unlikely to happen. Clear expectations. Instructions, procedures and relevant training. The opportunity to focus without interruptions. A complete game plan with structure, budgets, timetables, routines, etc.	To function with a sense of urgency, passion and excitement. Absolutely committed outcomes, especially deadlines. New, seemingly impossible challenges. Inspiration (e.g. via interaction with positive people, big benefits, recognition, etc.). To make a stunning impression. A fun and dynamic atmosphere. To solve problems by brainstorming and making decisions on the run. The 'bottom line' up front. Freedom to experiment.

Synopsis of the NEEDS of each *Instinctive Drive*™ to ensure action, fulfilment and decision making *(cont'd)*

(If these needs are not met, there will be procrastination, resistance or resentment.)

VERIFY	AUTHENTICATE	COMPLETE	IMPROVISE
Unconditional encouragement. Unconditional acceptance — this includes listening to them without trying to solve their problems (i.e. accept that they do not automatically require improvement or solutions). A foregoing reputation to eliminate the need for justification — this includes fame, profile, qualifications, image, etc. To get it right the first time. Conciseness and synopses. An environment where everybody's contribution is regarded as vital even though there may be obvious distinctions according to title, experience, remuneration, etc. Answers.	To leverage their effort (e.g. by delegation). To be personally involved in conceptualising, but not the 'doing' / implementation. Diplomacy and discretion from others and an appreciation for the 'invisible' contribution including subtle communication, past experience, lobbying behind the scenes, etc. This also includes being given the 'benefit of the doubt'. To be recognised for their mental rather than physical contribution, including the contribution of their 'personality'. To be free to act on their intuition and not have it automatically dismissed. To share their philosophies. To be able to pursue their idealistic beliefs and values.	To start and finish things in one go (a short-term approach). Variety and spontaneity. Goals rather than processes — they work things out as they go along. To pioneer and pave the way for others to follow. To keep their options open. To treat things as exceptions and be treated the same way, standing out from the crowd. Flexibility.	To be certain before committing. A logical approach to problem solving. A quiet, calm environment. To avoid being rushed or pressured. To eliminate risks. To separate diligence and striving from playing and fun. To derive ongoing value from their decisions.

Synopsis of TALENTS for each *Instinctive Drive*™

VERIFY	AUTHENTICATE	COMPLETE	IMPROVISE
Naturally quantify, compare and prioritise, then work through the top priorities with precision. Strive to develop a genuine sense of expertise and share it. See both sides of a situation and the relevant 'middle ground'. Investigate thoroughly and persevere with problems until they are resolved. Check and make sure. See ways to continuously refine and improve things. Justify their opinions or decisions with evidence. Function with fairness.	Always get personally involved. Communicate openly, honestly and literally. Deliver outcomes which are practical, durable and of high quality. Have a strong sense of personal endurance. Are loyal to a spoken commitment, regardless of subsequent developments, feelings and pressure. Demonstrate congruency between words and actions. Naturally use a tactile approach. Function with an 'anti-waste' nature, doing exactly what is required and focusing on the basics.	See and address ramifications to maintain harmony (the whole picture). Follow things through to completion with tenacity and focus. Deliver what is promised without taking shortcuts. Have a strong sense of anticipation and forward planning. Comply with rules and expectations, also demonstrating reliability and dependability. Function systematically and have a great memory for context. Combine their sense of anticipation and memory to prevent hiccups and chaos.	Take risks (and experiment) if necessary to usually find a way. Respond positively because their instinctive reaction is always 'yes'. Are quick on their feet and 'off the cuff', often appearing to create opportunities out of nothing. See problems as challenges, even if seemingly impossible. Inspire and persuade others to go beyond their comfort zones. Get enthusiastic and excited about things very quickly. Strive for simplicity in everything. Make a memorable first impression.

Synopsis of TALENTS for each *Instinctive Drive*™ (cont'd)

VERIFY	AUTHENTICATE	COMPLETE	IMPROVISE
Don't need to have reasons, a purpose or understanding to take action. Give unconditional encouragement and acceptance, including listening without advising. Look at things on their own merits, not blocked by past experience or comparisons. Move on quickly—don't hold grudges or get 'bogged down' in detail. Naturally trusting. Encourage answers from others. Treat everything equally and don't segregate. Communicate concisely. Give unilateral support.	Are very intuitive, naturally reading the unspoken language 'between the lines'. Are very perceptive of other peoples' feelings and adjust their approach accordingly. Strive for idealistic outcomes and are not suppressed by current realities. Leverage their time including delegation and non-involvement. Show discretion and diplomacy, varying their delivery and timing as required to meet outcomes. Influence and produce results without being obvious (i.e. working behind the scenes). Are loyal to feelings, motives and values more than the spoken word. Conceptualise and theorise. Embellish.	Are interruptible and therefore very approachable. Exhibit genuine flexibility, naturally willing to change direction. Act spontaneously. Focus on goals/projects rather than processes/effort. See where things are 'exceptions' rather than 'norms'. Tailor make their approaches and solutions. Pioneer—working things out as they go. Get started quickly. Naturally find quick ways to do things.	Commit only when certain. Identify the risks and work to eliminate them. Work to take the pressure off themselves and others. Perform to deliver a standard that won't need 'self promotion'. Work with and use logic rather than emotion/hype. Natural composure, even in emotional situations. Provide consistent energy and emotions. Meet obligations even if not enthusiastic or a deadline doesn't exist. Extract more value from things because they don't lose interest quickly.

Synopsis of the VULNERABILITIES for each *Instinctive Drive*™

VERIFY	AUTHENTICATE	COMPLETE	IMPROVISE
Think in terms of either/or rather than 'both'. Are naturally sceptical and critical (seeing the 'wrongs' before the 'rights'). Have firm opinions and can be confrontational which, although often right, when the other party 'loses', both lose. Get blocked by past experience, keeping scorecards and needing them to be balanced. Are seldom satisfied because of their thirst for continuous improvement. Freely give advice even when not actually required. Need valid reasons for everything.	Don't read the 'unspoken' language (silence, pauses, physiology, facial expressions, emotion, innuendo, history, etc) which can lead to misunderstanding and insensitivity. Translate literally when others expect them to read between the lines. Can stifle workflow because everything receives their personal touch. Frequently go overboard on quality, paying attention to all components, even those that don't really matter. Can be blunt and offensive, which can be inappropriate and insensitive. Often overlook finesse and aesthetics when only paying attention to the basics and essentials. Can appear to lack initiative when they perform exactly as requested.	Frequently worry about all possible ramifications, even those unlikely to happen, which can make mountains out of molehills. Have a great memory for context which can cause them to remind people of things that would be best forgotten, including 'I told you so!'. Stick to their routines and traditions, which can be boring and stale to others. Often stay with their own plans and timetables, appearing inflexible and uninterruptible. Are effort and process oriented and get frustrated when others criticise them for not achieving results even though they applied solid effort. Look for things to fit into existing patterns instead of treating them as the exceptions they may well be. Can be laborious with their step-by-step procedures.	Commit unnecessarily to tasks and people, frequently putting unnecessary pressure on others. Appear to lack conviction when they are easily persuaded or change so dramatically. Don't always deliver on their promises (which they deal with by trying to 'sell' a change in expectation)—compromising their credibility. Appear superficial with their overly simplistic solutions, causing others not to take them seriously. Can appear inconsiderate when they want everything done yesterday. Struggle to sustain the impact of their first impression. Appear flighty and prone to error when rushing from one thing to the next.

Synopsis of the VULNERABILITIES for each Instinctive Drive™ *(cont'd)*

VERIFY 	AUTHENTICATE	COMPLETE	IMPROVISE
Lose posture when caused to justify. Are indiscriminate with time and people, which can lead to conflict and inefficiency. Are non-confrontational. Assume and are very trusting, often appearing naive. Can appear superficial and half-hearted due to their conciseness. Often do not see problems until they are significant or inescapable.	Can cause others to feel ignored or unimportant due to their non-involvement. Are vulnerable to misunderstanding and conflict because they don't (consistently) fully disclose their true thoughts and feelings. Compromise their credibility and time management because of their idealism, apparent 'rainbow chasing' and frequent 'blindness' to reality. Can exaggerate situations out of context and read too much into things, especially when not dealing with them face to face. Often contribute so subtly that it can go unnoticed. Often are not taken seriously because of their constant hyperbole.	Don't anticipate all contingencies, which may have otherwise prevented obstacles or crises from occurring, compounded by their 'short-term memory'. Don't say things the same way twice, which can lead to inconsistent communication, affecting credibility. Are inefficient when repetitious tasks are tackled as one-offs. Get easily distracted and sidetracked on tangents. Appear to lack discipline when they don't follow everything through to completion. Can appear inconsiderate when they do not give sufficient advance notice or instruction.	Appear negative when they identify all the risks and reasons not to do something. Often ignore the 'psychology' and emotion of a situation. Appear slow or unenthusiastic when they don't act with a sense of urgency. Miss opportunities due to lack of self-promotion. Appear to lack conviction or 'attitude' when they don't commit absolutely. Often do not see or take opportunities of the moment.

Appendix B

Verification and development

The *I.D. System*™ is like your mental thumb print because *I.D.*™ is unique to each person. Put simply, if there were no mental thumb print for each person and, more importantly, no need to honour it, then people wouldn't be under stress. They would simply go with the flow — bending and adjusting to situations and environments as required, without feeling compelled to act in a certain way. But that wasn't what I observed.

Although people may bend and twist their behaviour to meet various needs and expectations, the more they depart from their natural instincts, the greater their stress and the worse their performance will be. More to the point, they would be forced — due to ill health — to either change their ways and return to their natural state or require medication to temporarily sustain their 'unnatural' path.

Although individuals I spoke to while developing the *I.D. System*™ didn't always verbalise their true feelings, when they did share honestly, the issue of incongruence always surfaced when they felt like they had been working against their grain. Even when interviewing subjects who appeared to be happy, fulfilled and successful, through my process of level 4 questioning I always arrived at a deeper, or core, truth about what drives people in life.

Like many others, I have heard countless stories about people who endure high levels of stress while others around them remain completely unaware. Sometimes even stressed people themselves can't see the symptoms — and it is only when they are diagnosed with health problems that they realise they have been paying a price that is too high and unsustainable. Ultimately they usually instigate change so they can go back to 'doing what comes naturally'.

I believe that intellect doesn't rule supreme; it can be temporarily fooled by other influences. As people, we must honour our *Instinctive Drives*™ if we want to be the best we can be.

Society has embraced the principle that people can be anything they want to be — that we can even change our natural make-up if we want to. My experience — both personally and now with more than 30 000 subjects — tells me that this is simply wrong.

By doing what comes naturally, we can reap the rewards and satisfaction that life has to offer.

A system — not just a questionnaire and profile

For all their significance, the *I.D.*™ questionnaire and accompanying profile is just one vital piece in a much more comprehensive system of separate but interdependent components. The whole *I.D. System*™ includes:

▷ The theories — such as those about intensities and combinations of drives and the correlation between *I.D.*™ and health — that have emerged from *I.D.*™ research and results.

▷ The Onion Skin model and the links between *I.D.*™ and attitude, drive and behaviour, drive and personality, and *I.D.*™ and stress.

⊃⊃ A library of strategies for each I.D.™ in a wide variety of situations.

⊃⊃ Link-up International's delivery methodology.

Other than the fundamental premise of the I.D.™ System™ —that it is evaluating drive and not behaviour—it is the I.D. System's™ status as a comprehensive system and its library of proven strategies that distinguishes it from every other model.

Proper evaluation of the I.D.™ theories and questionnaire requires that one is fully conversant with each of the components that compose the complete I.D. System™.

The *I.D.*™ questionnaire

When I began researching how to construct the I.D.™ questionnaire, I knew from my experience that for something to be statistically significant I needed a large sample size. I also knew that I needed to use a sample of the general population—not just one dominated by particular drives.

My anecdotal research with teachers indicated that they and the school system were about as close as I could get to a general population sample without needing to do thousands of tests. Accordingly, when I designed the first questionnaire it involved approximately fifty teachers and 150 close friends, associates, senior students and family members. I asked them to complete each version of the I.D.™ questionnaire until I could refine it to produce accurate results.

I also knew from my experience that I would need to establish a reliable pattern. But how many questions does one need to ask to establish such a pattern? I initially thought that fifty questions about fifty different scenarios would provide a reliable pattern. I provided options for each scenario that matched each of the four instincts—including four directions. Endeavouring to make the questionnaire process as user friendly as possible, I then removed questions to test how many of the questions could be removed without affecting the outcome. I ultimately narrowed the questionnaire down to thirty-two questions.

I then determined the options for each question from my own research. Each option was carefully designed to use words, phraseology or behaviours that would either repel or attract people driven to avoid or use a particular insist. I wanted each question, or scenario, to be relevant to people across all spectrums of life.

But the real challenge was in neutralising the four options so that no option appeared more correct, appropriate or somehow more popular than others. I wanted to be sure my company, Link-up International, and I were measuring what came naturally to people, rather than what people had been conditioned to believe. It was a painstaking process, but we achieved this by analysing the results of about thirty people at a time from a total group of approximately 200. We also continuously rephrased words until we could ensure that all options were neutral.

Each time we reworked the questionnaire, we chose a different set of thirty subjects so we could control the effects of repeated testing, use a larger sample size and give people enough of a break between questionnaires that they wouldn't remember their answers from the previous time they responded.

By the twentieth version of the questionnaire we were happy with it. Once we could see that the questionnaire was properly neutralised, I then designed an algorithm to score the intensity of each drive and a way of presenting the results that would make sense to all people.

So how do I know that the questionnaire is measuring what it purports to measure and that all instincts are being equally measured? How do I know that it is accurate and reliable? I did extensive research on testing for reliability and validity, and ensured that I applied what I learned to the development of the questionnaire.

Reliability

Arthur Aron and Elaine Aron had the following to say about reliability:

> The reliability of a measure is its accuracy or consistency. That is, when you apply the same measure to the same thing, under identical circumstances, how similar are the results? In psychology, results are not necessarily similar at all — for example, questionnaires given to the same people on different days often yield different results. Sometimes questions are ambiguous, so that a person may respond one way at one time and in another way at another time ... Psychological measures are often highly erratic from moment to moment.

☞ There are three types of measure for reliability: (a) test-retest reliability, in which the same group is tested twice, (b) internal consistency, in which, for example, scores on half the questions are compared to the other [Cronbach's alpha is the most common approach to internal consistency]; and (c) interjudge reliability, used for observational measures, which is the degree of agreement between observers [thus interjudge reliability is not relevant to the I.D.™ questionnaire] ... Test-retest reliability is often impracticable and often inappropriate, especially if, having taken the test once would influence the second taking.

Test–retest reliability

Test–retest reliability is an ongoing process. Although this test was also done prior to the I.D.™ questionnaire's public release in December 1991, to date, more than 300 people have retaken the I.D.™ questionnaire, from which five interesting and significant findings emerged for me and my company, Link-up International:

1 People who retook the questionnaire (usually more than six months after completing their first I.D.™ questionnaire) answered only four of the thirty-two questions exactly the same as the first time and yet their results were identical.

2 The vast majority of the 300 people who retook the questionnaire years later in different roles, relationships and moods still received identical results—further indicating that the I.D.™ questionnaire is measuring something that doesn't change over time.

3 Less than 10 per cent of 'retakers' received a result significantly different to their original score. In such cases, we observed three retest discrepancy factors: *prior knowledge of the questionnaire and the* I.D.™ *model, a heightened self-awareness* (from learning about their original I.D.™ result) and *an intention to manipulate* the outcome.

4 Greater than 85 per cent of retakers achieved a second result that was identical when it came to their strongest- and lowest-intensity instincts. (That is to say, their overall scores reflected a difference within one point between the time they took the first test and when they were retested.) The more intense their original score was, the more likely their second, retest, score would be identical to the first.

5   No matter what the circumstance or discrepancy between first and second *I.D.™* scores, in every case the candidate confirmed or demonstrated that their first *I.D.™* score was the accurate and correct score.

All these findings were a result of:

D> in-depth discussion

D> observation

D> testing the effectiveness of performance-improvement strategies relevant to each *I.D.™* score.

Furthermore, there is a mechanism—which remains private intellectual property—built into the questionnaire process that determines if a candidate completing the *I.D.™* questionnaire for the first time is attempting to fabricate the outcome.

Internal consistency

In the case of the *I.D.™* questionnaire, internal consistency was determined to the degree to which each option relating to a specific drive correlated with each other option for that same drive. If someone chose the Authenticate option in question one, what was the likelihood of that person choosing the Authenticate option in each of the other questions? The answer was significant if:

D> each of the options were in fact strictly and definably related to a specific instinct

D> people were driven by only one main instinct

D> all those people strongly driven by an instinct scored the same—or at least scored a similar result—in the other three instincts

D> intensity levels for each instinct were the same.

None of these situations occurred, however, because each option in the *I.D.™* questionnaire only relates to a specific instinct for that particular question, people can score the same in one instinct and then score very differently in the other three instincts and because every person is driven to either use or avoid all four *Instinctive Drives™* and to varying levels of intensity. Also, the direction of each instinct impacts on the application of the others—meaning that when two people score, for example, a seven in a particular instinct the application of that instinct will vary depending on their score in each of the other three instincts.

Internal consistency was instead achieved on a more qualitative (but more relevant) basis by only using verbatim language, and motivations and behaviours in the questionnaire that were specifically used by those people who were very strongly driven by an instinct and by testing each question as if it was itself a questionnaire. Accordingly, the traditional measure of Cronbach's alpha is not a valid or reliable indicator of internal consistency for the I.D.™ questionnaire.

Validity

My team and I were not just interested in the resulting I.D.™ scores for each individual we tested, but also in what those I.D.™ scores represented. It led to the requirement that the questionnaire be tested for its validity—that it measured what it claimed to measure. Arthur Aron and Elaine Aron also had the following to say about validity:

▷ The validity of a measure refers to whether the measure actually measures what it claims to measure.

▷ A measure that is not reliable cannot be valid. An unreliable measure does not measure anything. But even if a measure is reliable (accurate and repeatable), it is not necessarily valid for measuring what it is meant to measure.

▷ A test may not be valid, even if it is reliable because it may actually be measuring a tendency for the respondents to try to make a good impression or to say yes or some other response bias rather than the intended variable.

▷ Validity of a measure is more difficult to assess than reliability. There are several methods used. Content validity results when the content of the measure appears to get at all the different aspects of the things being measured. Usually this is determined by the judgement of the researcher or other experts.

▷ There are also more systematic means of evaluating the validity of a measure. Determining criterion-related validity involves conducting a special study in which the researcher compares scores on the measure in question to some other probable indicator of the same variable.

▷ One type of criterion-related validity is a measure's predictive validity—whether scores on a job-skills test taken when applying for a job predict effective performance on the job. Another type of criterion-related validity is concurrent validity. This refers to the procedure of comparing scores on one measure to those on another that directly measures the same thing.

▷ [Construct validity is] used in a variety of ways and often ambiguously. Even the textbooks on psychological measurement disagree about it ... Often it is used to refer to the measure's being used in a study in which there was a predicted result borne out by the study. Because the measure used was successful in producing the predicted result, it shows that the idea (or 'construct') behind that measure has proved itself under the theory.

Two types of validity were important to me and my team:

▷ Content validity (a measure of the validity of the instrument itself). The *I.D.*™ questionnaire possesses content validity to the degree that all motivations could be classified by four families (the four *Instinctive Drives*™) and that the options provided for each of the thirty-two scenarios, or questions, were drawn from each of those four families.

▷ Criterion-related validity (the validation of a measure based on its association with another related and external measure). Predictive validity — one measure of criterion-related validity — was used because it gives an accurate prediction of how a person will respond in a given situation, and that is used as a criterion (an external measure) for validating *I.D.*™ results.

After conducting this research, it was found that there is a significant correlation between people's *I.D.*™ and:

▷ their specific needs in order to perform at their best

▷ their optimum way of operating

▷ their specific motivators and demotivators

▷ their pathways to fulfilment

▷ the relevance and effectiveness of specific performance and communication strategies.

It was also discovered—with some qualification—that there is no significant correlation between a person's *I.D.*™ and:

⏃ their personality, attitude, mood or general behaviour

⏃ their level of ambition, specific interests or passions

⏃ their level or use of intelligence

⏃ likely leadership aspirations or achievements

⏃ their specific career options, direction or probability of career success.

Because there is currently no other comparable measurement for *Instinctive Drives*™, it has not been possible to perform a concurrent validity test (the validity of the inferences that are drawn from the results). However, construct validity—which shows that the idea, or construct behind the measure—was proved through empirical research that was backed by *I.D.*™ questionnaire results.

In respect to face validity, people who completed the *I.D.*™ questionnaire of their own volition agreed that the resulting *I.D.*™ was a true and accurate representation of who they are and how they perform. Some people initially participated quite reluctantly—for example, because of a sense of obligation to their employer—but in time, and with proper clarity, they too agreed that their *I.D.*™ was 'who they are'.

The basis of the *I.D. System*™

The *I.D. System*™ is not based on anyone else's model because they all seem to be about what people do—based on their behaviour, personality and preferences—and are grounded in the theory that people evolve and change with training, discipline and perseverance. My earlier work with people management stopped short of exploring drive and motivation, prompting me to believe that there must be something deeper—something driving what people do and observe.

I still intensely studied much of the history of psychology—including the noted theories of many highly respected psychologists and philosophers, including Socrates, Plato, Aristotle, Aquinas, Maslow, Freud and Jung.

The essential point of difference for me was that I was more driven to find answers to my own questions than to simply understand what was already documented. Rather than undertake formal training in twentieth-century psychology, I chose to conduct my own empirical research with people I lived and worked with on a daily basis—studying them and discussing why they did what they did. Thus began an intense and passionate life journey.

The *I.D. System*™ was initially based on 'I.D.™ theory'—a theory I had about what makes people tick. It was the result of my own personal experience, and my observations and fascination about what motivates people. It has since evolved into a much more factual motivational-and-performance science with proven formulas, continuous refinement and exciting new developments.

Independent research

In 2005 the University of Western Sydney (UWS) began several independent research projects lead by Dr Anneke Fitzgerald. These studies included:

▷ the independent validation of the *I.D.*™ model and questionnaire

▷ performance applications of *I.D.*™ in relation to leadership, team construct and effectiveness, and also to stress- and health-related symptoms.

The findings of this research have been published and are available via the Link-up International website at <www.linkup.com.au>.

Thanks to the stunning results of this research and the curiosity it has aroused in academia, additional research projects are now currently in progress.

Appendix C

Are you ready to be the best you?

By identifying your innate gifts and talents you will know what you naturally need to be the best 'you' you can possibly be. The insights that come from knowing your I.D.™ will also allow you to appreciate and manage your natural vulnerabilities.

Knowing and using your I.D.™ won't just change your life —it will positively affect the lives of your partner, children, friends, family and colleagues.

Complete Link-up International's I.D.™ questionnaire to receive your unique twenty-to-twenty-five-page I.D.™ report and two-page management summary report, identifying exactly what you need to be at your best—including your natural operating or leadership style and your needs, talents and vulnerabilities. It will also outline strategies for how you can operate at peak performance consistently. It's been said it's like reading your autobiography!

Visit <www.idcentral.com.au/discoveryourid> and enter the unique code NBSINSTINCT to receive a discount on your *I.D.*™ report.

For more information on Link-up International and the *I.D. System*™ visit <www.linkup.com.au>.

Index

If you found this book useful...

...then you might like to know about other similar books published by John Wiley & Sons. For more information visit our website <www.johnwiley.com.au/trade>, or if you would like to be sent more details about other books in related areas please photocopy and return the completed coupon below to:

P/T Info
John Wiley & Sons Australia, Ltd
Level 3, 2 Railway Parade
Camberwell Vic 3124

If you prefer you can reply via email to:

<aus_pt_info@johnwiley.com.au>.

Please send me information about books on the following areas of interest:

- ❒ sharemarket (Australian)
- ❒ sharemarket (global)
- ❒ property/real estate
- ❒ taxation and superannuation
- ❒ general business

Name:

Address:

Email:

Please note that your details will not be added to any mailing list without your consent.